RAW MATERIAL

RAW MATERIAL

The Autobiographical Examination of an Artist's
Journey into Maturity

by
Oliver La Farge

Facsimile of 1945 Edition

New Foreword
by
Marc Simmons
and
An Appreciation of a Father
by
John Pen La Farge

SANTA FE

New Material © 2009 by Sunstone Press. All Rights Reserved.

No part of this book may be reproduced in any form or by any electronic or mechanical means including information storage and retrieval systems without permission in writing from the publisher, except by a reviewer who may quote brief passages in a review.

Sunstone books may be purchased for educational, business, or sales promotional use. For information please write: Special Markets Department, Sunstone Press, P.O. Box 2321, Santa Fe, New Mexico 87504-2321.

Library of Congress Cataloging-in-Publication Data

La Farge, Oliver, 1901-1963.
  Raw material : the autobiographical examination of an artist's journey into maturity / by Oliver La Farge ; new foreword by Marc Simmons, and an appreciation by John Pen La Farge.
    p. cm. -- (Southwest heritage series)
  "Facsimile of 1945 edition."
  ISBN 978-0-86534-673-4 (pbk. : alk. paper)
  1. La Farge, Oliver, 1901-1963. I. Title.
  PS3523.A2663Z5 2009
  813'.52--dc22
  [B]
                                                    2008053234

WWW.SUNSTONEPRESS.COM
SUNSTONE PRESS / POST OFFICE BOX 2321 / SANTA FE, NM 87504-2321 /USA
(505) 988-4418 / ORDERS ONLY (800) 243-5644 / FAX (505) 988-1025

The Southwest Heritage Series is dedicated to Jody Ellis and Marcia Muth Miller, the founders of Sunstone Press, whose original purpose and vision continues to inspire and motivate our publications.

CONTENTS

I
THE SOUTHWEST HERITAGE SERIES

II
FOREWORD TO THIS EDITION
by
Marc Simmons

III
AN APPRECIATION OF A FATHER
by
John Pen La Farge

IV
OLIVER LA FARGE
(1901–1963)
by
Edith Bayles Ricketson

V
FACSIMILE OF 1945 EDITION

I

THE SOUTHWEST HERITAGE SERIES

"The past is not dead. In fact, it's not even past."
—William Faulkner, *Requiem for a Nun*

The history of the United States is written in hundreds of regional histories and literary works. Those letters, essays, memoirs, biographies and even collections of fiction are often first-hand accounts by people who wanted to memorialize an event, a person or simply record for posterity the concerns and issues of the times. Many of these accounts have been lost, destroyed or overlooked. Some are in private or public collections but deemed to be in too fragile condition to permit handling by contemporary readers and researchers.

However, now with the application of twenty-first century technology, nineteenth and twentieth century material can be reprinted and made accessible to the general public. These early writings are the DNA of our history and culture and are essential to understanding the present in terms of the past.

The Southwest Heritage Series is a form of literary preservation. Heritage by definition implies legacy and these early works are our legacy from those who have gone before us. To properly present and preserve that legacy, no changes in style or contents have been made. The material reprinted stands on its own as it first appeared. The point of view is that of the author and the era in which he or she lived. We would not expect photographs of people from the past to be re-imaged with modern clothes, hair styles and backgrounds. We should not, therefore, expect their ideas and personal philosophies to reflect our modern concepts.

Remember, reading their words and sharing their thoughts is a passport back into understanding how the past was shaped and how it influenced today's world.

Our hope is that new access to these older books will provide readers with a challenging and exciting experience.

Oliver La Farge as a young man. *Photograph courtesy of John Pen La Farge Archives*

II

FOREWORD TO THIS EDITION
by
Marc Simmons

"Indian Man"
The Santa Fe Reporter, February 1, 1979

When he died in the summer of 1963, Santa Fe author Oliver Hazard Perry La Farge was already ranked among the literary lions of Southwestern letters. Since that time his reputation has continued to grow and new honors have been added to his name. One of the most fitting tributes came when Santa Fe decided to name a new branch library after him.

The matter was attended by some controversy, partly because almost nothing that transpires in New Mexico's capital escapes heated debate, but partly too because Oliver La Farge was the kind of man who generated argument. His friend, the poet Winfield Townley Scott, once characterized him as "an aristocratic Yankee, a man of fierce pride who held his opinions strongly."

La Farge was much enamored of Santa Fe's Old World charm, as many other people of sensitivity and imagination have been. But his was not the usual quiet admiration for the place. He campaigned openly and with energy to keep crass commercialism and tasteless modernity at bay.

With support of like-minded citizens, he helped organize the Old Santa Fe Association and was a leader in getting a Historic Zoning Ordinance enacted. And in his weekly column, "The Santa Fe Bird Watcher," published for many years in *The Santa Fe New Mexican*, he repeatedly flailed away at the up-to-date boomers who were ready, at the drop of a dollar, to do away with what he called "the town's native style, unpretentious, priceless and vitally important."

In this respect, Oliver La Farge was more than a little out of step with contemporary America. He took a firm stand against the mindless doctrine of "change for change's sake" upon which so many of our social and economic premises continue to be based. Particularly in the fields of art and architecture, he noted, "nothing is more deadly than the innovations of the incompetent seeking to be striking." In condemning phoniness, fads and "daring new departures cooked up much as women's clothes designers and hairdressers cook up new styles for the fair sex," he stepped on toes.

When time came to choose a name for Santa Fe's branch library, more than fifteen years after La Farge's death, there were those who remembered and who objected to bestowing this honor upon him. Their complaints appeared in the press: Oliver La Farge lacked vision, he opposed progress, he was archaic, preoccupied with the past.

Unfortunately, the subject of attack was not around to defend himself, but others were ready to take up the cudgel in his behalf. Ultimately the Library Board decided to go ahead with its original intention, gracing the new branch with La Farge's name—on the basis of literary merit.

The man around whom this brief tempest in a teapot had swirled wore a number of hats in his tenure of 61 years: those of field anthropologist, linguist, professor, journalist, Indian advocate, lieutenant colonel in the Army Air Command during World War II, and editor. But it was in the area of literature that Oliver La Farge made his largest mark and won enduring fame. He was a writer to his fingertips and a lover of books to his shoe soles.

His first published volume put his name in lights before he was 30. The book was *Laughing Boy*, a novel of Navajo life, and it won the Pulitzer Prize in 1930. The background for the work La Farge had collected when, as an anthropology student at Harvard in the mid-1920s, he participated in summer archeological expeditions to the Navajo Reservation. From this experience he drew more than literary material. He gained a love for the Southwest and a sympathy for the Indian and his problems that were to prove a focus for his life thereafter.

Born of old New England stock and numbering the 19th century naval heroes Commodores Oliver Hazard Perry and Matthew Perry among his ancestors, La Farge also had a dash of Indian blood in his veins. Upon him, this slight aboriginal strain left a strong imprint. Owing to his dark complexion and craggy features, his mother affectionately nicknamed him "Indian Man."

After the success of *Laughing Boy* and the appearance of several scholarly works on the Mayan people of southern Mexico and Guatemala, Oliver La Farge was firmly established in the public mind as "an authority on Indians." A string of books on Native Americans that followed served to reinforce the image. His reputation, as well as his temperament and reforming tendencies, led him, perhaps inevitably, to become a champion of Indian rights and an exposer of abuses against them.

By the 1930s he was actively involved in the thankless and, as of then, unpopular work of Indian defense organizations. For many years he served as president and guiding spirit of the New York-based American Association on Indian Affairs. It was a cause that engaged him most of his adult life.

Just a short time before his death, already having trouble breathing, he drove the 80 miles from Santa Fe to Taos to confer with Indian leaders regarding the ongoing struggle to recover their sacred Blue Lake from the National Forest Service. Here was a moral issue to which he had long devoted his energies, and one whose successful conclusion he would not live to see.

Before the new spirit of the 1970s ushered in respect for Indian ways and culture, people who spoke out on their behalf were often subject to rough handling. La Farge tells in his autobiographical *Raw Material*, published in 1942, how he fared when subpoenaed to testify before the Senate Indian Affairs Committee in Washington.

Beforehand, his stomach churned and he could not even drink a cup of coffee. He knew all too well what pressure the senators could place on witnesses. During his testimony he relates, "I was taken beautifully to pieces." The same fate befell other pro-Indian witnesses who "went down in agony."

The Committee chairman, La Farge contends, was ruthless and sometimes unbelievably rude. "The more I heard, the sicker and angrier I felt. I think any American will get angry, regardless of which side he is on, when a senator starts working over a perfectly sincere witness."

The comments were typical of Oliver La Farge. The strong

sense of justice that weighed upon him kept him fighting. His courage sustained him. The Indians whom he had befriended and whose battles he had waged knew that he was one white man who could be trusted. At his open gravesite a delegation of Pueblos unashamedly wept.

While it was in the area of Indian history and literature that La Farge won his reputation, it bears mentioning that he produced one fine book on New Mexico's Hispanic population. At the Santa Fe Fiesta in 1936, he had met Consuelo Baca, destined to become his wife. She was a member of one of the old aristocratic families, the Bacas having been prime movers in the politics and economy of New Mexico for generations.

Hearing from his wife of the traditional life she had known as a child on the Baca ranch high in the Sangre de Cristos, La Farge set down in his *Behind the Mountains* a lyrical account of a way of life that had vanished. While it received no Pulitzer Prize like *Laughing Boy*, it nevertheless earned the affection of New Mexicans, who continue to regard the book as a regional classic.

Santa Fe has changed a great deal—more than most people are prepared to acknowledge—since Oliver La Farge died in August 1963. The small-town atmosphere with "its warmth and rewards" he often spoke of and admired is swiftly becoming a thing of the past. But with his name appropriately enshrined over the doorway of a library, perhaps the Modern Age will not be inclined to forget his love for the city and for the people of the Southwest.

III

AN APPRECIATION OF A FATHER
by
John Pen La Farge

It is difficult to know what to say when people ask about my father's career. The person asking has usually discovered an aspect of Father's career that had previously been unknown to him, which presents a puzzlement. The question, however reasonable, is not easily answered.

My father had a varied and complicated set of interests and talents which led him into a life of multiple careers, most of which he practiced simultaneously.

Oliver La Farge (b. 1901) was the scion of a number of old and important families of the East coast. The La Farges, per se, were far and away the most recently arrived. They had been royalist plantation owners who had escaped the Haitian revolt of the early 1800s. One family tradition has it that Jean Frédéric de La Farge became a favorite of the mistresses of the leader of the revolt, Toussaint L'Ouverture, and they helped him to escape the island.

In the United States, Jean Frédéric became successful in the import business in New Orleans, then Philadelphia, then invested in real estate in Louisiana and, also, founded a settlement that is yet known as LaFargeville in upper-state New York.

Other of Father's non-La Farge ancestors were Roger Williams, who founded Rhode Island as the first colony formed on the principle of religious freedom; Benjamin Franklin; both Commodores Perry— Matthew, who opened Japan in 1854, and Oliver Hazard, the "Hero of Lake Erie," for whom Father was named; and John La Farge, one of America's premier artists of the second half of the nineteenth century, an early visitor to Tahiti and to Japan (opened by his Uncle-in-law Matthew Perry), and who was, also, a major creative force who developed many new stained-glass techniques, including opalescent stained glass.

Father developed an early interest in the American Indians, partly from his father, the architect Christopher Grant La Farge, who had deep respect for their knowledge of nature and hunting, and who used Indian guides and canoers on hunting and fishing trips in Canada. Grant was, evidently, quite the expert with guns and fishing rod. Due to this abiding interest on Father's part (and due to his somewhat-Indian features, with high-cheekbones, dark hair, and feet that pointed straight forward), he was called, "Indian Man" by his mother, Florence Bayard Lockwood La Farge. It seems likely, as well, that his interest in the outdoors and those who enjoy its life was encouraged by Theodore Roosevelt, a good friend of the family's. Certainly, Roosevelt influenced Father's choice of anthropology as his life's work when he favorably reviewed Henry Fairfield Osborn's book, *Men of the Old Stone Age*, which fascinated Father.

Another friend of the family, and a cousin, Owen Wister, had gone west and also wrote about the West, so one may say that Father was surrounded by Western influences throughout his early life.

Grant's love of the outdoors was considerable, and he knew and admired Indians east, north, and in the Southwest. Indeed, he produced both drawings and paintings for anthropologist Elsie Clews Parsons's book, *American Indian Life*, and he spent considerable time with her on her expeditions to the Southwest.

As an undergraduate student at Harvard, Father majored in anthropology. Consequently, as a student he came out to New Mexico during the summers of the early twenties. New Mexico appealed greatly to him, and he became especially fond of the Navajos, whose sense of ruggedness and individuality also appealed to him.

His interest in the Southwest came as something of a surprise to him. Until he entered Harvard, anthropology, to him, had meant the Old World, partly because he had been entranced by *Men of the Old Stone Age* and like works. When he entered Harvard he discovered the university had a number of professors who knew much of American anthropology and who greatly influenced its future by re-directing their students' attention to America. Most famous among them, perhaps, was Alfred M. Tozzer, to whom Grant made certain his son was introduced soon after entering college. At least one of Father's biographers believes Grant pushed Father in this direction in order to continue, vicariously, his own fascination with Indians, and it was soon after this that Grandfather was commissioned by Parsons to illustrate her book.

Because of his work in the Southwest, during his time at Harvard, Father decided his interest lay not with the archeological branch of anthropology, but, rather, with the living branch, with ethnology, the study of culture and the distribution of culture.

Another engagement of that time was the nation-wide interest in the Bursum Bill. Protectors of Indian rights and Indian interests everywhere were outraged by a bill introduced in 1922 by New Mexico senator Holm Bursum. In effect, the bill would have legalized squatters' rights and the squatters' diversion of water for farming. Now, this sounds innocent enough without context, but in New Mexico, over centuries, both Spanish-Americans and, later, Anglos had moved onto Indian land and had used Indian water, squatting, sometimes for many years. As the Pueblo Indians had, from time immemorial, sought the best land, that is, the richest and most productive land, the temptation to squat must have been almost unbearable, especially as the Indians had little recourse.

At the behest of friends and interested parities, Senator Bursum had introduced his bill to make legal and permanent his supporters' claims. Immediately, the bill was opposed by all Indian rights groups, the two largest of which, the National Association on Indian Affairs and John Collier's Indian Defense Association, were joined into the Association on American Indian Affairs. Father was convinced to become its president, a position he held on and off until his death in 1963.

The Bursum Bill was eventually defeated and, in its stead, was passed a bill which set up a board that adjudicated all claims to land, fairly. Thereby, Bursum and his supporters received almost exactly the opposite of what they had wanted.

Father was one of a new kind of White interested in Indian matters. Before, there had been an assumption, both spoken and unspoken, that the Indian was a man on his way out, that his civilization was dying and would inevitably die, completely. Thereby, the government's policy, and that of Indian protectors, had been to assimilate the Indian into White culture as well and as completely as possible. With the 1920s, Father, and others, began to hope that Indian culture would not vanish, but could be preserved or, even, encouraged to grow healthy, again.

His twenties archaeological expeditions to New Mexico gradually began to shift Father's focus from the pre-historic Anasazi Indian to contemporary and living cultures, even as his Harvard

Hemenway fellowship paid for his archaeological interests. So it was. He decided to change his focus from the archeology to ethnology, the investigation of culture.

Father's change was followed by a master's degree, and its thesis, "Derivation of the Apache and Navajo Culture," in 1929, these two cultures being related by language.

Nevertheless, his interest in archaeology remained and resulted in several expeditions to central America, beginning in 1925, with Frans Blom, to study the Maya for the Carnegie Institution. Blom was another young Harvard Mayanist. Blom did the archaeological research on their journeys, while Father researched the Mayan languages, studying which language derived from which and their possible relationship to the Mayan hieroglyphs, many of which are untranslated to this day. The expedition was written up in *Tribes and Temples*, the first of father's three anthropological books on his Mayan work. It was during this expedition that Father found an Olmec head, one of his proudest moments.

One of the more familiar artifacts of Central America are the gargantuan heads, made by the Olmecs, a prehistoric Mexican culture. They are some 10 feet tall, made of black basalt, and feature a head with thick lips and wearing a helmet. Once thought to have been ball players, current theory is that they are the memorial heads of rulers.

In his work in Mesoamerica, as well as in his work with the Indians of the Southwest, especially the Navajo, Father demonstrated the same ability to make friends and to make people comfortable as had been demonstrated by his grandfather, John, during his travels to the South Pacific and to Japan. Both men had the ability to put people at their ease by treating everyone as equals, as not foreigners or as strange people "over there," but, rather, as though they were worthy of trust, no matter what their social station.

An example bears out this assertion. In Guatemala, Father and Doug Beyers, another Harvard anthropologist, stopped at a ranch for food and shelter. The ranch manager, a Ladino (and, thus, of a lower caste), told them he was sorry, but, not having been warned, he had, "nothing in the house."

Father wrote, "Barring this we lived like kings. . . he himself put off a business trip so as to guide us. . . his wife, without being asked, went through our packs and washed all our dirty clothes. . . "

D'Arcy McNickle, one of Father's biographers, goes on to quote in a short anthropological story from *The Door in the Wall*: "Ethnology," one character says, "is a slow process of gaining acceptance. And if you don't gain acceptance? You just go on being friendly with everyone, even the ones you would like to haul off and kick in the butt."

I stress this characteristic, as it played so much of a part in my own up-bringing. Santa Fe, Northern New Mexico, really, is a naturally diverse place where, especially in the first half of the twentieth century, one lived an "inclusive" life, perforce. There was no choice in the matter, except the choice to live in New Mexico. This life of "diversity" was not a matter of politics or of being politically correct; it was not a matter of rhetoric.

Protestant Anglos lived cheek by jowl with Catholic Spanish-Americans. The Indians, although they lived on the pueblos (rarely in-town, until recently), were an object of fascination. Not to be interested in two exotic cultures whose traditions and languages lived on, despite their being under stress, was to miss the larger part of why one lived in New Mexico. It was considered insane.

This feeling, this understanding, has changed, now, but its import does not change.

Thereby, I was the product of a mixed marriage (as yet unusual), Protestant Anglo with a Catholic Spanish-American, Consuelo Otile Baca. Father's living was largely made from his dedication to writing, but also from his dedication to the Indians and to their welfare. I was brought up, necessarily, with appreciation of the famed "three cultures," nor would my parents have had it any other way.

This meant that I went to grade school with the widest range of children. Today, Santa Fe is considerably divided by income, and, thereby, the old style of family-compound living, traditional to the Spanish, is going by the boards, and so is the heterogeneity of the neighborhoods. Then, my school had children whose parents were wealthy, were poets or artists, were businessmen, or investors in uranium mines, or mad scientists; likewise, there were children whose parents were the poorest of the poor, were plumbers, or butchers, or unskilled workers.

Aside from an invaluable non-academic education, I gained quite an insight into people, into people of different cultures, and into what one must necessarily tolerate.

This last was one of the more constant lessons of my childhood. My father, especially, balanced my fundamental and inescapable understanding of his upper-class background and of my mother's aristocratic New Mexican family with an understanding that the poor

Spanish-Americans around us and at school had worth in proportion to their character, not according to their pocketbooks. More (and to my father, deeper) the Indians—who were poor to the extent of having neither running water nor electricity—were people he admired deeply and fervently, and he stressed that their nobility transcended any consideration of class.

In 1926, Father joined Blom in the recently created Department of Middle-American Research at Tulane University, where he wrote monographs on subjects such as the syncretistic Guatemalan religion (an unusual combination of their ancient shaman–based religion with an over-layer of Catholicism) and commissioned such artifacts as a purpose-made Navajo saddle for the museum, while continuing his research into the Mayan language.

New Orleans was the proverbial eye-opener for Father. There he discovered another kind of person entirely: artistic, bohemian, creative, outside of the east-coast upper class, outside of the mainstream of American society, as well. These people gave him a sense of what was possible in life if one did not have to conform to bourgeois American expectations or to any expectations, altogether. This discovery shaped a good deal of his life from that point forward, culminating in his permanent move to Santa Fe, just before World War II (a move interrupted only by war service).

In New Orleans, he met and socialized with such people as William Saroyan, William Faulkner, Sherwood Anderson, Noel Coward, artists Enrique Alfarez, Caroline Durieux, and Angela Gregory, and Bill Spratling. The first four were writers of great note. Spratling was an architecture professor at Tulane, who went to Mexico and, as a designer of jewelry and silver, revivified the creative spirit and silver industry of Taxco. His designs and his studio are, even today, major influences on Mexican design.

In 1930, Father became a board member, later president of the organization that eventually became the Association on American Indian Affairs. With this move, Father became permanently committed to more than an anthropological interest in the Indians, but also, to fighting for Indian rights and welfare, professionally.

It must also be said that Father's interest in Indian rights was encouraged by example within the family. His uncle John, Grant's youngest brother, a Jesuit priest, had committed himself to racial relations and anti-racism early in the twentieth century. Indeed, Fr. John's writings on racism were so well appreciated that he was commissioned by Pope Pius XI, along with two other Jesuits, to write an encyclical condemning racism, in general, and anti-Semitism, in particular. Unhappily, the encyclical was never promulgated due to Pius XI's death in 1939.

Fr. John's example stood before Father as a guide as to how one might live one's life so as to realize one's moral values in concrete fashion.

During the twenties and thirties, among his activities on behalf of the Indians, Father composed the first Navajo alphabet and, with John Collier (later Commissioner of Indian Affairs under Franklin Delano Roosevelt), composed a constitution for the Hopi tribes, one which, I believe, they have not, yet, ratified.

Because of his anthropological work, Father's interest in creative writing was relegated to a secondary role, although one of his short stories, "North is Black," was chosen for a collection, *Best American Short Stories for 1927*.

However, this creative outlet for his imagination was too valuable to be let go by the board, and he continued writing when he could.

The next phase of Father's life, then, came when he published *Laughing Boy*, in 1929. The book is a novel about the life of a Navajo youth, Laughing Boy, and his bride, Slim Girl. Building on his anthropological background, the story became and remains enormously popular. The book is magical because it is a look into the romantic exotic—the life of an unassimilated Indian—a life which was unknown to almost everyone, as seen through that which is common to everyone, a love story. Indeed, the book was so highly regarded, so unusual, so tactile in its descriptions that it won the Pulitzer Prize for 1930.

The substantial success of the book, followed by the O. Henry Prize in 1931 for "Haunted Ground," gave father the high profile to sell everything he wrote, both short stories and novels. In part, his success came from his approach to writing about American Indians, an approach that eschewed the more popular sentimental and mannered view of their lives, in favor of a style both realistic and anthropologically accurate. For a portion of the thirties, Father rode upon that success, having, as his brother, Francis, recalled, black-tie dinners every night, and living the high life. Eventually, however, he became wearied by his success and the shallowness of his life and by having to write upon Indians whether he wanted to or not. At some point, he decided there were too many other topics on which he wanted to write, too many other stories, so he made the brave and deliberate decision to stop writing about Indians, to stop his effortless success, to become a writer who depended upon his work, not upon his fame.

As Father later recalled, this ended the gravy-train. Although he remained a highly respected author and was widely read for the rest of his life, he never again achieved the success or comfort of what one might call his "Laughing Boy period."

The change brought both good and ill. For good, he was freed to write as he wanted, to conduct his life out of the public eye, to live free of the expectations of the famous, of his class, of the east coast. However, he later said with some bitterness, he was continually asked, "Have you ever written anything else?"

Also for ill, Father divorced his first wife, Wanden Matthews, and, thereby, lost considerable contact with his first two children, Povy, and Pete.

Father continued his work in all three fields—Indian rights, anthropology, and creative fiction. Gradually, his work on anthropology lessened as the other two fields demanded more time and effort and generated more rewards, that is, a living.

In New York, in 1939, Father married my mother, who had gone to the city to find her fame and fortune. Of the six children in her family, Mother was the only one not to go to college, not because of inability but because of lack of interest. Mother was a self-described "party girl," more interested in having fun than in academics—she did well in both, but was especially able in the former. New York City promised unrealized horizons, and Consuelo Baca soon found success as a beauty and as a hat-check girl at Jack and Charlie's 21 Club. Father became fascinated by the Spanish exotic with a brain and a love of books, proposed, and they were married. Soon thereafter, they returned to their best-beloved area, New Mexico, and lived in Tesuque Village, just north of Santa Fe.

The next detour in Father's career came with World War II. As a self-described "Anglomaniac" during the Great War, he had wanted to fight for "dear old England." He had been, however, too young, at sixteen and seventeen years of age. Frustrated at not having been able to contribute, Father was determined to enter the lists when America entered the Second World War. As his health had become somewhat precarious, and as he was no longer a youth (he was 39 in 1942), he failed the physical to enter the armed forces. He was not to be stopped. Father then went to Mother's gynecologist and was passed. He entered the Officers' Training Corps, then served in Washington–where Mother spent the War working as a secretary–and overseas in the China-Burma-India Theater as the official historian of the Armed Transport Command. From this came an unusual book about the birth of that organization of the armed forces, *The Eagle in the Egg*.

After the War ended, the two returned to Santa Fe, where they bought the house I yet live in, and where I was born.

It is worth taking a moment to consider why Mother and Father wanted to live in Santa Fe.

First, of course, New Mexico had been the home of my mother's family, the Bacas, for centuries. Mother loved her home state, and, also, missed her family. Second, Father loved New Mexico, the home of the exotic cultures of the Spanish and of the numerous Indian tribes. Third, because of the last, there was no place better for Father to conduct his business of Indian rights work, for here there were not only many tribes but, also, many Whites both knowledgeable and interested and committed. Last, and least obvious, Santa Fe had been an artists' colony since the early twentieth century. This made for a conducive environment for Father's work as a writer and, also, as a person.

Santa Fe had begun to attract artists in some number in the 1920's, after the Great War ended. What the artists found was what had been discovered by the anthropologists and trappers before them in the nineteenth century, a frontier state which not only afforded them physical room and freedom but, also, a population that was open-minded and had a live-and-let-live attitude. For those who did not fit in elsewhere, Northern New Mexico, in general, and Taos and Santa Fe, in particular, offered freedom from restriction, from convention, and from expectations of either family or society.

Santa Fe had attracted a society of painters, sculptors, writers, poets, eccentrics, and patrons of the arts who appreciated the opportunity and the honor of being in the presence of creative talent. Many of these same patrons were also the same people who were interested in saving, and conserving, and encouraging the Indian and Spanish cultures, both of which were struggling to find their places in the twentieth century, even to survive.

Now, it may not seem particularly exemplary that Santa Fe offered a place to "be one's self" in today's culture. Today, one is encouraged to be "true to one's self," to be an individual, to be a rebel, to consider one's self unique and important on a regular basis. One must remember, however, that up until the Baby Boom turned the nation upside down in the sixties, for good and for ill, that these attitudes were much muted and that society emphasized one's duty to family and to society. The pressure to fit in and to conform was, at times, overwhelming. Small-town culture, with its suffocating atmosphere of convention and conformity, was yet the Culture of the United States. This is not to say that this was all wrong or bad, merely that it was so. There was, however, a place where one could escape these influences of convention and conformity, and it, too, was a small town—Santa Fe.

I don't wish to paint Father as a wild-eyed bohemian. I have known wild eyed, and I have known bohemian, and he was not either. Nor do I wish to paint Santa Fe as being full of either radicals or of great writers and artists, but there were both, enough of each to be intriguing, rewarding, and revivifying for someone who wanted to "escape."

In any case, what anyone of even minor curiosity would find was a culture of creativity and of imagination in which being one's self, for good or ill, was encouraged. Such an atmosphere was rewarding for patrons of the arts, as well, whether they patronized Anglo poets or wished to save the Indian or Spanish cultures. They often ran parties and dinner-tables at which the widest possible range of people were thrown together. In fact, Mother often stressed to me that a good party, a good Santa Fe party was one in which the gamut ran from elegant aristocrats to youths to dirt-poor artists to Indians. Her mother had taught her this after the family's move from the ranch at Rociada to Santa Fe, when Grandmother became Secretary of State in 1931. Grandmother had occasional "salons" at which all sorts were thrown together, especially with her young daughters and their friends. It was a primary principle of both my maternal grandparents that young people should be encouraged to listen to their elders, to learn, and to widen their horizons. This tradition was remarkably akin to the La Farge tradition, if rather less uproarious and argumentative. Then, because anyone who was anyone was introduced to my grandmother, her children were introduced to a wide range of people, indeed.

Further, Mother said, what mattered was not background, wealth, profession, ethnicity, creed, or other distinction. What mattered was what one brought to the table. If one was interesting and had something to say, one was welcome and others were welcoming. If one had nothing to contribute, status and wealth mattered not, that person was discarded.

For a writer, then, from a family famed not for its business acumen, its wealth, its power, or its influence, but, rather, for its creativity in all fields of thought and artistic endeavor, Santa Fe was a natural fit.

I could tell, from what he said, that father felt completely comfortable here—at home, in the truest sense of the term, natural and comfortable. He cared deeply about the town and threw himself into working for its benefit, not merely as a civic duty—another family tradition—but because he felt it vitally important that the City Different be kept from being ruined by commercial, development, or merely ignorant interests.

Father could always find his way back to his roots, when he wanted, and he went east each and every year for the annual meeting of the Indian association, where he stayed at the Century Club, in New York City. This was a journey he loved, if only because he could eat seafood, but also, because of family, and childhood setting, and a return to beginnings. This journey also reminded him of what he valued here and why he wished to return. Here he might not, as he did when a youth, dance at the Vanderbilts' under dripping candles, to go home in his tails with candle-wax on his shoulders, but he could relax completely into interesting, intellectual, and creative society, one with more to offer than insistence on convention as a beginning point.

One might say Father began one last career in Santa Fe, that was, keeping watch on Santa Fe. During the fifties, he threw himself into the work of historic preservation, preservation of both individual buildings and of the town itself, to the point that, with no prior training, he and a small group, including architect John Gaw Meem, Samuel Montoya, and urban planner Irene von Horvath, created Santa Fe's original Historic District Ordinance to preserve the look, feel, and authenticity of the oldest part of the city.

It is true, even then, even before our day, that the city and its claim to authenticity were under attack; thereby, it was considered the province of all good men to spring to her defense lest that sooner rather than later there would be nothing left to defend. As Father wrote during the battle for the doomed Nusbaum Building, "We can require that new buildings comply with certain style requirements. Fine. But pull out all the really old ones, everything that really backs up the city's claim to age, authenticity, and a special culture, and pretty soon it will look like a mouthful of false teeth, with a single old molar, the Governors' Palace, in one corner. Nobody, but nobody, will cross the continent just to look at a well-constructed set of dentures."

One may hear, here, his passion and his love for his adopted town, a town where he could live as he was most comfortable, in the midst of that which was being rapidly lost elsewhere, that which he had sought all over the southwest, all over North America, and had protected in the guise of the Indians, that which he had tried to tease apart in Mesoamerica—cultural integrity.

In his autobiography, *Raw Material*, Father wrote a superior account of one man's life. As Mother pointed out, it was superior because it was not a mere accounting of what, when, how, and in what order, rather, it was the account of how the raw material of one boy grew into a man, a man whose life both displayed and sought out true integrity.

John Pen La Farge. *Photograph courtesy of John Pen La Farge Archives*

IV

OLIVER LA FARGE
(1901–1963)
by
Edith Bayles Ricketson

El Palacio magazine, Summer 1964 issue.

Although Oliver La Farge was born in New York, spent most of his early years there and in Rhode Island, and was educated at Eastern institutions (Groton School, Harvard University, B.A. cum laude, 1924; M.A. in Anthropology, 1929), during the last two-thirds of his life he was strongly attached, intellectually and emotionally, to the American Southwest and the peoples and cultures of New Mexico and Arizona. His first acquaintance with the Navajo and Hopi Indians was made on Peabody Museum archaeological expeditions to Arizona, in 1921 and 1922 as a student worker, and in 1924 as director. Subsequent pack trips, some quite extended, in the Indian country of the Southwest, developed his knowledge of and interest in Indian people and their problems; and these experiences not only provided much material for his popular writing, but also shaped the expertise which he later put to such excellent use as a director and president of the Eastern Association on Indian Affairs from its organization, with time out for the war years, until his death.

During these "early years," roughly 1925 to 1940, he was also occupied with academic studies, which included research and teaching at Harvard, Tulane, Columbia, the University of Pennsylvania and field work in Mexico and Guatemala, which resulted in four substantial technical reports and numerous articles on ethnology and linguistics, chiefly of Highland Maya Indian groups. He was also writing fiction and, after the success of his first novel, *Laughing Boy* (Pulitzer Prize, 1930), he considered writing his profession and anthropology his avocation.

His novels and short stories dealing with Indians and their problems are pre-eminent in their ability to give the average reader an understanding of what it is like to be an Indian.

In 1941 he returned to New Mexico to establish permanent residence in Santa Fe, where he had lived briefly in the mid-1930s, but in 1942 he was called to Washington to become historian of the AAF Air Transport Command. He was commissioned captain in 1943, separated as lieutenant colonel in 1946, and received the Legion of Merit. His military service completed, Santa Fe was thenceforward to be his home, and he joined enthusiastically in community efforts to preserve its historic and cultural distinction. He served as one of the founding Board Members of the Museum of Navajo Ceremonial Art and was its Vice-President until 1958 when he became President. He was a member of the Advisory Council of The Old Santa Fe Association from 1948 until his death; and in 1956-1957 he served on the City Planning Commission. From 1953 until 1963 he wrote a lively and literate weekly column called "The Santa Fe Bird Watcher" for the local newspaper, *The Santa Fe New Mexican*.

Other honors accorded Oliver La Farge in his lifetime, not mentioned above, include the following: Fellow, American Anthropological Association; Fellow, American Association for the Advancement of Science; Member, National Institute of Arts and Letters; Member, American Academy of Arts and Sciences; Member, White House Advisory Committee; Honorary M.A., Brown University, 1932.

But the achievement for which Oliver La Farge will be long remembered, and certainly most widely, was in the field of Indian affairs. His concern for the problems of American Indians was genuine, personal as well as academic, and his zeal in their behalf, untiring. Newspaper tributes at the time of his death generally acclaimed him "one of the greatest champions of the rights of the American Indians"; tributes and expressions of sorrow from tribal officials and other Indian friends all over the United States poured in to his family and to the Association on American Indian Affairs, which he represented so vigorously. Expressions of respect and friendship came also from U.S. Government officials, with whom he often battled but with whom he also worked gladly and generously when he felt his aims and theirs were jointly for the betterment of Indian life, health and economy. In 1936 his particular task for the Bureau of Indian Affairs was the drafting of a constitution for the Hopi tribe, which was later adopted. He helped prepare an alphabet for writing the Navajo language, with the use of which members of the tribe were able to publish a Navajo newspaper. He was frequently called by tribal attorneys to testify as a technical assistant before hearings of the Indian Claims Commission. His unquestioned background knowledge of historical and actual conditions and his gift for precise expression made his frequent speaking appearances at Congressional hearings and other meetings truly memorable. The breadth and depth of his influence and active participation in nationwide Indian and Santa Fe community affairs has yet to be fully realized.

Considering his notable accomplishments in the diverse fields of science, arts, belles letters, history and humanitarianism, Oliver La Farge appears to have been truly a 20th Century "Renaissance man" . . . but anyone who ventured to make that suggestion in his presence would have been nicked very neatly by the rapier-like wit which he knew how to wield so deftly.

V

FACSIMILE OF 1945 EDITION

Raw Material

Books by
Oliver La Farge

ALL THE YOUNG MEN
LAUGHING BOY
SPARKS FLY UPWARD
LONG PENNANT
THE ENEMY GODS
AS LONG AS THE GRASS SHALL GROW
THE COPPER POT
WAR BELOW ZERO
(*with Cory Ford and Bernt Balchen*)
RAW MATERIAL

Scientific

TRIBES AND TEMPLES
THE YEAR BEARER'S PEOPLE
THE CHANGING INDIAN
(*editor*)

Raw Material

by
Oliver La Farge

Houghton Mifflin Company, Boston
The Riverside Press Cambridge

1945

COPYRIGHT, 1942, 1943, 1944, AND 1945, BY OLIVER LA FARGE

ALL RIGHTS RESERVED INCLUDING THE RIGHT TO REPRODUCE
THIS BOOK OR PARTS THEREOF IN ANY FORM

The Riverside Press
CAMBRIDGE · MASSACHUSETTS
PRINTED IN THE U.S.A.

PARA

MI

CONSUELO

Foreword

This book is one of two which were written on a John Simon Guggenheim Memorial Fellowship. Readers may feel that this is small credit to the Fellowships. To the artist or scientist, these awards, which give him a year's protection from the pressures of mere survival in order to carry out long-planned major work, are shining lights in a difficult world. The gratitude we feel is as fine a memorial as any man can have.

Parts of chapters 2, 5, 10 and 12 have been published in *Town and Country*, and parts of chapters 6 and 7 in *Harper's*. Chapter 4 was published in *The New Yorker*. I am grateful to these magazines for permission to include these passages in this book, and to their editors for numerous helpful suggestions.

Contents

1	In the Expectation of War	1
2	The Dream	7
3	Salt Water	23
4	Old Man Facing Death	36
5	Escape Within Me	42
6	The Eight-Oared Shell	49
7	The High Plateaux of Asia	72
8	Everybody's Business	92
9	American Splinter	103
10	Completely New	111
11	Incident in a French Camp	133
12	Firmer Than Stone	140
13	Indians	148
14	The Perfect Circle	164
15	Second Papers	191
16	Main Line	199

CHAPTER I

In the Expectation of War

THIS CATASTROPHE came upon us so slowly, remorselessly, and visibly that to varying degrees its imminence distorted us all. Essentially, we lost our assurance of security in 1929. It was not so long after that that we knew what was coming next, although we used many devices to deny it to ourselves. Expectation grew tenser year after year; the tension affected all our thoughts. It pushed some people into downright hysteria and caused us all to give serious audience on occasion to lunatics. The method and immediate timing of the attack on Pearl Harbor were a surprise, right in the middle of Sunday dinner or Sunday digestion, but the fact of War at last was not. It was a great relief. The catastrophe had arrived after our long waiting, we could relieve our souls with action, and immediately we began to see that what lay gleaming at the very heart of catastrophe was opportunity.

At the time I write this, giving this book its final licks for publication, the familiar writer's work has become a rare indulgence for moments of spare time. The pleasure of this occupation brings it home to me that for nearly a year now I have done nothing even remotely similar to what I have done all my life and that the whole routine of my living has been utterly changed. That change has become familiar, so that I have to take stock to realize, for instance, that there is anything out of the ordinary in not having to make any decision as to what clothes I shall wear, but simply to put on the uniform prescribed for this season, or that it is less than a year since for reasons of my own I, whose favourite means of travel was horseback, developed a powerful sentiment for the B-24 — the

Liberator — that grand, loyal plane with its ugly fuselage and its beautiful, long wings.

We all knew such upsets were coming, and we knew and know that while the extremes of war are temporary, a complete change in our lives, our world, is at hand. This, according to our natures, we dreaded with a greater or less admixture of hope. The waiting period led us to various activities. For my part, because of the coincidence of my own circumstances, it led to starting the experiment of this book.

It is a definitely odd undertaking, entirely a writer's conception, the experiment of a man immersed in writing. It was planned and a fragment written when war still overhung us like a dam which we knew had to burst but which still we hoped would not, and when already a thoughtful man could foresee that his life as a writer was likely to be interrupted. The draft of it was completed after Pearl Harbor, under the incitement of knowing that that interruption was certain and that the writer's life as we knew it might not return in our time. The last part of it was done in the assurance that I was to have the good fortune to go into uniform. The final revision is being made by a man who has fallen in love with a bomber.

The experiment itself needs some explanation, if only because of the cock-eyed form in which it has resulted. All writing is in one sense autobiographical, although nothing is more exasperating to the novelist than the peanut-minds which insist on reading literal autobiography into the sequence of his tales. The heroine of my first published novel was an Indian girl who had been at one time a prostitute; she then had worked her way up to being a kept woman, and finally all but wrecked her marriage by keeping up a little commercial sideline. Despite this remarkable background for a character whom, nonetheless, I succeeded in getting the general public to accept with liking and sympathy, literally dozens of idiots, mainly female, have told me that they were sure my wife was the original of Slim Girl. The only reasonable answer to which is, 'Certainly, madam, I got her out of a sporting house.'

Leaving aside that kind of ridiculousness, it remains that one cannot transcend one's own limits, one cannot really well describe an emotion of which one has never felt any part, or an intense feeling if one has never felt intensely in any manner. The greater the talent, the more nearly the writer can escape from the limits of his autobiography, or rather the more he can extend the contents of his autobiography into fields which he himself has not actually explored. Even in the most ordinary writing, there is again and again a synthesis made by the artist out of several related experiences of his own, through which (to the extent of his talent) he can extend himself into the being of a character undergoing an experience in itself unknown to him.

For my own part, certain things affected me intensely. Some I have already used, or shall use, directly, others indirectly in the manner I have just described. Where I had no such point of departure, I have fudged situations badly for lack of any idea of the truth of what I was trying to describe.

One can say that the artist is constantly making observations upon himself as the only *corpus vilum* to which he has real access, that he is his own chief source of material, since even his understanding of what he sees in others around him is conditioned by his capacity to put himself in their places, and that in turn by what he himself has undergone. His own experiences and perceptions are in the truest sense his raw material, and it is that with which I want to deal now. This raw material of my own work should provide a chance to bring out matter of interest with a greater directness than is possible when it is adapted for use in fiction. It has the appeal to a writer of letting him go directly after the points he wants to make, of an opportunity to have a shot at really telling the truth as he sees it, and with that a challenge to test the very foundations of his craft.

If these things have any validity, the result should have a relationship to the sketch-book of a painter. They are made up of an odd mixture which probably exists in the beings of most men with various differences and shifts of emphasis, the hodge-podge which makes up the raw material from which one's work springs, and I want to write about them while I am still too young and too unsuccessful in the serious meaning of success to have acquired that mellowness which is the hallmark of the satisfied, in an enterprise in which satisfaction is death.

Now as I teeter reluctantly on the threshold of middle age, my career is incomplete. I hold no brief for my own work: no writer (Saroyan to the contrary notwithstanding) can afford to approve of himself. Looking over what I have done to date, I find some sound craftsmanship, some passages to be proud of, much that is merely ordinary, and some work that makes me ashamed. Optimistically, I see in it enough to let me hope that I may yet learn to use words so as to reveal those fragments of truth which I may have been allowed to perceive, instead of using them to hedge around the truth and, as the deadly saying goes, 'clothe one's thoughts in words.' I suppose every artist is kept going by some such hope.

At this stage of incompleteness, letting go an orgy of first person singular lays one open to a charge of fat-headed belief in one's own importance. It's impossible to keep inserting modest disclaimers all through a work such as this. Since myself is the subject of it, once it gets going, of necessity the pages must be full of myself, and that's that. So let it go into the record now: the urge to undertake this job does not come from a belief in the subject's importance or unusualness. There will be no attempt at coherent autobiography, desirable only if the subject as a man and the story of his life be sufficiently interesting to justify an organized narrative, which is not the case.

The experiences to be analyzed are neither unique nor startling. If they have interest, it is the same interest one finds in good fiction: that this is the common stuff of all characters, that in it there really is raw material, the basic source of understanding. Of course, one would be an ass to deny that the human fondness for the pronoun 'I' didn't add a little to the urge, and then there is the pleasure of saying a lot of things that don't fit into most novels. But the *raison d'être*, or the excuse, for this account lies in the fact that a basic function of a writer, like a painter, is to describe and, if he have the gift, shed a new light upon the familiar.

These general motives have been reinforced and brought to a head by our present situation. Few of us can continue any longer on our own sweet ways, pursuing our favourite occupations. I don't think many of us would want to if we could. It seems more to the point to cast around for what each of us should be doing to help restore a world in which that same freedom will again be securely possible. In the pause before that plunge, one has a natural desire to get as much off his chest as he can.

Then, we are trying to understand ourselves and our country more earnestly than we ever did before. We feel the need of really knowing what both contain, and at the same time we see that everything is changing rapidly. Each of us is a document on America and on that change. We come of many and unlike origins and have advanced to different degrees away from particularity towards true union with our fellows; some of us had much further to go at the start than others. I grew up among the sheltered class of people of the northeastern seaboard, the people of the right schools, the right colleges, the right connections and acquaintances. That whole class, I think, is doomed to disappear, or at least undergo fundamental changes, but its influence has been great and is not yet ended. Its members have a much longer road to travel than do most people before they become Americans in the true sense of the word, but a glance at the White House shows that it can be done.

The motives, then, are mixed. The plan of this book appeals to me professionally, I see a chance to do something interesting. I want to record the America of one individual before it and I have changed so much as to make it hard to remember. What is coming is going to be so intense, so interesting, and I believe so much better that our own recent pasts are already receding into the quaintly archaic. I mean that literally. The Air Transport Command, to which I have the luck to be assigned, has one phase of the future already coming out of its bottle, only it is classified 'Secret' and it cannot yet be shown to people: I know what familiarity with that one phase has done to my whole view of the past. I want to record the old way while it's still hot, and to get it done while I still have a little time and leisure at my disposal.

The result should have a relationship to a painter's sketch-book, meaning by that the whole corpus of sketches, studies, notations of things seen, which tell so much about an artist's perceptions and his approach to his work. It emphatically should not relate to a writer's notebook. A writer with a notebook is comparable to a painter using a camera for his preliminary studies. Good writing stems from things so deeply felt, so sharply perceived, that they are unforgettable. If the writer must leaf through notebooks in order to find good situations, clear perceptions, the acute memory of expressions, tones of voice, words used, which alone make vividness possible, then he is not an artist, but at best a carpenter, at worst a jigsaw puzzle expert.

What I want to get at is a series of lines of internal experience, which of course must involve some incident, but are primarily of interest in providing keys to interpretations and failures of understanding, similar to what one learns of a given painter from his sketches and studies. Because I am not interested in autobiography, there is no attempt at completeness. The selection has been of material most suitable to the purpose in hand; in this the function of ego is as the lens through which perception came.

CHAPTER 2

THE DREAM

THE DREAM began in the first week of my freshman year and has continued ever since. I wake from it in a sweat of terror, for it is the champion of nightmares save only for the Second Dream, its brother, which, thank God, is rare. At first I dreamed it often; slowly in the course of twenty years it has become unusual, now it occurs in a blurred form, with interpolations from later parts of my life so that the edge has been taken off it, and it attacks me only at those depressed times when it seems that failure itself has touched me on the shoulder.

In its pure form, the Dream is simply that I am back at Groton. That is all there is to it. There are desks, apparently in Hundred House schoolroom; somewhere in the offing, but unseen, are the other boys. There is no action, just the elementary fact of being there. The memory of later time is wiped out, the only difference between dream and long past reality is that I have a heightened consciousness of what it is like to be there which would be possible only to one who knew how it felt to have escaped. There is no memory of such escape; as when I really was in School, that state of being stretches endlessly before and behind, graduation is an inconceivable ending past which imagination cannot reach.

I think this started with the sound of the great bell in Harvard Hall, so similar to Groton's rising bell, and coming at almost the same hour. I know that the first time, as I emerged from dream to consciousness, I felt the partial relief of remembering I was a Sixth Former now, a dormitory prefect with a study of his own and many alleviations. Then I opened my eyes to the bewilderment of green plaster walls instead of the expected, varnished pine of a cubicle. There was a picture on the wall. The realization, *I'm at Harvard*, swept over me as almost unbearable good news; at Harvard, and forever set free.

The Second Dream is only slightly more elaborate. I am at School again, apparently in my Fourth Form year. To me comes a group of boys, a Form or two above me, saying 'All right, La Farge, we know about you now.'

I understand them; at least they have seen through to my true self, and what they have found there has stamped disgust and indignation on their faces. I have been unmasked, and rightly, properly, they are going to visit terrible penalties upon me. My own feeling is a numb realization that the long-foreseen has come at last, and now there is no more evasion.

As I have said, this horror occurs rarely; it has not visited me for nearly five years, although now that I have written about it it may be called up in some form. But these two dreams and what they symbolize have been woven through all my adult life. There are certain things in me which I classify as 'Groton,' above all the twin motifs of insecurity and escape, which in many curious forms will recur throughout this account. The classification may be unfair.

About ten years ago, when it was still impossible for me to talk honestly about School and I avoided the thought of it as much as possible, I found the diaries I had kept there my last four years. A glance at them revealed calf love, turmoil, foolish adolescence, calling up those times and that state of being so vividly that I burned them. It was a stupid thing to have done, unworthy of a writer. If I had them now, perhaps I could recapture what it was really like.

It is difficult, perhaps impossible, for anyone to think clearly about his school days, whatever his attitude may be. He received his impressions at an age when detached, proportioned judgment could hardly be expected; later he must not only look back upon events grown dim, but into a personality which is no longer his, and which he may have lost the capacity really to understand. Perhaps none of what I have to describe can be attributed to Groton at all, but in one form or another would have befallen me anywhere; all I know is that certain things happened there, and that it is there I first can spot, tracing back, certain major lines of my life.

I am not interested in describing Groton. There have been lots of good jobs done on schools; this one was recently given very fair treatment by George Biddle. My purpose is only to pick up influences and motivations, samples of human behaviour, within my own experience and the aims I have already stated for this account in general. What I shall say about the place will attempt neither a rounded description nor justice; as strictly as in a novel, it will be one character's perceptions and emotions. Moreover, I understand that the school itself has changed greatly since my time.

Some generalizations are necessary as background to the special matter I want to follow. Groton was a school with a high code of honour and fair play. There was no homosexuality, and the bully of tradition, the big boy who tormented little boys, was smacked down about as fast as he appeared. By the standard of achievements, I was a fair success there. I had my letter in football and in rowing, occupied a position approximately equal to vice-captain of the crew, was elected to various secondary offices, kept out of trouble in my studies, won a variety of prizes, athletic and otherwise. On the surface it looks as if only some deep, innate weakness in myself could have made those six years terrible enough to engender my Dreams.

At Groton it was important to be regular. There were certain types of conspicuousness which were admirable, they fitted the general pattern and had been long prescribed. Apart from them, inconspicuousness, regularity, was to be sought. The collection of negatives and positives which governed our behaviour, the many precepts expressed to us, all served to sketch out a fairly explicit and detailed ideal — The Groton Boy. The Groton Boy was a concept and a goal, it is the key to an influence of terrific power, yet so subtle that it took years for me to perceive it. This Boy was perfect according to the standards of the school, which meant that intellectual capacity was of secondary importance but he should not be stupid, and any strong aesthetic leanings were out of the question unless they could be so controlled as to have no influence upon daily behaviour. He was the boy who fitted easily into every routine and institution of the school, a conformist, manly, honourable, courageous.

This is not just a product of my own imagination. I have discussed it with classmates and other graduates and found substantial agreement upon it. Further, we have even picked out certain boys in my own class who fairly well approximated The Boy, and also, checking a list of our own immediate time, found that those graduates who have accomplished something really worthwhile had not been in this group, rather the contrary.

For most of us it was a literal impossibility to become a Groton Boy, yet none of us questioned the validity of the ideal. Groton was the best school in the world, although if hard pressed, one might give precedence to Eton and Harrow. Groton's system and requirements were perfect, her standards unequalled; believing this, one had to believe that any manly young gentleman could and should live up to them eagerly. If he did, he would be a Groton Boy; to the extent that he failed, something was the matter with him.

The whole doctrine was grindingly conformist. The picture held up to us stressed not only what a boy did, but what he thought and felt, by which means real impossibility was achieved. Through six long years of school we tried, pretended, covered up just as hard as we possibly could, we put on masks and strove desperately to make the masks become our true faces. Some boys, I suppose, succeeded, thereby winning contentment and an end to their integrity.

The great struggle was not primarily of doing; the value of deeds lay in the key they gave to one's inner self. The struggle was in *being*, and it was in our being, in the essence of ourselves, that we were failures. If I not only do not do well, but my *being* is no good, the only thing for me to do is to crawl into a hole and pull it in after me. So we covered up desperately, and with amazing success. I was astonished to learn recently that three boys whom I had envied at school because they had seemed so much more secure and sure of themselves than I, all spoke bitterly of this aspect of school, all had been tormented by their own feeling of failure, and moreover had been similarly deceived in regard to me.

My younger brother and I were only one school year apart. We were intimate, and spent some portion of each day together, yet when we started comparing notes about a year ago, we had surprises for each other. But I do not claim that the experience of the others was the same as mine; as will be seen, my career had its unique elements.

My imagination was very lively, and my mind was always playing upon the things about me. For me, the concept of the Groton Boy resulted also in framing a picture of his antithesis. I doubt if this formulation was so clear in the minds of most, although the ideal boy and the utter skunk exist as folk-types to some degree in all schools and school fiction. This Ungroton Boy was sneaking and cowardly, he would lie, he was physically clean only when he was made to be, he preferred sitting in a fug of warmth to getting out and taking exercise. He was, in fact, put together entirely out of opposites. He deserved whatever he got at the hands of his fellows, for he was actively no good.

It was extraordinarily easy to identify oneself with this creature, since one naïvely accepted the idea that the 'healthy, manly' boy not only did what he was supposed to, but liked it. Taking cold showers in a cold lavatory in winter is unpleasant; I did it as everyone else did, and in my reluctance saw a segment of the antithesis. If I sat of an afternoon reading, so absorbed that I forgot all about going outside, and perhaps finally roused to find that it was late, that my hands felt rather sticky from nearness to the radiator, and myself unaired, I would again suspect that my true weakness had revealed itself, that at this point, too, I approached the archetype of failure.

As I say, I think that the clear personification of this second boy was pretty much my own; some of my early waking nightmares were beginnings of my own work as a fiction writer. They are part of the difficulty of an artist at such a school. It is not that young artists, artists-to-be, should not be disciplined. God knows they will be later in life, and if they have no discipline, in a much realer and grimmer sense, their work will never come to fruition. It was not regular hours, life by the bell, compulsory neatness, exercise, that made the trouble. Many of those things were particularly valuable for a person such as myself. But an artist, long before he dreams he is one, responds extremely hard. His perceptions are acute in the way they strike home upon him, occurrences excite him, he is likewise open to severe depression. It is not quite possible for him always to react as do the more typical Anglo-Saxons around him; he cannot always be circumspect.

One needed to be circumspect. The *tone* of the school, that indefinable, all-dominant thing, standardized acceptable behaviour in ways that went far beyond rules, regulations, and good manners. An artist was bound to offend, so was any sensitive, strongly reacting person, any natural intellectual with a probing mind and an emotional love of truth.

The description comes back over and again to conformity and insecurity, two major controls of our behaviour, with the figure of the Groton Boy looming above. The Groton Boy and the Groton code cracked down on bullies swiftly, effectively; I've seen it happen. But they gave extra impetus to the mass-bullying which exists in most places where boys are confined together in numbers. Oddity was inferiority, and with most of any given Form suffering from a bad conscience, life was made much more comfortable by tagging a few members as definitely inferior, either because of real oddities or imaginary ones insistently ascribed to them. The middle mass of the Form, each individually harassed by his failure to conform perfectly, to reach the ideal, was quick to clamour the dreadful offenses of the chosen victims.

This phenomenon is common enough and has been frequently described, but I don't remember reading anything about the mass-bully, the boy whose gift at getting the mob going, at coining slogans and inciting contempt, enabled him to operate with impunity as a sort of disease of public opinion, where old-style physical bullying would have won quick retribution.

To my knowledge, while I was at Groton two boys were run out of school by their own Forms by means of techniques which I myself was to experience. The boys also drove out a master, an inoffensive person, not really because they hated him, but because they found out how to get his number and could not leave it alone. It was a wonder some of the rest of us stuck it out.

If this were a treatise on schools, or on Groton School, there would be other points to follow up along this line, and many compensating things to be told. A matter of interest was the non-intervention of the faculty. The boys, victim and persecutors alike, shut up and covered up the instant a master appeared upon the scene. The School as a whole was a closed organization against the masters when it came to real penetration into its society, with the Sixth Formers as a rather uncertain liaison. Is it possible they did not know? Could they figure no way in which to deal with these traditional situations? So far I have no answer. It is not important here.

I could not have been more totally unprepared to enter such a place. There were not only the temperamental matters I described: home was in many ways a child's heaven, a happy, roaring democracy with a touch of anarchy, ruled by reason and justice tempered with indulgence. We were allowed to argue about anything that came up, and argue we did, particularly at table, be it over the depth of the channel in Narragansett Bay or what was the matter with the Darwinian theory. We were always getting up from the table to find a reference book. At times we nearly drove my father mad, for he liked quiet; how my mother survived I don't know. She got it all the time, and what was more, she treated our childish logics seriously, umpiring the disputes, barring the *argumentum ad hominem* until she had cured us of it, deciding when points were well taken, forestalling the resort to temper.

Even punishment was arguable; one might say that we enjoyed the right of trial by jury. Nor was it thought ridiculous for a ten-year-old to have an opinion, backed by reasons, on the values of Spartan culture (we disliked it, the Athenians were our meat) or the two-party system. We roamed the countryside on horseback or afoot, we occasionally stole sheets to make sails for our rowboats, we wrangled unbelievably, we were chronically late for meals, we read everything we could lay our hands on, and we stood in awe of no one save only my father. It was a good life, too good as a matter of fact, somewhere along the line discipline was bound to catch up with us. It certainly was no preparation for adjustment to a totalitarian community.

I had funny ideas about myself when I entered Groton. One was that I was a pretty fine physical specimen, a good athlete, tall. A day or two after school opened we had our first gym class. We were told to line up according to height. There were three outstandingly tall boys in the Form; I figured I came next to them or one below. But something, I don't remember what, had already suggested to me that it was well to be cagey, and there flashed through my mind the Bible story about 'Friend, go up higher.' I decided to place myself modestly in the middle of the line and have the satisfaction of being moved up by the instructor. This I did.

The boy next below me objected, but I paid no attention to him.

The instructor looked over the line, and with only a mildly humourous remark moved me to where I belonged, fourth from the bottom in a Form of about twenty-five. There was a laugh against me.

The incident was tiny, but significant. It has remained specific and clear-cut in a memory of a period which is mostly vague, primarily the memory of a growing bewilderment and uncertainty rather than of events. While the Form was still discovering itself, uncrystallized, I had been unfavourably prominent. Those things mount up.

I was awkward, small, not strong. My feet were too big, and pigeon-toed. They flopped when I ran, and I was slow. These physical realities were slowly but forcefully brought home to me, both through competition and through comment. Add spectacles which dominated my face, a cowlick, and a chronic incapacity (I still suffer from it) to keep ink from getting on my fingers and thence on my nose, and you have a classic picture. As increasingly the possessor of these attributes was made to be conscious of them, you can see how easily imagination could find in them points of identification with the antithesis, the Ungroton Boy.

I drifted through First Form year in reasonably safe obscurity. I watched a couple of would-be bullies slowly beaten down by public opinion, and without ever figuring that he was a bully too, saw the mass-manipulator at work. In the course of that year, he made life at Groton impossible for his chosen victim, a nice enough boy, really. The principal factors in hounding the victim were that he had a few warts, that he spoke with a Middle Western accent, and that the manipulator — let's call him Robinson and have done with it — baptized him 'Shulk.' The word, which intrigued us, counted as much as anything. I rather liked Shulk, but I held that in check. We all have our cowardices, and I was acquiring the commonest form in that milieu. After all, security for the insignificant lay in joining the mob.

Shulk's studies went to pot and so did his appearance. Next fall, at the beginning of Second Form year, he did not come back, so Robinson had lost his principal subject. He didn't quite know where to concentrate, and as a matter of fact, during the fall term he and I co-operated occasionally in bedevilling, by the manipulation system, a boy who had shown aspirations towards being the simple, physical bully of tradition. This boy was, of course, already formally tagged and in bad, an offender against the code, so that Robinson with his usual skill was following a socially prepared line of attack.

At Christmas I got my first suit with long pants. It was a brown tweed, a good colour and becoming; I think my father helped me choose it. About half the Form was still in knickers; I came back for the beginning of the Winter Term feeling cocky. That first day, unpacking in the dormitory, inspiration came to Robinson. I don't remember just what set him off; there was some chance connection, it was not quite whole cloth, there would always be a thread. Perhaps I had wrapped something in toilet paper when I was packing. I was quite capable of doing that in all innocence.

'Bumwad Inky,' he said, his eye lighting up. (Inky is my ancient, family nickname.) 'Bumwad Inky in his bumwad suit.'

I recognized that hot look in his eyes, the way his face lighted up, his weaving motion. I should have socked him then and there, but I was even smaller and feebler than he, I knew I should be licked, and I lacked the simple guts.

Through the day he worked on his new idea, through Bumwad Inks to Bumptink, to Bump, and finally to the *chef d'œuvre* of his career, Bop. I am describing a genius in his own line. He immediately associated this elementary noise with the action and alleged sound of my awkward feet, and at the same time he kept the original meaning alive. I fought him, and was licked, that evening, and several times more in the next few days. It was too late then, I was Bop.

That first night when I went to bed, I knew that it had happened. My mind being what it was, I had already figured out the existence of definite classes within the Form, and particularly the bottom one, the slums, containing the two or three wretched individuals on whom there was always an open season, the exposed failures, the — dread word — *unpopular*. I had seen, too, that another group stood just within the bounds of belonging, and could at any time be pushed down into the slums. I had been one of those, I knew; now I had joined the outcasts.

Robinson developed the toilet paper thesis in many directions. I wrote my letters on it, used handkerchiefs of it, and so forth. As we began to be interested in girls, he spied on the outgoing mailbox until he got the name of one to whom I wrote. He built her up into my toilet paper complement, although most of the Form thought this was going too far.

In time the original meaning faded, but it was always ready in the minds of the other boys, to be called up by some happy, chance connection. The force of the name lay in its mere sound; one could shout it, one could whisper it, there was a very definite technique for mouthing it in silence so that a master would suspect nothing, but its bearer would know what was going on. It could be chanted very softly in unison when I rose in class to recite, it could be indicated by a faint movement of the lips and a gesture of the hand if I came late into the schoolroom, if I went up to receive a prize. From that day forth, anything I undertook which exposed me to public notice, no matter how creditable or how accidental, had to be carried out in time to that name.

Robinson was a remarkable boy, and an unhappy one himself. I might as well give him what credit is due him. Here is another use he made of mass manipulation:

In that same Second Form year there was one real bully in the school, old style. He was in a higher Form, a very big, slow boy, slow-moving, with a puffy face, small nose, and full lips. He took small boys into the cellar, I believe, and twisted their arms, gave them Dutch rubs and hot potatoes. He never bothered me, so I can't say for sure. Anyhow, his reputation was foul, and to some extent his own Form had washed its hands of him. That was a most unusual thing; under our caste system, a Form ordinarily was absolutely solid against any freshness from lower Forms towards the very least of its members.

One rainy Sunday afternoon when there was nothing on earth to do, Robinson organized a gang of small boys against the bully. They surrounded him like jackrabbits around a bull and then began yipping. With Robinson to lead them, what they said had plenty of sting. At first he couldn't believe it, it was an unbelievable insurrection, there were even new boys in the pack. He charged this way and that, and got no one. No older boy, no Form mate intervened. He tried to take refuge in the library, but they tortured him out of there by silent waiting and by coming right up to him, there where he dared not grab one of them. They drove him round and round the school.

He stopped to drink at a fountain, never dreaming that any of them would dare touch him. Robinson ran forward and smacked the bully's head down so that he cut his lip on the mouthpiece. I remember him in the latter part of that afternoon, walking desperately along the corridors, his mouth bleeding, his face soaked with tears, alternately threatening, and begging the kids to leave him alone.

In my Third Form year an incident occurred which had little effect upon my general development, but which I want to record because it remains one of the most purely happy memories of all my time at Groton. Also, it shows what every novelist knows, that events which in a novel are condemned as being 'too good to be true,' too cut to pattern, happen in real life.

A boy — call him Jones — in my Form had not fully recovered from a long, serious illness. He was delicate then, later he became quite otherwise, but at this time he had to stay out of all violent things. We struck up somewhat of a friendship, and I admired his courage in the face of his handicaps.

There was another boy who might as well be Brown. He was about my size, but he was officially stated to have the most perfect physical development in our Form, one of the best in the school. I did not like him.

On my birthday, when my usual hangdog condition had been somewhat lightened by the addition of another year, Brown took it upon himself to harry Jones. I forget the details of it, save that it was a low, crude kind of teasing and insulting, clearly based on a sense of Jones's helplessness. I knew my friend well enough to be sure that if insult bore too hard on honour he would fight regardless of his own capacity, and I dreaded the thought. I was also conscious of all the literary and folk-precedents for my part in this scene. Sure that I had a licking coming to me, I tackled Brown.

A Fourth Former who turned up promptly organized the fight, which was staged in the big, east entrance hall of Hundred House. We had quite an audience. Brown seemed formidable, cool, self-confident; he acted as if he had taken boxing lessons, which he had. I was scared to death, throwing as good a bluff as I could, and searching desperately in my mind for some way out of this mess.

So we went to it, and I know that part of the time, kid style, I was flailing with my eyes shut. I found, surprisingly, that the punishment was not too hard to take. Suddenly the Fourth Former's voice said, 'Go on in, Laf' (my rare, alternative, good nickname), 'go on in and finish him.' I shook my head and really looked. Brown was covering up, making no attempt to hit me. There were thirty good seconds left of that round, thirty seconds of deliriously swinging one haymaker after another into whatever part of his head he left uncovered. The whole thing was astonishing, wonderful.

From the point of view of the Form it was a real upset, and I suppose it did help my standing. For myself, it decreased somewhat my belief in my own cowardice. But on the whole it does not seem to have affected the flow of events much, at least not in any way that I could perceive.

In my Fourth Form year I was becoming a tolerable physical specimen. I had no idea of this. My incapacity and awkwardness had been so thoroughly drummed into me by then, via my nickname and otherwise, that I had a fixed mental image of myself which remained dominant, though slowly giving way, until I was thirty, and of which I find traces still remain. Yet actual trial showed that I had some capacity for high-jumping, so I worked at it.

Any endeavour of mine was a source of joy to Robinson and hence to my fellows generally, with the delighted anticipation of my failure; this one was made to order for him. A high-jumper must figure his take-off exactly. At a chosen distance from the bar, where he has made a mark, he sets down a certain foot, from there, running fast, so many counted steps (I always used seventeen) take him to just the spot for his jump. He should be able to do it blindfold. All Robinson and his playmates had to do was to stand on either side of the jumping pit and chant 'Bop — Bop — Bop' in time to my takeoff. There was no way for me to avoid them, unless I gave up, and that would have been to give them the perfection of triumph. Thus I did my practising that spring, save when the instructor or some alert Sixth Former was around.

I should like to call this little game to the attention of all those hearty, clean-cut masters who consider that because Higgins, who is desperately unpopular, is also a rather snivelling little rat and doesn't care for athletics, the boys are probably right in chivvying him. It's not easy to go out for anything at all when experiences like this are certain to follow.

Competition in the Spring Meet was keen, not only for individual prizes but to win points for one's Form, in the hope that it might capture the school cup or shield or whatever it was. Now I had to exhibit what I had learned to do, and really test it. Robinson and his helpers rallied around the pit, mouthing the silent chant of my name which they knew I could not fail to catch. The athletic instructor had no flies on him; he spotted that they were interfering with me in some way, and chased them off.

That was a great relief. Then I began piling up points for the Form, and thereafter, of course, not even Robinson would have been mad enough, then or later, to expose himself to a charge of harming my jumping. It was my first taste of athletic success, and it was very good.

The victory alleviated but did not really alter my opinion of myself. It did not lead me to think I might be well made, or an athlete. Success was an intense surprise. I went out for high-jumping as I had for everything else before, and did for many years to come, with the conviction of inadequacy and eventual failure. My mistakes and failures seemed in character; my successes, surprises, glorious exceptions.

In me was raging an endless conflict. In part I accepted the doctrine of my failure in being, in part I rejected it, and all of me longed to believe it was not so. By the process I have described, I kept on proving to myself my greater or lesser identification with the Ungroton Boy. I went out for almost everything from football to dramatics, always reluctantly, always expecting it would end in jeers and ridicule, save for the one clear line of writing which nothing ever touched.

I went out for things partly because I was damned if I would admit myself licked, and not to try was to admit it, since I knew I feared the jeering as much as I did merely not succeeding. This stubbornness was reinforced by a different urge, a truly hopeless quest which continued through college and far beyond. There was the desire to prove to the world, and to myself, that I really was like others, the vain attempt to replace a failure in being by achievement in doing. So long as I was convinced of my internal inferiority, so that winning my letter or being editor of the school magazine merely seemed surprising exceptions rather than parts of my real pattern, no honour won could do me any good, but each one turned to ashes as soon as it was in hand, leaving always the restless ambition to go higher and prove at last that I was really all right; the next achievement would do it. At the same time, and running directly contrary to all this, was a vast elaboration of all the techniques of escape. Escape, and the wedding of escape to this urge for doing, produced the dominant motifs of my adult life and in one form or another will run through many sections of this story. This now is merely the anatomy of an inferiority complex — I suppose it's that — the formation of an individual.

By my Sixth Form year my record of performance had, in fact, formed a pattern which in the eyes of the others showed me as far from unsuccessful. I did not become exactly popular, but I was accepted, I formed certain friendships, I carried some weight. I enjoyed my change of status, but I thought I was merely fooling public opinion, for I knew that I, myself, had not changed from the person who had been so despised. The idea of the mask had become a conscious one; from there on for fifteen years or more I was to live with it.

We went on to Harvard, to the bliss of a new start among strangers. Without word from me, by common consent my classmates from Groton dropped my hated nickname. It was a very decent thing of them to do, the biggest assist they could have given me, and it must be remembered of them. So far as I know, none of them has used it since, save only Robinson. I hear that he speaks of me so, and I look forward to meeting him sometime and hearing him say it. I have changed greatly from what I was at Groton, and I should no longer hesitate to push his face in for him.

But Groton and the Groton Boy were not easily shaken off. The Dreams showed that. I strove ridiculously at Harvard for surplus honours. Thus, having joined one utterly sufficient club, I was glad to get into two others for which I had no use at all, simply because it might prove to me that I was really all right. Being President of *The Advocate*, the college literary magazine, I nonetheless submitted wormlike to all the hazing involved in heeling for the *Lampoon*, although I didn't have much respect for it, didn't like most of the editors on it, and knew that they didn't like me. They had to elect me finally, whereupon I dropped the thing like a hot potato. At no time had I really wanted it, in a way I had committed an indignity against my own publication, which I loved, and all because to be editor of *two* magazines seemed more outstanding.

Along with all this running furiously and getting nowhere, were the familiar phenomena of the inferiority complex, the touchy arrogance, self-assertiveness, and withdrawal, the behaviour which made people think me a swelled-headed nuisance, and so forth. That's all familiar stuff, there is no point in going into it.

The chase after honours died away after I graduated. Some part of the torment of unreality in which I lived was dissolved by hard contact with the real world. More durable, more difficult to lose, was the drive for conformity, the Groton Boy, evolved now into an adult concept. I suppose the world is full of people trying to prove to themselves that they have the assurance and capacity of their neighbours, in whom they read qualities which frequently aren't there at all. If the men around me talked casually of how drunk they got once in Belize or were funny on the subject of the Alcalde of Puerto Santa María, I would equally casually exaggerate about some drinking I did in Huehuetenango and mention the frontier guards at Nentón, but always I felt that their places were remoter, stranger, more wonderful than mine. If men spoke confidently of women and love, I did the same, imagining them Don Juans of a thousand amours, seeing myself as a weakling, unable to win women, carefully covering up my lack of mistresses. And by myself, I would strive after affairs, on the peck all over the French Quarter or wherever I happened to be living, in order to convince myself that I, too, had what it takes.

The large and small failures which are a part of everyone's life had for me the heavy weight of fulfilled expectation. I thought that only I missed out so badly, and with each occasion there was the feeling of here I go again, the hopeless one.

My Groton Boy, grown up, was a curious blend of the standards of school, of New York gentility, and of fellow explorers and fellow artists. It would be hard to make logic of him, but his influence was powerful. Under it, I was particularly prone to aspirations towards conservative gentility which actually were alien to my make-up; to live uptown in a presentable apartment, have friends out of the same drawer as myself, give dinners of six and eight deftly served, accompanied by the right wines, and to be asked to the small, fashionable parties (white tie) — a death in life, which I eagerly embraced as soon as financial success enabled me to, and of which it took a series of disasters to cure me.

I have said that I managed to keep the one, clear line of my writing free of almost all that happened to me. That is fairly true, no more. It was a great disadvantage to an artist to be born a La Farge and have gone to Groton. Counting in a great-grandfather who painted miniatures, I was of the fourth unbroken generation of artists, and they had all been gentlemen. My distinguished grandfather being long dead, his legend insisted upon the genteel character of his work and one was supposed to live up to him. The pressure to do the kind of writing which only a gentleman would do, to be, God help me, in good taste, was terrific, and the Groton Boy of course insisted on it. It cost me a constant struggle to write the thing as I saw it, and on many occasions I failed. Only recently have I really unloaded this influence.

As a matter of fact, my grandfather was far from being always an admirable man. He had some bang-up faults, and did some thoroughly disagreeable things. He was a gentleman in his ordinary converse because he was bred that way, but as far as I can find out, when he painted he painted, and to hell with everything.

And so say I, but I've been a long time getting there. It is only recently that I have been able to eliminate the fatal consideration of whether a given piece of writing would be, not only artistically sound, but creditable to myself. I was eighteen years out of school before I could force the name 'Bop' across my lips, and the first time I said it I was astonished at myself. I think I am rid now of the things I have classified as Groton, but I may be fooling myself. I do know that even two years ago it would have been impossible for me to set those three letters down so calmly and so often on these pages.

Nowadays the Dream comes seldom, and then in an imperfect form. In it I know that I am in fact grown up, that they have no right to keep me there, I am aware of my present self, and the whole thing blurs off into more ordinary, thinly nightmarish confusions. And it is at least five years since I have had the Second Dream.

CHAPTER 3

SALT WATER

At earliest memory, at the farthest back that I can take myself, the waters of Narragansett Bay were long familiar. From then till now it continues — stability, security, happiness, the perfect opposite to what I have been describing.

The shore is always a place on which a group of boys, or one boy alone, can become utterly absorbed and self-forgetful. Exploration of the little basins, the animals, the rocks, is never completed or exhausted. As soon as we could swim, we put out in rowboats for ourselves. With a complexity like Worry Wart's in 'Out Our Way' we rigged sails for anything that would float, slowly learning how to make the most unlikely tubs move to windward, acquiring unconsciously the feel of wind, boat, and water.

Growing a little older, we progressed to canoes, and then to sailing dories, the most seaworthy of small craft when properly handled, and the most easily capsized. Although we thought little of it, we must have become pretty skillful, for now I can see that in all innocence we performed some surprising feats. We had no intention of being foolhardy, but, for instance, felt as boys will that we really should get home somewhere around the time at which we were expected, rather than lying over in a safe place, waiting for a bad blow to pass. It never would have occurred to any of us to tie canoe or dory up and telephone for someone to fetch us by land. Out of this simplicity arose two occasions that I can remember, when we had sizable audiences down on the shore watching to see if we should be swamped before we reached shelter.

It is only the later mentions of the onlookers that made me see that we had in fact been in danger. My mother was most anxious to avoid building up fears in us, she wanted her children daring, and so she swallowed her own fears without a murmur. When, for instance, we had brought a canoe across two miles of open water in a full-bodied northwester, she would confine herself to pointing out rather mildly, that it would have been all right if we'd stayed on the other side of the bay, provided we had telephoned her. Beyond that she did not blame us, nor did she praise, since she hated a stuck-up boy as much as she did a coward. She followed this policy in all things; when I walked into the house with a handful of puff-adders, when she found all the children playing tag on the stable roof, when we brought my cousin in with a bullet through her foot.

When I became a constant searcher after escape, here was a marvellous form of it. There was nothing about a boat that could remind me of Groton. I had the actual, physical fact of flight, and no fear either of interruption or that what I was engaged in could seem contemptible to anyone. I felt at home and sure of myself on salt water as I never did on land. Here was not the conflict with people, which I feared, but with physical problems the handling of which had been so learned that it ran in my blood. For an imaginative youngster, small boats are extraordinarily satisfactory. The pretense that one is a pirate, an explorer, or master of a clipper, is half borne out by the realities of one's occupation; the smell of water, the motion of the boat, one's small activities in navigating, all bolster the story. And then, no adult, no sensible person can come crashing in to shatter the dream; usually, one is completely out of call. The sea was safe, the sea was peace.

In time we graduated to the *Windigo* and were allowed to take her out alone. Now a new element of delight came in, the sense of mastery. There was no doubt in the minds of any of us that she was a most superior boat, that to sail her competently was an achievement. We were right. The world is loaded to the Plimsoll line with descriptions of beloved boats; of this one I shall tell only what is necessary for understanding of what follows. Anyhow, if I tried to do her justice, I'd be taken for a liar.

She was a smart nineteen-foot sloop, built to special order by Lawley in 1897, and when she left the ways she was the latest word in her type of vessel. Sturdily built, with care she was ageless. We made changes in her from time to time, and she passed her fortieth birthday still young, sound, dependable, superior. She was not built for racing, but leaving racing boats aside, she was unusually fast, very handy, and able to stand up to a terrific pounding. More than once she won through in weather when no boat her size had any business leaving snug harbour. Her chief fault was that she was headstrong; she always made the steersman work to keep her from heading up into the wind, and sometimes in a heavy blow, running before the wind, she could not be held on her course. This fault saved us once from real disaster so I can't kick about it too much.

What I am saying is bare truth and understatement. She was a queen. As to her appearance — I was aboard of her so much that I always saw her from the tiller end, so to speak, and thought of her in terms of sturdiness and solidity. It happened from time to time to me (and to my brothers) that I would see an exceptionally pretty little yacht coming down the bay, and notice how handily she came about, how trim she was, what a lovely run and sweet bow, what graceful lines. There, I would think, was the loveliest craft I had seen in a long time, and then she would come nearer and I would see with true surprise that it was the *Windigo,* that that was how she showed herself to other boats when her sails were set and she had come to life.

The sense of mastery in handling this boat came not only from her virtues, but from the fact that her proper crew was two, and three was the minimum for racing. Even for a grown man with long arms and legs to manage her smartly by himself called for fast work. We had to develop techniques of steering with one foot, or managing the tiller with what amounted to a prehensile tail, while attending to other duties. (This skill with the feet, leaving the arms free, became useful when we were of an age to take girls on moonlight sails.) Not to be able to take her out alone, put her through all her paces, and get the best out of her, would be a disgrace, so we all learned how. No allowances were made to excuse slovenliness, nor did we expect any. There is seldom a time in coastal waters when a boat is not in sight of knowledgeable people, on the land or aboard other boats, and pride demanded that the *Windigo* be not betrayed. We learned to jump fast, to do several complicated things in rapid succession, to perform two mutually exclusive operations simultaneously.

On land I might be clumsy and slow on my feet, slow in my reactions; at school I might be the sad specimen whose development into a high jumper, an oarsman, were incongruous exceptions, but afloat I was something else. Bop was completely shed, and at the helm of the *Windigo*, now at last I was altogether Oliver La Farge as he longed to be, competent, sufficient, sure of himself.

Imagination could still run free, but it did so less and less as the all-sufficient occupation and endlessly changing beauty of sight, sound, smell, and motion absorbed me. Here reality offered the absorption and self-forgetfulness I sought eternally. In moments of fast manoeuvre, in narrow waters and tricky shoals, there was the use of body, mind, and training all together; in foul weather there was the great satisfaction of violence and effort to the extreme of one's capacity. The satisfaction of violence, the extreme — genteel up-bringing does not mention it, οὐδεν ἀγαν and *nil admirari*, balance, control, refinement are the doctrines, but here in a boat a shade too big for me, with half a gale blowing, I first found what I really wanted. I found it again in football and in rowing, then in drunkenness, in horse racing, in cohabitation, and — though this may sound strange — best of all in writing when the passage comes well and the racing hand cannot keep pace with the thoughts and there is no consciousness of anything beyond these two.

Not until I had finally shed Groton and laid the super-civilized ghost of my grandfather La Farge did I really absorb the fact that, along with the cultivated pleasures, these violences were necessary to me. But I did recognize early that I enjoyed them. It began with a lesson the sea and *Windigo* taught two of us.

'We' for purposes of salt water are the three brothers and a cousin who is indistinguishable from a brother. The *Windigo* came back to us after being laid up on account of hard times, shortly before the end of the war. For the first time my cousin and I were allowed to take her out unsupervised, and we were all of a twitch to get her when my elder brother wasn't around and see what we could do with her. We set sail on a still, heavy afternoon, in erratic, light airs to the portent of which we gave no heed. We set all her racing canvas, the spinnaker to balance the mainsail, and the biggest balloon jib forward. She went well, then an odd flaw of wind from a crazy direction set the sails to cavorting and flapping, the appearance of the water became strange, and we woke up. Looking to the north, we saw a great, purple-black thunderstorm bearing down on us.

By fast work we got in the fancy sails and stowed them, and hoisted the very small, sturdy storm jib. We knew we had no time to reef the mainsail so we let it stand. Hardly had we set the jib when the blow hit us, and our hands were full.

That wind did not kick up a sea, but rather pressed the waves flat, cutting their tops off and covering the bay with a layer of driven, silver mist. The piercing rain was all but horizontal, hissing and stinging. Having no slickers, we stripped, and the flying water struck like needles. We had much more sail up than the boat could stand, so that it was all we could do to keep her from going over. She raced through the water, heeled over to the very edge of disaster, while we perched high on the windward rail taking the wind and rain on our backs and hoping to keep her steady. We were heading for the only possible shelter, to make which we had to carry the wind about abeam. We saw the silver-spotted water, the driving spray, the foam under her lee rail, and the upper corner of the white mainsail stretched drum-tight, with the broad lightning flashing and twisting behind it against the pall of the sky. It was the most beautiful sight I had ever seen. We were both of us as worried as we could be, but at the same time we were stimulated, excited, happy.

Then in one intensely beautiful moment before it went to rags, the mainsail ripped across from luff to leach. Immediately the pressure was taken off the *Windigo* and she rode easily. We got the remnants of sail in somehow, and made shelter under the dependable canvas of the jib. The glory was over; there remained wet and cold, concern over whether the anchor would hold, the necessity of swimming ashore and going home soaked, in dripping clothes, to tell my father what had happened. I was sure he would be angry, it never occurred to me until I actually faced him, that he would think it amusing. All that was rather dismal, but for a brief time I had tasted sheer delight.

That was short and spectacular, and we were at an age which is inclined to be fearless to the point of idiocy, but the nature of this delight was made certain by longer, tougher experiences. My younger brother and I, now of college age, were caught out in

Vineyard Sound heading for Vineyard Haven, in a blow of real power. It was a northwesterly storm in which, not far from us, a four-masted schooner sank at her anchors, and which did enough damage along the coast to get into the papers. We knew more by then, and we were better equipped, but we had underestimated the wind, thinking the *Windigo* could handle it easily with the mainsail double-reefed and her ordinary, large jib. Also, when we were well away from land, the wind increased on us.

We were serious enough about it. I assumed my technical authority as older brother for the only time in all our cruising, to the extent that I insisted on staying at the helm. We were in a region of shoals and reefs which we had never sailed before. I knew that sails could blow out and masts carry away, and if any such thing happened, we should be driven onto the coast of Martha's Vineyard, harbourless and rock-strewn. To reach shelter, we had to get around the clifflike point of East Chop; until then, disaster lay to leeward of us. It was no place for an accident and the prospects of losing the boat were excellent. I was no more competent than my brother, but if she went, I was responsible, so I should steer her.

This meant that when we saw she could no longer carry the big jib, my brother had to go forward to take it in. The only help I could give him was to hold her nose as straight as possible into the wind and waves, and with that, of course, she swooped madly down the slopes and shipped water by the bucketful around his feet and legs. There is no pleasure whatever in remembering my brother up there on the deck, water swashing round him, balancing to the dives and rises while he worked. He was quick about it, as a matter of fact, but to me it seemed an age before he was safe in the cockpit again.

On our course, we carried the wind a little forward of abeam, so that the seas were striking about against the highest part of her windward side. These seas ran steep and high enough so that again and again we shipped green water into the cockpit, no more than the pump could readily handle, but constant reminders of what could happen. There is always something rather sickening about seeing green water pouring inboard. We were, of course, under a constant, generous bombardment of spray. My brother was moved to song, and I was particularly irritated because his favourite tune was 'Oh, do it again,' the words usually coinciding with a new dousing. It was a long, slow fight, the water being much too rough for us to make good time under the little canvas we were carrying. It was exhausting at the tiller. Yet both of us enjoyed ourselves enormously.

We rounded East Chop finally, and bore round into Vineyard Haven. The Haven is a great V, directly open to a northerly wind. But the chart showed a semicircular breakwater across the narrow part of the V, with a passage at each end of it. I chose the western passage as being the nearer. To make it, we had to run dead before the wind.

Now we began to move. Now we really moved. With storm and sea behind her she tore like a runaway horse, she made you want to shout. But I have said she was headstrong; with the pressure of that much wind on the mainsail and no jib to counterbalance it, it was impossible to hold her on her course. I had to let her swing round to the eastward, spilling a little wind out of the sail, and run for the eastern entrance to the harbour. We made it in grand style, came round, and anchored with deep relief.

Later, according to our custom, we rowed around the harbour and explored it. We went, of course, to the western entrance we had failed to make, to see what the passage was like. *There wasn't any western entrance.* The breakwater there was so low the tide covered it; the chart showed a passage, it looked like a passage, had we been able to hold our course we should have piled up at full speed on solid rocks in a foot of water, and there would have been nothing left of the *Windigo*, perhaps not much of us.

We came to know the sea and to rely upon it. My brothers and cousin know it far more widely than I, though travelling to the tropics on smallish steamers does teach one something if one has a little background. We knew its curious dual character of friend and foe, though both terms are incorrect since, kind or murderous, the sea is utterly impersonal. On its surface, there is no relaxing, no room for forgetfulness. A moment's inattention or a single rotten rope may turn pleasure into swift disaster. It is a curious relationship one has with these elements, water and wind, which one exploits and manipulates, and which are yet so deadly a team. The very qualities that make them potently hostile are those from which one receives riches, it is a relationship of conflict, defense, and use almost impossible to describe. I found it again in the desert, had a glimpse of it underground in the mines. Mountaineers know it.

In time, one has one's particular part of nature taped out. A desert rat learns the desert's gift for making a man lose himself, for producing waterholes that have dried up and trails which fade to nothing. A seaman learns the equivalents, the answers to them, the margin of uncertainty with which he must always gamble, and the limits which even the sea cannot overstep. And then one day the sea breaks its bounds and the world goes mad. It happened to us, along with thousands of others, in September, 1938.

Our place is on the west shore of Narragansett Bay some four miles above its mouth, the bay at that point running about two miles in width. The shore is steep-to and rocky. At high tide line we had a sea wall of heavy rocks and cement, about five feet high. Above the wall the ground, covered with a thick growth of trees and bushes, sloped upward another nine feet to the level of the lawn. Some thirty feet inland, there was a terrace slightly under three feet high, then from that it was another twenty-odd feet to the house, a big, frame building standing among bushes, vines, and sizable trees, with a roofed verandah running along its east (seaward) and south sides.

South of the house, about fifty feet from it, was the 'South Acre,' a tangle of wild growth including massive grapevines, a stone wall, and large trees, running solid for actually more than an acre along the shore. The *Windigo* was moored slightly over a hundred feet off shore, the mooring being an extra large mushroom anchor, a good deal bigger than is usually considered necessary for a boat of that size.

There were in the house at the time of the storm, my father, who had been confined to bed for months with a bad heart and had only recently been allowed to come downstairs (he had been told that he could be taken for a motor ride the first fine day); my mother, seventy-four years old; my two children, Oliver, aged seven, and Povy, aged five; their nurse, Miss Wiseman; the cook, Mrs. Clows; and Ellen Allen, the maid.

The first sign of unusual weather was the high barometer, reading 30.1 Tuesday afternoon. At 4 A.M. on Wednesday I was awakened by the strange sound of the wind, which was blowing with unusual violence out of the east. Instead of the usual soughing noise in the trees, it maintained a steady hum which had a frightening quality. I went down to see if the boat was all right; she seemed to be safe enough. The barometer had dropped more than a tenth. It continued dropping through Wednesday morning, and reached a low of 28.81 about three on Wednesday.

Wednesday morning I was disturbed by the hard blow from the southeast. My brother Christopher came over from his farm, and we went aboard the boat. We figured it to be blowing about half a gale, and everything was all right. We had no idea that the hurricane might hit us; the last reports placed it somewhere off Hatteras, following the usual course. We thought we might be getting some sort of a backwash from it, that was all.

At 2:30 in the afternoon the wind was about east-south-east and increasing in violence. The skiff fetched loose from its running mooring at the end of the dock and was pounding on the rocks. I saw that the *Windigo* was dragging her mooring straight in towards shore, so sent for my brother again. By the time he arrived we had the skiff well up on the slope of ground behind the sea wall, beyond the reach of any possible weather.

The seas by now were coming against the rocks with too much violence for launching the little boat again, or even if we could get her out, we didn't see how we could land in her afterwards, so the only way to get to the *Windigo* was to swim. I was afraid of it, but my brother dove in off the end of the dock without apparent hesitation, so of course I followed. It is possible that he was able to do this because I was behind him, that neither of us could quite have made it alone. The swimming was surprisingly easy; it always is, if one is outside of the breakers. It did take quick work to scramble aboard, for the boat was pitching and wallowing violently, smacking down into the water each time the cable brought her up short.

We passed the anchor forward, working pretty much on all fours as it was difficult to keep our feet. The only thing we could do was to throw it as far out as possible, and this my brother did, which meant that he had to stand up and hang onto the forestay. The *Windigo* pitched wildly, and he lost his balance, spinning around the forestay with a curious, contorted gravity as if he were performing an acrobatic stunt, then he went overboard. I couldn't get to him. I thought the bow would smash down on his head as he came up, but he rose clear and climbed back on board. We paid out plenty of line, hoping that the anchor would take hold when she had dragged a little farther.

Swimming back was an alarming thought again, it looked as if it might be tough getting onto the dock without being battered, and I was glad that again by precedent my brother went first. But this, too, proved easy if one waited for the trough between two waves, and climbed fast.

My father and mother watched all this from upper windows, and I know they were both frightened, particularly when Christopher went around the forestay, but they made no comment, save that my mother expressed her satisfaction that we had had nerve enough to swim out.

By 4:15 the wind was obviously worse than a gale, the upper part of the house was rocking, and what we took to be rain was working in through the upper windows. We moved my father to the living room to be more comfortable, and my brother and I spent much time going from window to window, trying to stop the leakage, and nailing shut those that tended to blow open. The noise of the wind in the living-room chimney became very unpleasant, and we were all unquestionably nervous.

The first indication of the real nature of the storm was when I saw a canoe which we had left on top of the sea wall suddenly appear on the lawn. Then I went out to close the shutter over the east window of the living room to keep the water out, and discovered that what we had taken for rain was salt spray. This spray was coming in the dormer window at the top of the house as well.

The maid served tea as usual at five. She told me calmly that Mrs. Clows wanted to see me. When I went to the kitchen, Mrs. Clows asked if I had seen what was happening. Looking out of the kitchen window, which had an exceptionally clear view, I saw that the shore front was gone, the dock and boat were gone, and waves were breaking on the lawn and reaching almost to the foundations. She suggested that we might want to move my father and children, and said she was at our service for anything we wanted.

All three servants were magnificent. The nurse, Miss Wiseman, gave the children their regular supper in the dining room on the lee side of the house, and kept them happily occupied most of the time, avoiding panic. Ellen Allen was equally good.

To finish with the *Windigo*, none of us saw her strike. We were too busy to keep a steady watch; we hardly wanted to. A man who watched the destruction of the ferry slip and harbour from a high point did see her end. He said she was the last to go, and was fighting and riding the waves until she pounded. He stated, 'I never saw a boat make such a gallant fight.'

Mrs. Clows sent for me again, and suggested that I look in the cellar. I did. The place was full of water, inky-black from the coal down there. It rose and fell as the seas came in and drew back. That sight seemed final.

At this point, Miss Alice Biddle, our neighbour from up the hill, arrived in the kitchen with her adopted daughter and her man. They said they thought they could bring their car down across the meadow, which was treeless, and thus we could get my father out in a covered car. Even if it stuck, he would be safe. So we decided to try it.

I went into the dining room on my way to the living room when my son, Oliver, came running in crying, 'Daddy, Daddy, the house is falling in.' It was exactly what I had been expecting; I did not have to look to be able to see the foundations give way at the windward corner and the living room capsize. I told him very crossly not to be a panicky fool, and fairly leaped through the door.

What had happened was that the entire verandah had caved in. It was not blown down, but washed out. I arrived in time to hear my father give a wordless exclamation. My mother looked all around, and said, 'When I rebuild the verandah, I certainly shall not roof all of it. See how much lighter the room is.'

Miss Biddle got her car down at six o'clock, by which time the barometer was rising almost as fast as the minute hand of a watch. The wind had hauled to the southeast or even more southerly. This shift brought the seas farther around the west side of the house, so we evacuated from the north, the kitchen door. We carried my father to the car in a 'queen's chair.' My brother and I were so afraid of what we were about to do that for what seemed many minutes we could not get our hands arranged properly. I don't know what my father thought while he stood there, waiting for us to stop fumbling. We carried him the hundred feet to the car without accident, and his heart stood up all right. When he was in, he told Miss Biddle that the doctor had told him that he could go for a drive on the first fine day.

My mother and the children, with baggage, went across the fields in the station wagon. We all reached Miss Biddle's house in entire safety. Mrs. Clows had brought thermos bottles of coffee and chowder. She and Ellen Allen made trip after trip back to the house until they had everything they needed, and served us dinner with broiled lobster at nine o'clock.

My brother and I returned to the house to get additional supplies, particularly from the windward portion of it where we did not want the women to go since the seas were striking there, and to make a final patrol. During the whole time that Christopher had been there, it must be remembered that his wife and children were cut off at his farm two miles inland. They were safe enough from water, but there were big trees around the house, and the wind alone was ample to do serious damage. He set out for home on foot at about a quarter to seven, when it was quite dark. Driving was out of the question. He made the distance in about two hours, dodging falling trees in the woods, and wading for two hundred yards waist-deep where Narrow River had flooded the road, with plenty of down timber in the water to add to his difficulties. He got home all right and found the place undamaged.

The storm died swiftly after the tide turned. The ebb tide went out like a cataract, among other things dragging a bell buoy two miles out of place. The bottom of the bay was greatly changed. By ten o'clock the night was quiet, and one could walk along the shore to look at the damage.

The storm took about thirty feet of land from our place all along the shore. At that, we were lucky. The foundations of the house remained sound, and we moved back into it a couple of months later. On the lawn was piled enough lumber to build another house, mainly from docks and boathouses. Rocks so big that they could be moved only on rollers, with a car pulling them, were piled as far as fifty feet back of the new shoreline, and half our land was six inches deep in sea sand.

It would be pointless to try to describe the general damage even in this one village. There were iceboxes on the shore and the woods back of the little harbour were full of boats. The windows of my brother's farm were obscured by salt the next morning. The salt spray turned all the woods, even six miles inland, to the dead brown of late winter overnight. The grass on the steep slope of my brother's farm was flattened out as if water had rushed over it, *but pointing up hill,* from the pressure of the wind.

No one at Saunderstown was killed, which made us nearly unique for this part of the coast. The worst thing about the storm was the looters, who came down the next night, before the troops took over, and cleaned out everything they could. The best thing was the behaviour of the people; no one complained, everyone was friendly and co-operative. Never before have I seen Yankees so smiling or so quick to exchange greetings. The first wailings were raised by summer people who came back to see what the storm had done to their estates.

CHAPTER 4

OLD MAN FACING DEATH

THE RELATIONSHIP and common interests of two artists came late with my father and me. For us three brothers the early one, the constant running through our lives, was the outdoors, first the boats and the horses, then fishing, hunting, and on according as our various experiences matched his one way or another.

For me it begins with candlelight and a whisper. Long before dawn there would be the step on the stairs and the yellow clarity of the candle reaching through the doorway, spreading along the wall, growing stronger. Then his voice, conspiratorial, eager:

'Four o'clock, Inky. Get up.'

He would leave the candle and slip downstairs, very quiet, a man to whom it came natural to tread lightly. I dressed in a hurry and followed him. A lamp and two alcohol flames burned in the dining room. In one copper kettle eggs were boiling, in another, coffee, which otherwise I did not yet drink. There might be only me, or a brother or so as well. The eggs would be served soft-boiled. We hated soft-boiled eggs, but it never occurred to us to say a word. It was part of the ritual, along with the smell of the flames and hot copper and coffee, and my father constantly glancing out the window lest a gleam of white in the east proclaim us laggards.

All in whispers and soft movements. Guns ready. Rubber boots. The marsh and gun-oil smell of shooting jackets. Quietly down to the shore, the definite quality of escape, the canoe grating slightly on the beach, then the lap of water and the long paddle to the marshes.

You had the sense of being taken into a man's world; as Kipling said, of crossing to the men's side. A boy might be very much a pupil under instruction but at the same time my father let him feel that he was an equal partner in the joint enterprise of hunting. There was a thrilling promotion to equality in a private world. All hunting was illuminated by his artist's response to beauty and his trained perception, which he knew very well how to convey. When the duck came, when a trout rose to the fly, when there was a hen grouse with her chicks in the springtime or a butterfly hovering in sunlight, he could pull you alert and into perception with his quiet voice. There was an eternally fresh excitement in his speech and his eyes.

The voice was always quiet. He used the wild country as Indians do, in co-operation and communion with it, finding any form of noise a baneful disharmony. The impossible union of liquor and gunning which some men attempt, the loud talk sounding over waters, closing hearts and ears and eyes to the essence of hunting, were abomination to him. He called such sportsmen yahoos and taught us to hate the donkey-laugh in the woods as much as we do the mere killers. The Indians know a way of belonging to the manless country. Their ritual expresses the communion of love between a hunter and the game he seeks to kill. There is a way of being which fills with pleasure even the entirely luckless days when no game is seen or killed. These my father had.

Learning from him, we were always conscious of his reserves of experience. Canadian Indians accepted him as an equal canoeman. He was utterly at home in Arizona. He had sailed with our own Rhode Island fishermen long before a power-driven smack was dreamed of. The wild goose, the mountain goat, elk, salmon, moose and caribou, snowshoes, pack-horses, tump-line and fishing smack were his familiars. We became men and in one point or another achieved some single experience which we could match in talk with some part of his, but the older we grew and the more we learned, the deeper grew our respect.

This old man was practically indestructible. When he was seventy he decided I should have a real taste of Canadian-style duck-hunting in a canoe. He put me in the bow and took me up-river. With age he had shrunken very slightly, a light, slender man with no great appearance of strength about him. I knew he was good, but I did not expect the force of his final twist of the paddle at each stroke, the feel of the canoe leaping and turning under his hand, all in nearly perfect silence. The loudest sound, I think, was the fall of drops off his paddle as he reached forward. Coming back downriver I took bow paddle. He was nice about it, but the plain fact was that I was nowhere near man enough to make an adequate mate for his stern paddle.

It was about that time that the depression liquidated his architectural practice. It took some persuading to talk him out of starting over again from scratch. He had no intention of becoming idle and quickly found new uses for his skill and reputation.

It would not be quite true to say that he laughed off his first heart attack, but it did not stop him from travelling through Europe on a fellowship. The second one laid him low. He had fished that spring, killed his duck in the fall, then suddenly he was imprisoned in a small room with a good view over the bay. After months he would be allowed to walk about that floor, after yet longer he might be free to go downstairs, carefully.

For more than a year we visited with him in the room. Each of us received the same impression. Neither self-deceived nor a coward, he was visibly making himself ready for death. He let go, one by one, of minor interests and particularly of those, such as improvements in the place, which could be considered only in terms of years from now. He kept up those which were rewarding in themselves and out of them made himself a lively life. He entertained himself with us.

I still do not know if there is a smell of death. There was something in that room which had the emotional effect of a smell, one felt the presence of the old skull and bones. To him it must have been perched on the foot of the bed. It might come in ten minutes and it might not come for a year or more, there was no way of knowing. It could come quietly, instantly, or it could strike as a searing, unbearable pain in the full fury of a heart attack. None of this could be foreseen. It simply was always there, waiting. And he knew it.

In its presence he sat up radiating his great personal charm and his warmth at its most perfect. With me he talked intimately about my writing, following my ideas and endeavours with great interest, and endlessly we shared the tribes we knew in common or matched this odd thing about Guatemala with that of Canada. He was a very easy man to talk to. He offered the wisdom of his many years and at the same time he made himself contemporary.

When we came in from the river or the marshes we went to his room and gave him a blow-by-blow account. I started fishing at the big ben and put on a Queen of the Waters and a Whirling Dun. That big bastard was feeding under the log at the back of the bend, he rose to the Queen a couple of times but wouldn't touch it. The marsh marigolds were beautiful and there were some lady-slippers out. At the log below the reach there was a good one feeding. He took the Dun almost as soon as it hit the water, here he is. . . .

My father would listen, smiling, alert. At a lost fish or a missed shot he would exclaim with the same disgust as he had in the field, a success would give him the same pleasure. When he detected a flaw in technique he would advise as he always did.

Never, at any time, did he protest at being cooped up in that room. None of us, nor my mother, heard him pity himself for that, not even when we were on the marsh with a fine sou'wester blowing. He would damn the cook for a flavourless soup, row with my mother for ordering food he didn't care for, in ten minutes he could cure visitors he didn't like of coming to sit with him, when his vitality was up he could raise particular hell over small things. But he never complained about the big one, and whatever fear sat on him, he never referred to it.

The fear was there along with the courage to handle it. Death was in the room. You could not be there long and not know that. Coming down for the week-end and entering the room you were aware of it, it was oppressive and it filled you with wonder at this man. Then he made you forget it, and to the degree that you forgot it you recognized it again after you had gone. The memory of that time is made up of his warmth, wide-ranging talk, laughter, his quick response, and that eternal presence. The two elements were in balance with each other, one could not separate them.

He had a shelf outside his window on which he put feed for the birds. Some of them were becoming very tame. There was a rat which came up the grapevine onto the porch roof at sundown and raided the feed. He had also killed a bird. My father wanted to get him. How about laying for him with the twenty-eight?

I took the little shotgun down from the shelf by the door. There were shells in his bureau. I mounted the gun and loaded it. Now we were back in our private world. It was dusk and the rat would come soon.

'Quiet, Inky. Sit here on the bed. He's smart, if you move he'll spot you.'

The old voice, a whisper which you felt rather than heard and yet had the hunting timbre in it. The half smile and the lively eyes. We were hunting, sitting there in the growing darkness, he in the bed, I on it, waiting for a rat to show up. Hunting — my mind was divided, feeling his pleasure and thinking of the geese and duck coming in a howling snow-storm, of the big-horn and the moose and the mountain lion and the feats of skill and endurance. Hunting.

'Here he comes.'

You didn't need to understand the words, you knew the all-but-inaudible, thrilling tone since you first crouched in a blind with him and the V of duck showed in the sky. Raising the gun and the click of the safety was too much, the rat fled back down the vine.

'Shah!' It was what he always said, and he made an adequate curse out of it. 'They're so quick.'

'We'll try again tomorrow evening.'

I put the gun away and we went on with normal talk, but I was glad when I was called for supper. I needed time to cope with my sense of the pathetic.

His funeral was on the day before the season opened. That evening we spoke to my mother, and we all agreed that he would be most upset if we missed the opening day on his account. So the three of us went out and hunted for him. We felt tired, lax, and curiously peaceful. There was a great closeness to him in doing this, and none of us referred to him while we were out. We worked unusually carefully, and we had good luck. When my mother saw our bag, as many black duck as we had use for, she said:

'Oh, boys, your father would be so pleased.'

In a sense I have hunted with him ever since and discussed the problems that arose with him. Often I talk to him in Spanish, a language he loved and which was one of our common interests. Then he is the man of the first thirty-five years of my life, the woodsman who could always walk me groggy. At other times it occasionally happens that I think about my own death, and pray that it will be sudden. And if it comes slowly I wonder and doubt if I could turn the old skeleton into a mere visitor sitting to one side while I entertained myself by fascinating my friends.

CHAPTER 5

Escape Within Me

In trying to pick out and expose the multiple threads which were laid together to make a sort of a man, one can follow the usual novelist's method of taking the finished product, or the man in one of his key moments of transition, and describing him very fully over a relatively brief period. By detailed exposition of all the effects, a cross-section of the cord, one then infers the whole backward reach of the strands. The alternative method, which is unavoidable here, is to go back to the beginning, or near the beginning, of each one and follow it up. This means that for a few chapters yet it is going to be necessary for me to start at Groton. There must have been a lot of other influences. The all-important ones of my home, and especially of my mother, it is almost impossible for me to analyze, because they begin so early and were so taken for granted that I used to be quite unconscious of them, and even now I can perceive them only in spots. Then, too, one is always more aware of the hurtful or painful than one is of the helpful. The comfortable shoe that supports one's foot and enables one to walk far is forgotten even while it is on the foot; the one that pinches and distorts is constantly in mind.

Discomfort can become so habitual that one hardly notices it until there comes the intense relief of its ending. In one of his stories, Robert Benchley describes a pageant in which the pleasures of mankind were portrayed. Among them, along with the usual list, he includes a pleasant-looking, plump, middle-aged woman representing the Pleasure of Taking off Tight Shoes. It may be that part of the motivation of this book is a celebration of that pleasure. However that may be, Groton must come in some more. That long unhappiness had too many effects.

I had discovered day-dreaming before I went there, and it was partly something my mother said once about telling one's self stories that channelled it into the form of the told story in the narrative past. Being at that time pretty well satisfied with the world around me, these stories became primarily the exploration of a new, delightful faculty. I was anxious to inflict them on my brother. They gave me a feeling of power, of making something. I didn't need to escape, and I tended to lay them in the present and close to home.

By the time I had become Bop at Groton, I was steeped in the sense of failure in being I have described, I was unutterably lonely, thoroughly unhappy, and escape I needed desperately. The School was not geared to provide much. There were books, and a truly rich library. But a little boy's time was pretty well mapped out and the hours he could spend in there were sharply limited. Nowhere else through the day was there any approach to privacy. We dressed together, washed together, ate together. To walk alone to Chapel or the Schoolhouse, or to walk alone on Sunday, was to brand one's self as very queer (I'm not sure that Sunday walking alone was allowed) and to advertise to the world that one had reached an almost unimaginable abyss of unpopularity. In my Form, two of the most successful boys made it their business to invite the unfortunates at the bottom to walk with them, thus saving them from final shame. In my Third Form year, after my younger brother had come to school and got his bearings, he made it his rule always to walk with me. For brothers, that was possible even though they were in different Forms. It was a heroic thing for him to have done and to have kept up without failure and without comment for four years, and one for which I am eternally grateful.

But as to privacy — it was forbidden to enter the dormitories save when going to bed, getting up, or getting ready for meals, when everyone else was there. We did not have studies until Fifth Form year, then most of us were paired, and not according to our own choices. The water-closets were partitioned off from each other, but they had no doors. One could get fragments of a sense of being alone by sticking one's head inside his desk or locker, but only for a moment. In a story I have described this as feeling like pressing a bit of cold metal against a burn. It did.

Solitude was a priceless thing; the more unhappy and disliked one was, the more priceless. It was genuinely dangerous to day-dream in public. The sight of a completely absorbed face was tempting to the other boys, and the good day-dreamer, who forgets where he is, may take a wrong turning as he walks or make some other gaffe which will bring the pack down on him in howling delight.

But there was night, after the lights were out. The law of the Medes and the Persians direly forbade any boy to enter another's cubicle, and few ever dared to try it. There was a curtain across the doorway. As far as the eye was concerned, one was alone.

Then, bit by bit, the whole being can relax from the constant tension of the day. It becomes possible then in the mind to be loyal to family beliefs and customs that one has denied, like Peter, in public, to indulge the fading remnants of one's perception of truth. But those things are in effect a prolongation of the long struggle, and one wants surcease. Then day-dreams are the answer.

They quickly changed character for me. The desire to tell them to someone disappeared, and with it the feeling of creative power. This was escape, pure and simple. I did not keep on for long with dreams of athletic prowess, prominence, success, but turned entirely away from School to the remotest and most distant subjects. As far as preparation for a writer's career was concerned, I had taken an important wrong turning.

One subject came early into the dreams, a subject on which the whole School was united — the First World War. We were, of course, Anglomaniacs, and as far as we were concerned the war was a clear-cut matter of a crusade between Galahads and Huns. We ate our atrocity stories whole, and we quite literally worshipped the Allies. I remember only one master who tried to give us a little balance — Guy Ayrault, a splendid history teacher. He wanted us to remember that there were good things in German culture, he wanted us to have some faint perception of weaknesses, even faults, among the Allies, I think he tried to prepare us for the shock the post-war realities were going to give us. All he got for his pains was the label of pro-German, which was a deadly insult. We were going into the war as one man, if possible in the English Army, we trained and studied for it. The men in the war were heroes purified by fire; we, too, should join them, we would gladly die, or if we lived we should in the end be part of that ennobled army which was to remake the world.

The whole generosity and fire of adolescence had been enlisted and allowed to run wild, resulting in some nasty, souring shocks later. Doctor Peabody held to a very excellent policy of preventing, as much as was humanly possible, the sexual-religious confusions which might be expected in a Church School full of healthy adolescents, but I don't think he realized how readily the same thing could be attached to the war instead.

For me, the war came into the day-dreams in a big way. It stood at the end of School like a fixed star. Give me a subaltern's pip or a second lieutenant's bar and I should cease to be Bop, the failure in being would be wiped out, I should be changed and newborn.

The nights came, and I slipped into the haven of bed. Bed and sleep acquired a new significance, a new preciousness, for here was surcease and escape. I have noticed ever since that when things are going badly and I am unhappy or worried, my capacity for sleep increases and I can't seem to get enough of it. Secure in the dark, I built my dreams, in warmth and rest and comfort, dreams of war and glory, of home, of pure fantasy. Girls began to come into them, the new curiosity of sex, a little talk picked up here and there of the pleasures of Paris in which even heroes, apparently, might indulge. So the sexual day-dream started.

This was a yet more complete means of escape than any I had ever known. It caught up the whole mind and the emotions, it completely enfolded the dreamer in a fantasy that could not possibly be farther removed from life around him. Nor did it take a boy of fourteen long to discover that he could implement his fantasy with an action which brought the whole thing extraordinarily close to realization. There was that dream, and thrill, and the miraculous release, a new sweetness of relaxation followed by a certainty of deep sleep. There was heartburning, fear, and shame, and a long, violent struggle with one's self, made, not easier, but more difficult, by superstitious beliefs and by the feeling that this foul act set me off yet further from my fellows. There were periods of something that I named to myself as 'diabolism,' the belief that I was utterly vile, destined only to vileness, that therefore it was inevitable and right for me to do the vilest things. The situation was not aided by the fact that the other boys found me out and let me know it. It never occurred to me that any of them might also be guilty: I thought I was unique.

The idea that sexual activity can be an escape mechanism is a new one to me. It's only since I became able to think back to Groton days with a little detachment that I've seen it. I wonder how much it is recognized. To me it seems important, and I know beyond the shadow of a doubt, that not hard exercise, hard mattresses, cold air, or any of those things, but happiness and a feeling of success enable a man to be continent.

Of course this development yet further distorts one's approach to the whole matter of love and love-making. Any New Englander, even from comparatively liberal Rhode Island, graduated from a New England church school, may be expected to approach love-making with reservations of shame and of a formalized morality which is not so much hostile to the act itself as it is to any kind of complete release and surrender to sensation, but he is yet worse off when he has added to this a special sense of the vileness of his own indulgence, and has, unwittingly, associated sexual pleasure with escape from reality.

Here is a character-situation which is material for fictional treatment, and could be developed without offending reasonable taboos. I have already described the curious perversion of the Groton Boy complex after I had become a man associating with men of action and artists, which made me see relations with women, not as a thing existing in and for itself and myself and to be approached with simplicity according to my own deep desires, but as another quest in that hopeless effort to compensate by doing, by recording achievement, for a failure in being. Add the development described here, and you have a man essentially unfitted for a sound relation with any woman.

A man grown up, especially one who has a talent for loneliness, feels increasingly not merely the desire for fun in bed, but for a complement and companion in the other sex. The Indians among whom I have lived always felt rather sorry for me when I was a bachelor. This was not because they felt that I lacked for gratifications, but because to them an adult, single man was incomplete. Their sense of this rounding out of an individual by marriage is very deep and, I think, partly explains the great harmony prevailing in their homes. When I appeared among them married, those who cared for me manifested their pleasure, and I could see that I entered into a closer relationship with them. Indians are conscious of this; we all have it instinctively. It is the foundation of real love and a true relationship. It does not exclude or minimize the act of passion, but deepens it and makes it greater by setting it into its context. So long as I remained an escapist and my war with myself continued, this fundament of life was closed to me. I do not think I was unique.

I realize that in these two complaining chapters I have made a terrific attack against my old School; I have blamed it for wrecking my life at its core, so thoroughly that it is a miracle if, in my late thirties, aided by change, misfortune, and the blessing of great friendships, I have been able to equip myself with a passable juryrig. I must record that I am fully aware, and mean in every way to have it understood, that this wrecking was achieved, not by Groton alone, but by close collaboration between Groton and myself.

How much by myself? Someone else than I must determine that; I can't. A document on the subject exists in the chances I had to recover, of which I failed to take advantage. Harvard was release and great happiness. There I knew success, prominence, my first true friendships, and real joy of the mind, but I seem to have had no good of it in this sense. From Harvard chance took me out of the normal circle of my kind, to live in New Orleans and in Latin America. I entered settings which were the complete antithesis of everything that I claim distorted me. And I remained distorted.

As a matter of fact, I nearly got cured during that period when I was a free man making his own way in a free world — but not quite. The well-trained horse comes docilely to be saddled. Out on pasture, he may make a little play of escaping but he expects the rope to catch him. He believes that he likes his burden. I thought I was in New Orleans and poor and struggling only because fate had forced me to be there, and as soon as success and money came my way, I made a beeline for the expected life of a Groton graduate. With this I became entirely surrounded by the established projection into adult life of the standards and ideas of the New England private schools and their relatives, and I backslid with great speed into the being who had finally made at least a three-quarters adaptation of himself to Groton. I dressed very correctly, and I persuaded myself that cocktails were a barbarous, American device and that of course I preferred a spot of dry sherry before meals. I made the final, complete capitulation of exploiting the achievement which should have set me free, to turn myself at last into a really successful Groton boy. To top the whole thing, I attained the almost incredible dishonesty of registering my son for Groton as soon as he was born.

How much was myself, and how much was those six years of moulding, abetted by Harvard and polite society? I know that during those years of fat prosperity I was constantly doing things (some of which surprised me, and some of which made me ashamed) in violent conflict with the way of life I had chosen. For a moment my writing faltered, but only for a moment, thank God, and out of it from time to time emerged statements that my choice was wrong which I myself failed to recognize. All the time that I was so happy over my attainment of the ambitions implanted in me, I drank much too much.

So there's the evidence. I'm not particularly interested in an accurate distribution of blame. Quite likely Groton was not an instrument, but merely the setting of my troubles. The interest lies in a character, the anatomy of an escapist who was more than anything else in flight from the dreadful implications of his inability to achieve what he had been taught to believe was success, and in the curious fact that when by his own endeavours he suddenly was able to have all of that, not only did not really want it, and was nearly destroyed by it, but had the idea of *failure in being* so deeply implanted in him that even if he had wanted it, he could never have allowed himself to enjoy it.

CHAPTER 6

The Eight-Oared Shell

I WONDER why there has been so little that could be called literature written about games. There has been some good, standard writing about them — Dorothy Sayers in *Murder Must Advertise* astounded me by making a cricket match interesting — but offhand I can't think of any first-rate writers save Homer, Virgil (who didn't do so well), Hemingway, and Sir Thomas Malory who have really cut loose on games. Yet they can be passionate, beautiful, and fine material.

Personally I prefer the sports, properly so-called, the activities deriving from the closely related occupations of primitive travel, seafaring, and hunting. Most writers seem to feel the same way. Perhaps they lend themselves more readily to our purposes because the line between the sports and the ancient, deadly earnest business is so dim. You can get just as thoroughly drowned cruising off Nantucket for pleasure as you can navigating a shipload of merchandise, but it is also possible for a boy literally to die for Dear Old Podunk, and what's more to do it willingly, which seems to me to be something writers should want to investigate.

A boy's athletics are set against a powerful emotional background. Perhaps one of the reasons that good writers have failed to exploit them is that they have begun with the adult's common habit of forgetting what they were like when they were boys; they substitute for memory the accepted folk-picture of shallow, standard emotions, and by thus depriving the game of the furious background which gives it depth destroy its values and its interest.

High-jumping has its own values and attributes, and ran a curious course for me. My elder brother, who had been school champion in his time, put me up to trying it and gave me some instruction in my Fourth Form year, when in my own mind I was still the hopelessly clumsy, flopping Bop I have described. As I said before, practising went on under great difficulties, but there were times when I was able to do it in peace, there was the Physical Director's encouragement, the dawning discovery that I could move well and precisely, and finally the comment of a few of my classmates that I was pretty darned graceful going over the bar. It was the conquest of my limbs, the consciousness of having brought my body into order, and the fulfilling pleasure of performing, over and over again, a complex, beautiful action made all the more thrilling because it had some of the quality of flight. A really good high-jumper performs excellently well and to its extreme a single one of the many evolutions of a dancer — look at a slow-motion picture and you will see it. If he has any temperament at all he is bound to get satisfaction from the act.

But as I grew older and came up against ever stiffer competition my own temperament entangled me. Regardless of medals and the fact that I had found a gift by which I might even conceivably reach that impossible pinnacle of winning my H, I came to loathe the game. It was perfectly unsuited to me.

At the instant of jumping one unleashes his strength in a powerful kick and follows it with a further, disciplined effort as he rises. For one half second the jumper exerts the force that is in him. The rest of the time he either waits, or moves gently. This is worse than baseball.

I am left-footed. My take-off was exactly planned. From a little distance back of my first mark I trotted forward, at the mark I put my foot down precisely, then ran quickly, but not hard, for seventeen steps which should bring my left foot down at a fixed spot in front of one end of the bar. For an instant I turned myself loose. We assume that I cleared the bar. I trotted back to the starting point, put a sweater round my shoulders, and waited for my turn to come again. While I waited I watched the others and mentally jumped with each one. Anyone who failed to clear the bar in his three tries was a load off my mind but there were always some who did it easily. By this time ten minutes had elapsed, seeming like an hour. I was no longer warm, I pranced around to get my legs loosened up, the man ahead of me jumped, failed, jumped again, made it, and here I was again facing the thing once more but this time the bar would be two inches higher.

Again I keyed myself up, intensely conscious of a watching audience now centred upon me alone, at Harvard even more painfully conscious of being one of a team and therefore responsible to others, something quite different from individual competition for a medal. If I was sufficiently strung up the chances were ten to one that I would put my jumping foot down too far from the bar, for all my prepared take-off, that before I crossed it I would be well above it, and would hit it as I came diagonally to earth. I would clear it on my second try, and feel like a fool.

Now the bar reaches five feet, where I am no longer sure of myself, and the agony is intensified. I know perfectly well that the highest point of my jump is almost always well above that, but that's not enough. Over-eagerness will send me into the air too soon. Despairingly I must make myself go easy and still give everything I have in the one split second. It reaches five feet two, a modest height in fact. The waiting is torture, standing ready to jump is an agony. It would be a great relief to drop out, to knock the bar off three times and have done with this wretched business, but you can't do that.

I've never had an opportunity to ask any high-jumper who stayed with it and became Varsity material to what extent he suffered from my tremors. None of them seemed to. But nothing I can remember that was supposedly undertaken for pleasure was ever as profoundly disagreeable as this business of key-up, let-down, wait, key-up, let-down, wait.

I don't see how a good story could be written solely about high-jumping, or about any game for that matter, but if and when writers ever decide to do an honest job of exploiting the rich material lying in the transition from boy to man (not the sensitive-little-boy story, which has been pretty well handled a few times, nor the Tom Brown-cum-Stalky stuff, but the real, universal story) I can see how jumping could be made important for the main character and some pretty good things be done with it.

The games I wanted were those in which a boy could spend himself utterly, the games of violence, and I found my satisfaction in football and rowing. For that I suppose I owe a debt to jumping which gave me the narrow margin of confidence needed to try for the greater games.

I'll die for Dear Old Podunk. It isn't entirely tripe, certainly not in a preparatory school. Football is violent, in its periods of action it is the use of everything you have to the limit of your capacity directly against the bodies of your opponents. For the linemen it is pure physical conflict, formalized, disciplined to serve an objective, but nonetheless violent, and it is comradeship. These are strong things, part of the juice of life, they reach into the very origins of man. Call them forth, add the pure singlemindedness of your schoolboy, and you get something between ecstasy and a crusade.

We were constantly told, English style, to play the game for the game's sake, not for winning. I don't know if the English really achieve this or not. We were Americans. We wanted passionately to win, but the winning would have been null and void, it would have carried all the emotions of defeat, had it been done by cheating or any unfairness. As to dying, actually it's not usual for anyone to be killed in schoolboy football and we didn't think about it much, but we certainly were prepared to be severely injured.

In Sixth Form year with the final, Saint Mark's game looming ahead and the distraction of the war removed, these emotional sources were brimming high. We must win the Saint Mark's game or live out our lives under a cloud. If you had asked us who won in 1911 or in 1896 we couldn't have told you, but as far as we were concerned the results of our game would be eternal. Next spring we would die and be born again as college men but that meant no more to us than the rewards after death mean to the average man at his full strength; our life was in the School and it was drawing to a close but before it ended there was its climax in the Saint Mark's game.

Football drew me into one of those intense friendships that belonged to my age. In my Form was Jones who was a good deal of a poet, with ambitions to be a writer, and plenty of sensitivity. He outgrew these things, unfortunately, but at that time he and I saw alike and reacted with equal violence. Jones was first substitute quarterback, I was first substitute tackle, and both of us were too light for our positions. We had to make up by sheer ferocity and attack what God had failed to give us in flesh and bone, and both of us were doing pretty well at it. We became allies in our common goal of winning our letters and winning for Groton, an alliance based primarily on our ability to tell each other what we really felt, for under the School code the expression of such emotionalism would have been dangerous. We were pretty sure that most of the rest of the Form who were on the team felt as we did, and I suppose that in pairs and groups according to their loves they expressed themselves in their own terms. Ours were blended with my adoration of Keats and his of Shelley, with what we were getting out of the *Iliad*, with all our feeling about writing and about life.

He was convinced he could never be anything more than a very minor poet, I that I could never really get anywhere in fiction. This seemed related to the fact that we were substitutes, that we very well might not get in The Game, and writing and life and game and friendship united in a common understanding that we would spend ourselves without limit, beyond all limits, a mutually understood dedication which was perfectly genuine however ridiculous it may seem now.

People, including writers, smile at these young exaggerations but the boys do not; that this high state is transitory is no more important than is the brief duration of intense pain or fear under special circumstances in later life. While these emotions last, they are dominant, complete, and as deep as anything that is felt later. For many people these are the only real emotions they will ever feel, this is the end of their time for being truly open to deep devotions which overwhelm the thought of self — which is why a group of boys or girls always seems so much more *promising* than what they eventually will become would justify. The great unhappiness of many boys at school derives partly from this same intensity and lack of perspective, so does the extreme courage and devotion of boys taken immediately from schools into armies, the seventeen- and eighteen-year-olds who fight like hell and die like heroes.

There is nothing that graduates forget quicker. The universal flight from it has prevented this remarkable part of everyone's life from being the subject of great writing. We knew that they forget, for we were constantly exposed to fatuous graduates who talked to us through the veil of their glossing folk-memory and thought they were speaking with inward understanding of where we stood.

Doctor Peabody, we felt, understood us, but the graduates made us sick.

In schools like Groton, Sixth Formers take their position very seriously. This is one of the best things about that semi-English system. It may be tainted with a Kiplingesque Sahib complex, but it carries with it a real sense of responsibility and a duty to the commonwealth exceeding personal inclination. This, too, fed the stream of our mounting feeling as the football season wore on. A recent graduate and former football captain came up to give us a pep talk, big with his Varsity status and bringing with him the unpleasant habits of College coaches between the halves. Good Lord, how fast he had forgotten in a few years! In language which to us was revoltingly foul he heaped insult upon us, attacking the core of our beings, our sincerity, our will to fight. The whole technique of insult and emotion is old stuff on Varsity teams, but we had never heard anything like it, and it was not at all what we needed. He aimed to get us fighting mad — he did, at himself. We who ate, slept, and breathed the Saint Mark's game threw out any application to ourselves of what he said, feeling simply that his mind had become corrupt.

Jones and I talked it over hotly, and we swore then that we would remember, we would engrave in our memories what we really believed and felt while we were in School; however much we might change we would remember that we had changed and what we had been, and we would not return some day, fatuous and lying, to sicken the boys who came after us. That particular graduate did me a favour, putting me in a habit to which I have kept ever since of marking down what I was feeling and thinking in a given state of evolution and, when my turn came to talk or write about it, to the best of my capacity throwing myself back to that past self, rather than recording the external, easy memory of acts performed with the changed emotional interpretation natural to the different man I had become.

I start writing about football and am carried off to a complex of surrounding emotions; they are the essence of it. One follows the emotions more easily in the quiet moments off the field but they continued into the game. Unfortunately, the career of a substitute tackle does not provide much dramatic action; it is too monotonous and inconspicuous.

The game against the Harvard Second Freshmen sticks in my mind. We were a Harvard school, we knew what Harvard Freshmen were — the boys from the Form immediately ahead of us, our own kind, familiar, but grown in stature. It wasn't a featured game but the team took it seriously.

Because I was so light I was kept on the bench. The Freshmen outweighed us considerably, and we soon became aware of a surprising thing — these weren't the newly graduated private school boys of our acquaintance, these were a bunch of toughs. Actually, for all I know they may every one of them have come from Saint Paul's, Saint Mark's, and the rest, but for the first time were facing the sportless grimness of college football, something diametrically opposed to our crusading devotion.

For the greater part of the game I watched Harvard push our line around. They got a lead on us, not a very big one. One regular right tackle was taken out, worn out or slightly injured. The coach looked past me and picked another boy, younger but big, as heavy and hefty actually as the Harvard lineman but not yet well-knit. Size had it. I watched him go in.

I saw right away that he didn't know how to get low to the ground. I watched his arms swinging, I watched his stance, and I knew that he was literally a pushover, but there was no way on God's earth that I could, under our code, tell that to the coach, then or later. The Harvard quarterback threw a play through him, I saw his opponents catch him underneath and turn him over backwards and the play went through for a nice gain. So they did it again, and a third time, then shifted to the other side of the line, and then came back and did it again.

By this time I was in a quiet agony. It was fairly late in the game, it would be a bad omen if I didn't get in at all, and I knew I could do better than that even if only a little. At last, at last, the coach sent me in. I was perfectly conscious of weighing only a hundred and fifty pounds, I knew very well that I must look like a humourous mistake to the other team. I knew that I had a God-sent chance to show that it was possible to make up for lack of weight by other factors, and I knew that the coach would not have put me in if there had been any other alternative.

Now I was facing those big men. Lord, what a difference a year or so can make! The stubble of their chins, the formation of their mouths, their hard expressions had an authority and ruthlessness which made one feel like giving up, like being careful not to provoke them. And I had never seen so huge a line. They towered.

I was loose-jointed, supple, a good tumbler. I had made getting low my special art. The only earthly hope I had was to work around these men's ankles, and I did it.

Everything is quite clear up to when that first play came at me. I was frightened of these men. I remember just how my opposite number glared at me, his contemptuous muttering of threats, and that there was miscellaneous cursing in the talk of the College men as they got set. From there on I know only that I caused a lot of men to fall on top of me, I discovered that being charged by a College man was no more painful than being charged by anyone else, and that on the whole I held my end up all right. I could hardly give any more detail about most of the games I was in. But when I was playing I was indescribably happy; absorbed in violence, my troubles were forgotten.

As I write about it and in so doing recapture increasingly that past state, I realize that in fact, by the time we came onto the field for the Saint Mark's game, I would have died for dear old Groton unhesitatingly. I don't mean a boy's fantasy of being desperately injured and carried off the field to a comfortable heroism, but that if by some miracle it had been given me to make a winning touchdown at the price of my life, I'd have gone ahead and done it. So would the others. Actually, my contribution was to sit in mounting agony on the bench on a cold, blowy day, watching an uninspired game with Saint Mark's in the lead, and the ball moving to and fro across a narrow range in our territory, with a great deal of kicking. It was a game without brilliance or breaks, an increasing ache of desperation.

On the benches we watched it minutely, detailing every play, what went wrong, what worked, and why. Our coach was chary of substitutions, but at last, in the second half, left tackle was replaced, and shortly afterwards Jones went in as quarterback. I was truly glad of that, but meantime I stayed on the bench.

When I had been in the Lower School it had seemed to me that it would be an ample achievement to make the Second Team some day and wear its black jersey. Even up to my Fifth Form year earning the convict-striped jersey of the First Team had seemed ample;

a chance at my letter was beyond my dreams. I had my striped jersey all right, I'd been in every game of the season, and I was fully aware of what it would mean to me, Bop, to win my letter and be one with the immortals, the godlike men who had worn that sweater when I was a First Former. But right tackle was doing well, and it was not for the good of the School that he be taken out. Through the dragging quarters of the game I wrestled between my ambition and my devotion. Dick must stay in, they needed him in there. I must want him in, if I didn't, I was a traitor. He was limping a little; after one play, he turned and walked, testingly, in a circle behind the line. My heart jumped up and then I took hold of myself. I made a sincere, silent prayer that he be all right. Some other miracle must make it possible and beneficial for me to go in.

I claim that the school that can teach boys to think like that has no little virtue.

The coach called to me. In a white excitement which actually caused the colours of what I saw to become faded, I crouched beside him.

'I may send you in in a moment. If they don't kick the first play after you go in, tell Jones to try a long run around left end. Do you understand?'

'Yes, sir.'

I did not. I was incapable of understanding words.

'Repeat what I said.'

'If they don't kick the first play after you go in, tell Jones to try a long run around left end.' Like that. It was not until the game was over that I figured out what he meant.

They kicked that play. He told me never mind about the message. Then he sent me in.

You are not allowed to speak to anyone until one play after you go in, but your team slaps you on the back, welcomes you, tells you to come on, let's break it up. Some of them called me 'Bop,' one or two used the rare 'Laf' which always made me feel good. The Saint Mark's quarterback began to call signals and I took my place.

Now I knew what I was doing, I was at home, on the defensive facing boys my own age and only reasonably bigger than I. I had learned something from that Freshman line, it had increased my toughness. The boys opposite me looked mild in comparison. A couple of games before somebody had stepped on my face and his cleats had scratched it magnificently; I believed I looked ferocious and I capitalized on this, swinging my arms and looking my opposite number in the eye with the grim contempt I had learned from the Freshmen. I don't know whether I had any effect or not. But I can testify that I was at that moment a sort of explosive charge all ready to go off.

I expected them to throw a play at me and they did, skin-tackle, and the end and I stopped it dead. Their next play was around their right end, and I remember the details of my part of it better than any other of my career. I sideswiped the opposing tackle with my open hand and bowled him over, and found myself behind the line going full tilt. There ahead of me, to my left, the Saint Mark's interference was running close to the line of scrimmage, behind them was the runner with the ball — unprotected from me, but an impossible distance away. It seems to have taken place at great leisure and either standing still or in slow motion. I told myself, heart-sinking, that I couldn't do it; not I, Bop, could catch that man for the glory of a tackle behind the line. It was no use. The next thing I knew I was floating through the air, and the next I had thrown him for a handsome loss. There was that strange, comfortable sensation of a good tackle, finding oneself sprawled on the ground and hugging a pair of padded knees, and triumph, and the team pounding me on the back, and an intense surprise at myself. What I had done I had done in entire despite of my own conscious decision.

This has happened to me a few times since. If I'm sufficiently keyed up there wakens in me something with a little more courage and more effectiveness than my normal, organized self, and I do something which I have just realized I cannot do.

That spring Jones and I made a solemn compact to take elementary Greek and to go out for football at Harvard. The point of the elementary Greek was that we had studied under one of those unfortunate, depressing men against whom a class of boys can hardly help ganging up, and as a result we had learned almost nothing. We could hardly conjugate $\dot{\epsilon}\beta\epsilon\iota\nu$. But we received credit for Greek in entering Harvard, so that if we took Greek A it would not count towards our degrees. As for football, we both knew that we were much too small to get anywhere at college, but we adored the game, and we agreed to be unsung worshippers together.

We released each other from the Greek part of the pledge as soon as we reached Harvard, for Greek A that year was being taught by the self-same teacher who had bored us so at Groton! As for football, my part ended quickly. For a boy of my weight to go out for tackle was prominently absurd, but I could face that; what sickened me was the coach, not so much his foul language as his foul attitude, the complete absence of love of the game, of anything but an ugly, snarling training of slaves to win — or so it seemed to me, fresh from Groton. To my intense relief I sustained a complicated shoulder injury which still hurts occasionally, and retired to leisure with my arm in a sling.

When my shoulder healed I went out for rowing — fearfully, for perhaps that dearest sport, too, was fouled and uglified at college and the coach would ask us for Chrissake what kind of a bunch of pimps we thought we was anyhow. Five minutes after I took my place on one of the machines I met Bert Haynes; in a day, like hundreds of other Harvard men, I adored him. I had no further thought of football.

I took up rowing through a series of accidents, chief among which were the fact that Groton was one of the very few preparatory schools to have crews, that I was a duffer at baseball and hated it, and that Harry Morgan, who was captain in my Fifth Form year, asked me one winter's afternoon what sport I was going after in the spring. I told him high-jumping. He remarked that that wasn't much of an occupation, I should come out for rowing. I was astonished for I had never pulled an oar save in skiffs on Narragansett Bay and I still held firmly to my picture of my weedy, gawky self, the weakling with eyeglasses who had achieved, not strength, but the skill to manipulate his limbs over a bar. As a matter of fact, he was short-handed. He told me I could have a place on the second crew.

All this, remember, was the year before my football climax. It must have been the year in which I solidified my growth. The photograph of my crew taken that spring shows that as a matter of fact I shaped up pretty well, and I suppose that influenced Morgan, but I don't know why he gave me that vacancy on the second crew instead of promoting one of the men from the third (a four; there weren't enough candidates that year to make a third eight).

It took me a few days on the rowing machine to be broken of the habits one forms rowing fisherman's style in skiffs, then apparently I caught on fast. When one has never been in a shell, the practice on the machines seems stupid, a pure grind. The more one knows about rowing, the less this is so. I worked away in the second eight, very pleased to be there and much afraid that I should be dropped to the third four. Then one day someone on the first crew fell ill and I was taken up. I was delighted but assumed that this was temporary.

I don't remember now whom I replaced. But when the warmer weather came and the ice went out of the river, it was in the first boat that for the first time in my life I laid my hands on the loom of one of those grand, long, racing sweeps. By a month later I realized that in fact I was on the first crew, not just subbing but on it, and that barring disaster I should have earned my letter by the end of my Fifth Form year. Rowing was the third major sport; it ranked below baseball and football, but it was major and it carried a letter, and here I was in on it. The thing had come gently; an oarsman is fairly sure of his place in advance of the final race although upsets do happen; you grow without half realizing it into the assurance that you know how to row and pull your weight in the boat. By gentle stages I became good, by school standards, in a major sport, gradually I was knit with the other seven oarsmen and the coxswain in the union of a crew. Without anything dramatic happening I became an Athlete, a Letter Man, I acquired Face.

More than that, I discovered rowing. For most of us there is no hope whatever of continuing after we have left college, but the love of it remains. A few weeks ago I met a Yale man who had rowed there while I was at Harvard. I don't remember how the subject came up, but we began talking about it, then we drew away from the rest of the party and lovingly, happily, rowed over our whiskeys until our wives dragged us home. This has happened to me many times. No writer has told the nature of rowing in an eight-oared shell to landsmen, none who haven't rowed understand what it is we remember, the crash of the oars in the locks, the shell leaping

THE EIGHT-OARED SHELL — 61

at the catch, the unity and rhythm and the desperate effort, so when we meet we babble with joy.

What is the nature of it? To begin with the setting — the green-banked river or the Charles Basin ringed by the city, both are beautiful. The shell swinging through open country on a fine spring day is hard to beat. Down on the Basin the water is oily, in the late afternoon it catches the deepening sunset, after dark the advertising signs over the factories are reflected on it, twisting as if the lights were darting snakes, and the swirl of one's oar is shot with colour. There is the slight excitement and the echoing change of sound in shooting under a bridge, there is the fresh day on the river as you carry your shell down to the float. Rural or urban water, rowing is set in beauty to begin with.

There is the nature of the stroke itself, the most perfect combination I have ever known of skill and the full release of one's power. It takes more than a dumb ox to make a fine oarsman, the traditional 'weak brain and strong back' won't serve. To my mind it begins with the 'recovery,' the forward reach to get ready for a stroke. You are sitting on a slide, a seat on rollers, which runs on a track about two feet long, set variously according to the type of stroke your coach favours. Your two hands are on the loom of your twelve-foot oar, balancing it neatly. If you lower them too far, you sky the blade of your oar and the shift of the centre of gravity will make the boat rock and cost you precious headway; if you raise them too high your oar will touch the waves and you may cause a jolt that will throw the whole boat out of time. So your hands are balancing delicately — next time you see a good crew rowing, watch the oars moving together clear of the water on the recovery, see how narrow that long shell is and realize the miracle of balance that keeps it steady while those big men swing aft and the long sweeps reach forward. Or watch a green crew, see the oars at eight different levels and the shell wallowing from side to side.

You are moving your hands, your shoulders, and your tail aft (you are facing aft) at three different rates, to bring each to its stopping point at the same time. If you rush your slide to the end of its run, that sharp motion and possibly the abrupt stopping at the end will check the motion of the shell (you can see it happen) and you yourself will fall into the position of your maximum effort with a jerk which will put you out of balance. Hands, shoulders, slide, must move *in related time* one to another, and in perfect time with the other seven men, so that at the right moment you are leaning forward just far enough for reach and not too far for power, your slide is all the way aft, your legs and knees are ready, your back is arched, not slumped, and your balancing hands are holding firmly to the oar. In the very last part of your swing your outside hand — the one towards the blade — has turned the oar a quarter circle, so that the blade, which was parallel to the water, is perpendicular to it.

CATCH! A slight raising of your hands and arms has dropped your blade into the water, and instantaneously your shoulders take hold. That simple action is not quite so simple. If you have not done it minutely right your oar may skitter out above the water, slice too deeply into the water to help the boat, or you may catch a crab — entangle your oar in water so that you can't get it out. That last is virtual shipwreck, it may knock you out of the boat, and it will almost certainly lose a race. Once you and seven other men are driving with all your forces it is too late to attempt to turn or guide your oar. You must have dropped it into the water so accurately that it will stay with the blade just submerged all the way through your pull and come out willingly. That is part of the turn of your outside hand and the act of slightly raising your arms. This raising of your arms must be neat; you don't let your oar into the water on a diagonal after you have begun to pull (that is, you don't and stay on a good crew), nor do you succumb to the natural tendency which you will see in any fisherman's rowing, to let your hands dive slightly as you get ready to catch on hard, causing the blade first to rise slightly in the air and then to hit the water with a spanking motion.

An immeasurably short time after your shoulders, your legs start to drive. Now your arms are merely straps attaching your hands to your body, legs and shoulders and back for all they are worth are pulling on the oar, everything you've got is going into it, but you have taken care that your tail, driven by your legs, will not shoot on the slide ahead of your shoulders.

You have driven through almost to the end of the catch, your slide is almost home, your shoulders are back. Now your arms come in, and just as your knees come down locked, your hands touch your stomach. Here is the prettiest part of the stroke, the shoot of the hands to start the recovery. Remember, your oar is still deep in the water rushing powerfully past your boat; if it becomes caught in that, it turns to a wild machine. As your hands touch your belly they drop, shoot out, in a motion 'as fast and smooth as a billiard ball caroming,' at the same time your inside wrist turns and the blade is once more parallel to the water — feathered. The shoot of your hands and arms brings your shoulders forward and you commence your recovery once more.

All of what I have described happens in a single stroke by a good oarsman. This stroke, its predecessors and successors, is performed in a unison with seven other men which is more perfect than merely being in time, with the balance of the body maintained also in relation to the keel so that the boat shall not roll. At a moderate racing rate it is performed thirty-two to thirty-six times to the minute, all of this, nothing omitted, and in a rhythm which keeps the time of the recovery not less than double that of the catch.

This is not the whole of rowing, but it is the basic part of the individual's job in it. Unite it to another fundamental and you can have a crew.

The other fundamental is unison. I have said that a crew does not merely keep time; it does something subtler than that, it becomes one. This it cannot do if there is bad feeling between any of the men in the boat; a single antagonistic personality can keep eight oarsmen accurately following stroke's oar and the coxswain's counting from becoming a crew rowing together. Crews are not made up on a basis of personalities, but according to the coach's estimates of individual capacities, it is after they are rowing together that they become friends. My crews at Harvard contained men with whom I had nothing in common, men by whom I should naturally have been bored or antagonized, and who should have disliked me. As we rowed together we became fond of each other. It had no lasting value, but for the duration of our rowing, we esteemed each other dearly. As this feeling grew, so did our boat shake down and become one, and so did we increasingly care for the foul-mouthed, brilliant little devil who was our cox and in a race the instrument, voice, and control of our unity.

You have three or four years of rowing back of you, and from them the assurance that you are a sound oarsman, a sound waterman, whether or no you are going to be good enough to win a seat in the particular boat you've set your heart on. You have spent a month or so rowing on the machines, indoors, with a tentative crew made up of four or five fellows with whom you rowed last year and some newcomers, all of merit. The ice has gone out of the river, it is raw and cold but tolerable. Today you will take to the water.

This oar is yours. No man but you will handle it from now till the end of the season, barring disaster. (I saw a Princeton crew once whose managers carried the oars down for the men. One hopes it was a rare exception.) You take it from the rack and look it over, a good, spoon blade, not too wide, a sound piece of white ash, the leather in right condition. You ask the manager to roughen the handle for you a little, and watch critically while it is being done, then you take it down to the edge of the float. The others do the same, the cox brings down his rudder and megaphone.

Here is your shell, resting upside down on its rack, a long cigar of wood so thin that it bends readily under your finger, surrounding a skeleton of wood and metal that will stand up under the force you hope to bring forth. This, too, has its attributes and properties, some visible as you look her over, some yet to be learned. You take your places, the cox gives his command. Tenderly you lift her out, she's fragile. Four men on a side you carry her down to the float, and freely curse anyone who gets in your way. (Even those Princeton men carried down their own shell.) At the edge of the float you wait. The cox shouts 'Up!' The shell rises to the height of your arms, and all eight of you are standing under her. Then over — gently now — bending all together you lay her in the water. This tossing a shell is a good ritual in itself, one of the many graces of rowing. It is your first genuine act as a crew together.

You put in the oars, take your places, settle yourselves. There's a lot of arranging and adjusting to be attended to. Then you shove off, and you're out in the stream.

It's months since you've been in a boat. You are nine men who know their business individually, but collectively you hardly exist yet. Suddenly you feel self-conscious, almost afraid. This feeling is as much fear of a foully bad start and an affront to your art as it is of the mechanism of yourself and your oar, but there is a fear, something big is coming which may go wrong, and you are stale....

You all swing forward and the boat does not lurch, a good sign. The cox's voice is familiar, he urges you profanely to get off to a good start in front of those heavyweight bastards who are now coming onto the float, and you feel soothed. You start. The eight oars get in fairly well together, the shell leaps, it keeps running well as you swing for the next stroke, it leaps again. You had forgotten; for all your years of rowing you had forgotten the power of those eight sweeps driven together, the initial leap and run of the boat, the settling down to a smooth, even swing. The power of that first stroke is always astounding, so is the way the oars crash in the locks, and you are going, and you feel like a giant and you want to shout.

These are parts of what the oarsman loves, along with the sunny days and the girls who stand on the bank and stare at the near-naked men (don't think the oarsmen don't spot them), and coming in at night listening to the sounds of other crews and seeing the reflections of the guiding lights under the bridges dripping off your oars, and the increasing sense of strength and competence from day to day, and the growing union with eight other men into something mystical and strong — values of strength, skill, physical beauty perceived, and the spirit. There are all of these in this sport which I loved, as there must be in those beloved of others.

But a boy weighing a hundred and fifty pounds had no future in University rowing. I treated myself to it the fall of my Freshman year as an indulgence, I did well, but I saw that the competition was too stiff for me, and high-jumping offered me a gambler's chance at my H. I went out for Freshman track. I jumped against Andover. I had some future. There was a rumour that Harvard was going to try out these new hundred-and-fifty-pound crews that were having such a success at one or two other colleges.

It was raw, cold, early spring. As I walked over Anderson Bridge I saw the first Freshman eights getting into the river. Some damn fool stepped in the bottom of a shell and put his feet through it. Another boat got away cleanly and started going, rolling a bit but not doing badly. I could hear the cox's commands. Some upperclass eight came downstream from Newell Boathouse and passed right under me; those fellows could row. The coach followed in his launch, megaphone in hand. What he was saying was anciently familiar. After all, what the hell was an H?

I told the track coach I was going out for rowing. He seemed to disapprove, so I told him my family wanted me to. As a matter of fact, my family wanted me to do what I wanted, but I put on an act and lied because he was a pretty decent fellow and I could not face telling him that as far as I was concerned high-jumping was the bunk, and I'd rather row in the lowest crew on the river than win my letter leaping over little sticks. I went down and signed up for rowing, feeling like a man reborn. So it happened that I was in the first hundred-and-fifty-pound crew ever to take the water from Harvard.

I find, in writing about rowing, that I tend to concentrate rather technically upon the sport itself with the attendant danger of losing that very background of its relation to a boy's life which would give it validity. This is partly because the average man who reads this has played football, and many women have at least had the game explained to them and have learned how to watch it, while the essentials of rowing are widely unknown. Then, while I partook of the comradeship of my crews, there were no intimate friends among them, nothing compared to my relationship with Jones and football. More important, rowing became for me an occupation, something complete in itself into which I entered and from which I returned to ordinary life, it maintained its own, unbroken stream winding through the other currents of my existence. I believe you will find this true of anyone who is truly devoted to any game.

But it had to relate to all the rest. At Groton it brought a tolerable relationship with boys whom I respected and who carried much weight in the School; it brought self-assurance and a realization of strength; it brought the curious, traditional honours of athletes. There is a lot more to the preference of boys in most schools for athletic over academic honours than mere over-emphasis on athletics. The little, new boy, looking about him for gods, finds them at the outset of his first term in the football giants. He sees these big, self-confident, deep-voiced men in their daily goings and comings as well as in the games, among them are the holders of many other honours, Prefects of the School, leaders of this and that.

The man who tells him to SHUT UP when he tries to whisper after dark—and refrains from reporting him—is a quick-running half-back. Those who win academic honours and prizes come to light much later in the year, they have no letters broad across their chests as they go to and fro, in many cases they are quiet boys whom ordinarily one hardly notices. One may see them receive their prizes, but one does not watch, breathless, while they earn them and fight for the School. I can name off now the gods of the Sixth Form in my First Form year and tell who threw a long, magnificent forward pass, who knocked out a triple with two men on base. I saw them 'tossed'—picked up by their team-mates and half thrown in the air while the boys gave them the long cheer. And then, and then, one spring day, with *my* letter broad upon *my* chest, I was being jounced up in the air amid laughter, and it was my name on the end of the long cheer. Those gods stood around me in my mind, those great men, and I knew I was a good oarsman, and my crew had won, and it was legitimately mine, and I knew what it was to love a game and be good at it, and here was a new strength in myself.

Rowing at School was fun, but rowing at Harvard was magnificent. There was more of it, it was more intense, and it was better rowing. The hundred-and-fifty-pound crews were step-children, born of hesitant concessions by doubting authorities; at first they could hope for no insignia, they accepted cast-off shells and unwanted, used oars and liked them. They were made up of boys who were perfectly willing to row in a soap-box if necessary so long as they could row and count from time to time on a full-fledged race. We won recognition slowly, better boats, decent oars, a minor sports letter. Not until after my time did the lightweights get the same breaks in equipment and general treatment that less conservative colleges gave their rivals. We didn't care. For three years we rowed under the brothers, Bert and Bill Haynes, who themselves adored rowing and held it a prime part of their work to make us love it, thereby making us love them. We consciously rowed *for* them. We became a crew that could make the real Varsity stretch over a short distance, we were made use of to pace the Varsity for starts and sprints, one splendid afternoon we beat the Junior Varsity handily in a regular, two-mile race.

We loved it from the bitter, all-but-winter days when ice formed on the oars to the long, grass-smelling spring afternoons when we went far upriver and then, before turning back, leaned on our oars and made the age-old jokes about going a little farther and seeing if we could stroke the Wellesley crew. The rowing after dark I remember especially; I've tried to describe it a little, I never became entirely used to the beauty of city-ringed water and the mystery of the bridges.

One night in the early spring there were a great many crews out on the Charles River Basin. We were heading upstream for home, taking it easy, and I remember how clearly the voices of coxswains and coaches, the sound of the oars, came to us from many sides. Our cox was peering ahead a trifle nervously. Presently, to one side of us, we heard a practice race coming downstream, two class crews and the coaching launch behind them, with their coxswains making lots of noise and the coach calling from time to time. To play safe we lay on our oars. It was full dark, the water around us pearly in colour because of the city lights, the distance a very dark-grey haze rather than black, the sky above having the tawny quality so common over cities. A big sign on the Cambridge bank blinked on and off, flashing a red and yellow reflection across the basin almost to the side of the boat. Against it we caught a glimpse of the racing crews, the two long, ruled ink-lines of the shells and the figures in them black, small outlines in motion, sliding across the flash of light in an instant. There was some other race going on somewhere, and at a safe distance behind the class crews several more were being given a workout.

It seemed to us that the sounds of boats and of racing were getting too close together in the darkness below us. Then suddenly we heard a coach boom out in a new kind of voice, 'Easy all, there! Easy all! Hold her all! Look out, Tech crew! Look out, you there!' And into this the coxswains' voices shouting, and other coaches, commands, 'Hold her, Starboard! Hold her, Starboard! Hold her all! Look out, for Chrissakes, look out!' There was miscellaneous yelling, and then a sound as if someone had jumped on an unusually large bass viol. It was a wonderful crash, and it was almost immediately followed by another.

Like reinforcement coming into battle the second set of Harvard racers swept past us, going full tilt. The shouting broke out again, more tumult even than before, and there was a third crash. Then there were a lot of orders and questions being called in the night.

Someone said, 'What the hell?'

'They ran into a bunch of Tech crews coming out from their boathouse.'

'Let's go down and pitch in.'

Ridiculous of course, but one halfway felt like that. A wind from distant, ancient seas seemed to blow across us, the sound of many oars in their locks, the shouting, the crash of galleys ramming ...

Cox ordered, 'Forward all!' We settled into position. It was time to row home, but the quiet paddle upstream seemed strangely tame.

In the due course of time it is given to you to row a race. Not a practice race against one of your own, but the real article, and the oars of the boat taking position on your port hand are painted, not crimson, but a fine, shining blue. The feeling of it starts before then, when you take your shell down and toss her better than you ever did before, and you and the managers are in a different, special communion over the free running of your slide, the grease on your oar where it passes through the lock, the comfort of the stretcher into which your feet are laced. The love you bear each man in the boat is stronger, warmer, than it has ever been; it is positive, almost visible. Each man looks smilingly at his neighbour — a curious combination, already the tension and the earnestness is on their faces, but with it comes this affection. You shove off and paddle along to the start taking it easily, perfecting your form, the cox saying just what he always says, everything ordinary, everything calming.

Starting an eight-oared race is a frightful job. There is the current, and then there will be a slight cross-wind, something you wouldn't notice if you weren't trying to hold two or more boats as light as cigar-boxes in perfect line beside each other. You jockey and jockey, the good effect of the paddle wears off. You get into position, the starter has asked 'Are you ready Harvard? Are you ready Yale?' and one of the shells swings, and it all has to be done over again.

At last you are set. A racing start is entirely different from the ordinary process of getting a shell under way. This time you want to make her fly at full speed from the first stroke, you want to develop speed just as fast as is humanly possible, and faster. You have practised many times the series of short, hard strokes and the lengthening to the full, rhythmed swing but it remains tricky, a complex set of motions to be done so rapidly and hard that it's unreasonable to think it can happen without something going wrong.

Beyond that lies the race, the test itself. You know what a gut-wracking process it is, you are too tense about the outcome, you doubt if you can stand up to it. What's ahead of you is too much. There are many things that can postpone a start and several that can cause a race to be called back within the first ten strokes. You pray for them all to happen. You are so taut inside you twang. You are afraid, not of anything, just afraid.

The pistol cracks. You carry out those first three, scrambling strokes neatly, you begin to form the full, balanced stroke as you go on to complete the ten fast ones. All those fears and tremors are gone and you are racing. Coxswain's voice comes, intentionally soothing, carrying you over into the regular swing and beat of the long-term pace your crew must set, you are eight men and you are one, the boat is going with a sizzle, smoothly through the water, and out of the corner of your eye you can see the blue blades flashing alongside you.

The effort settles down and mounts again. There are races within the race, spurts when one crew tries to pull suddenly ahead, and the other answers, the sustained, increasing efforts, the raised beats of the crew behind, the somehow easier but intense drives of the leader. Cox tells you you are past the halfway mark, he tells you you are near the end. The start tests a good crew, the last stretch proves it. You are tired now, everything is coming to a final settlement very soon, you must row harder, faster, and still row smoothly and well. You have got your second wind and used it up, you are pooped out and you know you are at the end of your strength, you simply have nothing left in you. The beat — the rate of the stroke — goes up. Cox is yelling, pleading, advising, cursing. And you are staying with it. On the recovery the captain grunts out something unintelligible but urgent. Near the end other men may wring out cries intended to be 'Come on!' 'Let's go!', hardly recognizable. There's not much of that, it's against your training and besides wind is too precious, but the pent-up feeling is so strong that sometimes it must have an outlet. This is a good crew, a real one. As the beat is raised, as the reserve behind the reserves of strength is poured in, each stroke taken as if it were the last you'd ever row on earth, the crew still swings together, it is still one, that awareness of each other and merging together is still present and still effective.

Three-quarters of the way through you could hear them on the referee's launch and whatever others are permitted to follow, shouting, 'Come on Harvard! Come on Yale!' Now you vaguely know that they are still shouting, but you can't really hear them. There is some sort of sound around the finish line, you do know that a great many people must be making a lot of noise, but you don't hear that either. You are conscious of something arching up from the banks which, without looking at it, you *see*, and you know it's cheering. Your eyes are fixed on the shoulder on the man in front of you and (I rowed starboard side) the blade of Number Seven's oar, but the one thing you do know is exactly where the other boat is. Then here it comes, the final spurt, and you cease to hear or see anything outside your business. Faint and hardly noticeable the pistol fires, then cox says, 'Easy all,' and you loll forward.

Done. Like that, done, over, decided. And you are through, you are truly empty now, you have poured yourself out and for awhile you can hardly stand the effort of your own breathing but your tradition despises a man who fails to sit up in the boat. You have known complete exertion, you have answered every trouble of mind, spirit, and being with skilled violence and guided unrestraint, a complete happiness with eight other men over a short stretch of water has brought you catharsis. You may find it in storms at sea, in the presence of your art, on a racing horse, in bed with a woman, but you will hardly find it better or purer than you have found it here.

CHAPTER 7

The High Plateaux of Asia

IN PLANNING the experiment of this book, as frequently happens with experiments, I did not fully foresee what turns it would take, certainly I did not realize that it would be inescapable to start so many of these descriptions with the period of growing up. Along with our forgetting the true nature of the years from ten to majority we seem to forget the power of their influence not only on general character but on many specific matters, reaching all through life. If we postulate, as most men do, that on graduation we were that rare specimen, 'a normal, healthy boy,' with the creation of that standardized fiction we cut off our lines of thought, requiring the man we have become to spring, fatherless, from a plaster cast.

Also, I had not realized until I reached this point how little a boy is of one piece. This account shows despair and triumph lodged within one frame, often concurrently, it shows a number of coexistent elements which one would expect to be mutually exclusive, and it shows that life at Groton was not, as I remember it, grey, but most remarkably mottled even though many of the hues were sombre.

A number of factors entered to pave the way for one of those flukes which direct the course of one's entire life. We frequently recognize what an amazing accident it is that a given man should marry a particular woman, the couples themselves are usually aware of this and will comment on it, and we all acknowledge how fundamental in its effects this accident is. The public won't let novelists depict most of the other major developments of life as prey to equally pure chance, fiction dare not be as strange as truth, and as a matter of fact most of us don't realize what featherweight dips of the balance of events control our lives.

There is always a build-up, of course; one's situation has evolved to the point at which it is susceptible to chance if chance occurs. I had a bookish background, my mother encouraged us to read widely and to cultivate doubt of authority and intellectual curiosity. We had the habit of reading and weren't afraid of studying matters supposed to be beyond our years. One learned to be cagey about this at Groton; an intellectual interest, a highbrow taste was dangerous for anyone, an unpopular boy might have an unpleasant time if his fellows caught him busy with too deep a matter, but with a really good library at our disposal, it was possible with reasonable precaution to follow one's interests and educate one's self.

A little train had been fired in my mind at Saint Bernard's, where I studied before I went to Groton. In that remarkable school they were not afraid to expose children's minds to college-level concepts, the instruction there was intended to form an education. Among other things, I was given a vague idea of the relationship between English and Latin, the formation of French from Latin, the march of Romance words into English. There was the idea of language not as a finished thing but as an orderly, continuing process.

The idea of process and order, causes and effects, meets a desire in the minds of many children trying to puzzle out the world. To that was added something, again vague, which caught the imagination and spoke to the same faculty which makes a writer — the vision of ancient, far-off, tremendous happenings, of the march of primitive, great, bearded men out of Asia, the wagons and the cattle in motion as whole nations marched slowly, blindly to new lands, of wars and new migrations, tide on tide. Here too were beginnings and a process, the common roots from which by a turn to the right or the left in the long march could come the Greeks or the Vikings. It was not just a coincidence that Socrates' pun, $\nu\eta$ $X\epsilon\upsilon\varsigma$, worked when translated into English; back of that fact lay what I did not then think of as evolution but in which I sensed ordered change for reason, and it reached to the high plateaux of Asia and campfires beside the wagons where the imagination could range and the mind wonder.

It was a little train and a stimulant not well understood, it was a long time before the train reached explosive material.

It happened that my mother sent me at Groton a clipping of a review by Theodore Roosevelt of Osborn's *Men of the Old Stone Age*. She knew I'd shown a boyish curiosity about Stone Age man and sent this to me because it was written by one friend about the work of another. The review was an article in itself and made me want the book. I was fifteen (this happened shortly after my fight with Brown). Once I got my hands on the book the direction of my life began to be determined.

It was now that the spark of that early train reached the explosive. The real concept of evolution, the answer to Sunday-paper claptrap about the missing link, process and cause and sequence carried far back of the Aryan-speaking migrations, the mind's desire for order and understanding combined with a tremendous field in which the imagination could roam, not with the curious unsatisfaction of your pure day-dream but purposefully, deductively, with a backbone of fact and a lure of theory — in other words, speculation.

I did not merely read this book, I studied it. Although I ended by taking a couple of degrees in Anthropology I never sat in a formal course on the Stone Age of Europe, yet the grounding I got from this book was so firm that later it was easy for me to fit in the changing theories and new discoveries as I learned of them, so that I still have, for an ethnologist, a pretty fair, generalized grasp of this branch of my science — as much at least as if I had taken the usual undergraduate course on the subject.

The book took me into Darwin. From *The Descent of Man* I learned how to wiggle my ears, practising assiduously during Sunday sermons in Chapel according to the principles Darwin laid down for the restoration of obsolete muscles. Then Osborn's *Origin and Evolution of Life* came out and I fell upon it.

Men of the Old Stone Age began with a creature, *Pithecanthropus Erectus*, who was nearly enough human to swat his fellows over the head with a club. The new book began at the beginning. As a matter of fact it was largely beyond my comprehension but I was ignorant enough not to realize that and I found it, too, exciting.

Without realizing it at all I was discovering what every good scientist knows and finds so difficult to communicate to other men: that when approached without prejudice, questions which people have *learned* to classify as dry, dusty, and even repellent, have not only the fascination of difficult puzzles, mental exercises, detective stories, but tremendous colour and romance and vast spaces calling for the imagination to sweep in. It was there for me in the transition from anaerobic to aerobic bacteria and the pinpoint, the inconceivably minute line and inconceivably enormous change from a chemical reaction to life, in the archaeopteryx and the cynodont pointing the way to the shape of animal life as we know it today, in the mutations of de Vries and Waagen.

What happened to me happens to lots of bright boys. As I have said, the book was much too deep for me. I could understand it in spots and I could get from it an over-all picture, a generalized idea which was crudely correct. I was so ignorant and my mind so untrained that it was easy for me to gloss over my misunderstandings and plain incomprehensions by a glib surface reading of words and again and again short-circuit ideas with which I could not hope to cope by fantastically naïve reinterpretations of the text.

Even that was not come by easily. *Origin and Evolution of Life* was a formidable presentation of a formidable subject. I have since retreated gratefully to the confines of Anthropology and content myself with a somewhat amateurish defense, at times, of Wood-Jones's theory of arboreal man. I soon found that I was reading whole pages without retaining a word. This would never do, a remedy must be found. There was some 'required reading' in our courses at School but no training to equip one for *teaching one's self*. I hit on what I believed to be a totally original notion — I made myself take notes on every page I read. Recently I ran across the notebook, a small, red one which could be concealed in the pocket quickly, with its page by page, naïve summaries (but not much worse than undergraduate work), the diagrams carefully and almost neatly copied to scale.

Behold the schoolboy — I'm almost finished with him now. He is sixteen, he has recently spent an agonizing week in Coventry, he is the Bop I have described. High-jumping is just beginning to become his achievement, at night he finds refuge from misery in the escapes and wild fancies told of earlier, his clear ambition is a uniform, a commission, and the front line, and he would gladly die in action. He also dreams of making the first squad in football and considers winning his letter too high an ambition to torment his mind with. He is romantically in love with a girl he met last Christmas. He sits, bespectacled, a cowlick rising umbrageously from his head, ink on his fingers and on his nose, secretly summarizing an advanced work on biology and evolution into a small notebook while his studies go to pot. All these elements and many more go to make him up, and it is he by the thousand whom masters, parents, graduates and writers, summarize so quickly and so glibly.

When I was ready for college I thought of becoming an historian. I had fallen upon Hakluyt's *Voyages*, read them nearly straight through, and embarked upon a two-fold study of Elizabethan seafaring and the history of the sailing vessel. This might have been the most natural choice I could have made, its alliance to writing is obvious, and already my secret ambition was to be a writer. Had I made it, my life would have been unthinkably different. But, I had read *Men of the Old Stone Age* first. The other was a delightful occupation, Science stood forth as a vocation. Even in that there were manifold choices — Paleontology, Evolutionary Biology, Physical Anthropology and Archaeology, all were pertinent to my interest. *The Origin and Evolution of Life* had been just a little too tough for me, *Men of the Old Stone Age* reread was well within my grasp. I chose Archaeology, and specifically the archaeology of palaeolithic France. In this I was conscious of a gentle pressure, my mother's feeling about a professor in the family. My real decision was that I should start in this direction and see what happened.

The authorities at Harvard tested the strength of my interest by the simple method of sending me on an expedition to Arizona, to see what long hours wielding a shovel in the hot sun would bring out of me. Various other factors came into play at the same time that the Navajos dawned upon me, and without even being conscious of having made a vital change I settled upon Ethnology. I also fell in love with the Southwest and made the first steps in breaking out of the protected, secure provincialism of the nicely brought up Northeastern American.

Through my own indiscipline I got in bad with the powers that were in Southwestern research, and at a critical time found it impossible to get a post in that work. By sheer chance I met a Dane, Frans Blom, who was going to Mexico and Guatemala for Tulane University. He took a shine to me and hired me as his assistant. He was a fine scientist, a real explorer, and a natural teacher. New Orleans became my home, my specialty the Mayan Indians of the high, mountain country, Spanish became my second tongue, so much so that I can no longer speak Italian and my French is sadly corrupted. Those Indians remain my special subject to this day; had I continued earning my living as an anthropologist I should have visited those mountains year after year; as it is, I know them better than I do the northern half of my native state and had Pearl Harbor not occurred I should be there now. Thus one 'choses' his career.

What is Science? What is the special nature of a scientist as distinguished from a soda-jerker? Not just the externals of teaching classes, unconsciously using a trick vocabulary, seeking information about such things as the distribution of plumbate pottery in northwestern Guatemala, but the formation within the man that gives a writer something he can set his teeth in? There's been a lot of rot written about scientists in fiction. The reality can be found in rare works like Eve Curie's. When I think of the hard-drinking gentlemen and delightful companions who are my colleagues in Maya research I find them quite unlike the folk-picture.

The internal nature of science within the scientist is both emotional and intellectual. The emotional element must not be overlooked, for there is no sound research on no matter how odd and dull-seeming a detail without it. An emotion shapes and informs the scientist's life, an intellectual discipline molds his thinking, stamping him with a character as marked as a seaman's although much less widely understood.

We can get at the man partly through his work, considering it in its wide context although much of the time the man himself, in his intensive study of a single tree, not only can't see the forest but forgets all about it. He is an ant, putting forth great efforts to lug one insignificant and apparently unimportant grain of sand to be added to a pile, and much of the time his struggle seems as pointless as an ant's. I can try to explain why he does it and what the long-term purpose is behind it through an example from my own work.

Remember that in this I am not thinking of the rare, fortunate geniuses like the Curies, Darwin or Newton, who by their own talents and the apex of accumulated thought at which they found themselves were knowingly in the pursuit of great, major discoveries or theories. This is the average scientist, one among thousands, obscure, unimportant, toilsome.

I have put in a good many months of hard work which ought by usual standards to have been dull but was not, on an investigation, as yet unfinished, to prove that Kanhobal, spoken by certain Indians in Guatemala, is not a dialect of Jacalteca, but that on the contrary Jacalteca is a dialect of Kanhobal. Ridiculous, isn't it? Yet to me the matter is not only serious, but exciting. Why?

There's an item of glory. There are half a dozen or so men living today (some, alas, now our enemies) who will respect me for adding to the linguistic map of Central America the name of a hitherto unnoted dialect, spoken by about twelve thousand people. Bear that matter of the respect of six or eight men in mind, it will come up again.

There's the nature of the initial work. I have spent hours, deadly, difficult hours, extracting lists of words, paradigms of verbs, constructions, idioms, and the rest from native informants, often at night in over-ventilated huts while my hands turned blue with cold. (Those mountains are far from tropical.) An illiterate Indian tires quickly when giving linguistic information. He is not accustomed to thinking of words in terms of other words, his command of Spanish is very poor so that again and again you labour over misunderstandings, he does not think in our categories of words. Take any school-child and ask him how you say, 'I go.' Then ask him, in turn, 'thou goest, he goes, we go,' and so forth. Even the most elementary schooling has taught him, if only from the force of what he has seen on a printed page, to think in terms of the present tense of a single verb, and he will give you — in Spanish for instance — 'Me voy, te vas, se va, nos vamos,' and so on. Try this on an illiterate Indian. He gives you his equivalent of 'I go,' follows it, perhaps, with 'thou goest,' but the next question reminds him of his son's departure that morning for Ixtatán so he says, 'he sets out,' and from that by another mental leap produces 'we are on a journey.' This presents the investigator with a magnificently irregular verb. He starts checking back, and the Indian's mind having moved into a new channel, he now gets 'I am on a journey' instead of 'I go.'

There follows an exhausting process of inserting an alien concept into the mind of a man with whom you are communicating tenuously in a language which you speak only pretty well and he quite badly.

Then, of course, you come to a verb which really is irregular and you mistrust it. Both of you become tired, frustrated, upset. At the end of an hour or so the Indian is worn out, his friendship for you has materially decreased, and you yourself are glad to quit.

Hours and days of this, and it's not enough. I have put my finger upon the village of Santa Eulalia and said, 'Here is the true, the classic Kanhobal from which the other dialects diverge.' Then I must sample the others, there are at least eight villages which must yield me up word-lists ample enough to show about where they fit in the general pattern, there are two from which my material must be as full as from Santa Eulalia. More hours and more days, long horseback trips across the mountains to enter a strange, suspicious settlement, sleep on the dirt floor of the schoolhouse, and persuade the local boys that it is a good idea, a delightful idea, that you should put 'The Tongue' into writing. Bad food, a bout of malaria, and the early morning horror of seeing your beloved horse's neck running blood from vampire bats (Oh, but yes, señor, here are very troublesome the vampire bats), to get the raw material for proving that Jacalteca is a dialect of Kanhobal instead of . . .

You bring your hard-won data back to the States and you follow up with a sort of detective-quest for obscure publications and old manuscripts that may show a couple of words of the language as it was spoken a few centuries ago, so that you can get a line on its evolution. With great labour you unearth and read the very little that has ever been written bearing upon this particular problem.

By now the sheer force of effort expended gives your enterprise value in your own eyes.

But the real drive is greater than all these. Suppose I complete my work and prove, in fact, that Kanhobal as spoken in Santa Eulalia is, first, a language in its own right, and second, the classic tongue from which Jacalteca has diverged under alien influences, and that further I show just where the gradations of speech in the intervening villages fit in. Dear God, what a small, dull grain of sand.

Follow the matter a little further. Jacalteca being relatively well-known (I can, offhand, specify four men who have given it consideration), from it it has been deduced that this whole group of dialects is most closely related to the languages spoken south and east of these mountains. If my thesis is correct the reverse is true, the language belongs to the Northern Division of the Mayan Family. This fact, taken along with others regarding physical appearance, ancient remains, and present culture, leads to a new conclusion about the direction from which these people came into the mountains; a fragment of the ancient history of what was once a great, civilized people comes into view. So now my tiny contribution begins to be of help to men working in other branches of Anthropology than my own, particularly the archaeologists, it begins to help towards an eventual understanding of the whole picture in this area, the important question of, not what these people are today, but how they got that way and why, and what can we learn from that about all human behaviour including our own?

Carrying this bit of research thus far brings me to the limits of my capacities, but its results would presumably be exploited by men of greater attainments. Sticking to the linguistic line, an error has been cleared away, an advance has been made in our understanding of the layout and interrelationship of the many languages making up the Mayan Family. With that we come a step nearer to working out the processes by which these languages became different one from another (my beloved processes again) and hence to determining the archaic, ancestral roots of the whole group.

So far as we know at present there are not less than eight completely unrelated language families in America north of Panama. This is unreasonable, there are hardly that many families among all the peoples of the Old World. Twenty years ago we recognized, not eight, but forty. Some day perhaps we shall cut the total to four. The understanding of the Mayan process is a step towards that day; it is likely that one day Mayan will prove to be anciently related to at least one of the others. We know now that certain tribes in Wyoming speak languages akin to those of certain others in Panama, we have charted the big masses and the islands

THE HIGH PLATEAUX OF ASIA — 81

of that group of tongues, and from the chart begin to see the outlines of great movements and major historical events in the dim past. If we should similarly develop a relationship between Mayan and, say, languages of the Mississippi Valley and Labrador, again we offer something provocative and helpful to the archaeologist, the historian, the student of mankind. Perhaps some day we shall show a provable relationship between some of these families and certain languages of the Old World and with it cast a new light on the dim subject of the peopling of the Americas, something to guide our minds back past the Arctic to dark tribes moving blindly from the high plateaux of Asia.

My petty detail has its place in a long project carried out by many men which will serve not only the history of language but the broad scope of history itself. It goes further than that. The humble Pah-Utes of Nevada speak a tongue related to that which the subtle Montezuma used, the one narrow in scope, evolved only to meet the needs of a primitive people, the other sophisticated, a capable instrument for poetry, for an advancd governmental system, and for philosophical speculation. Men's thoughts make language and their languages make thoughts. When the matter of the speech of mankind is fully known and laid side by side with the other knowledges, the philosophers, the men who stand at the gathering-together points of science, will have the means to make man understand himself at last.[1]

In this description I have allowed myself some fantasy and a bit of exaggeration to convey in a crude way the concept, the drive, that underlies the scientist's work. The emotions of curiosity, of combativeness against difficulty, and the pleasure of using one's faculties for all they're worth are involved, these are rewards along the way, but the great, guiding emotion is in this vision of future understanding, something to be attained by other men and for the far future, towards which he can make his little contribution, of which he can now and again catch a thrilling, prophetic glimpse.

This enterprise goes on under a severe discipline of emotion as well as mind. The investigator is interested in disclosing the truth, not in proving himself right, which means that from time to time

---

[1] In the back of Hayakawa's *Language in Action* is an article by my colleague, the late B. L. Whorf, which gives an exciting glimpse of the broad understanding to be reached at the end of countless tiny studies.

he has to accept agonizing sacrifices. Thus, I might complete an unassailable job of proving my Kanhobal idea and be ready to publish it, or even have published it, seen it generally accepted, cited by other workers, my own reputation enhanced. Then one day there might be brought to my attention a forgotten manuscript by Fray Juan de Fulano, written in 1678, containing a brief grammar and vocabulary of the language of the people of Santa Eulalia which proved conclusively, in a manner that no logical analysis of modern data could overthrow, that in the sixteen-seventies the Santa Eulalia Indians spoke pure, slightly archaic Jacalteca clearly related to the Southern Division of the Mayan stock.

Of course I could burn the manuscript and keep my mouth shut, just as I might murder my mother for her insurance. As a matter of fact my best out is to publish the manuscript myself, and myself destroy my own theory. If I am a good scientist, about halfway through the moral struggle I shall become intrigued with the wider significances growing out of this proven, Southern relationship, my mind will begin to follow lines of argument, I shall see a rather nifty little publication, requiring some six months of absorbed work to prepare, to be entitled *The Evolution of an Atypical Highland Mayan Dialect in Post-Columbian Times*, and along about the time when I should be coming to a rather noble decision I shall have forgotten about the decision in the resurgence of the scientist's fundamental emotional drive.

It's more painful when a colleague makes the upsetting discovery. If he be a good fellow, and the matter to be upset one of importance, he'll communicate with you and offer you the privilege of helping him tear down your own evidence. It takes some of the sting out of the proof that La Farge was wrong, misinterpreted some of the evidence, and overlooked a couple of important bets, to have the article showing this contain expressions of gratitude to you for your help and quote a letter from you making a contribution to the new thesis.

It happened that when I was a pup anthropologist I ran across a copy of a manuscript supposed to have disappeared, and following a lead unearthed three more versions of it, a grammar and vocabulary of the now extinct Chol language of Guatemala compiled by a Fray Morán between 1670 and 1690. The Choles occupied a keystone position geographically in the Maya Area, so that the question of their speech and its relationships is an important one. The last and best word on the subject was an article *Choles und Chortis* published in 1915 by Doctor Carl Sapper, one of the great veterans and deans of our field. In his article he spoke of the 'lost' Morán Manuscript.

A brief study of it showed that Doctor Sapper had been quite mistaken. Crudely speaking, he had tried to reconstruct Chol of 1600 from six words recorded by the leader of a Spanish military expedition plus a list of words he had made in a modern Chorti village. Chorti *used to be* the same as Chol except that it substituted *r* wherever *l* appeared in the other language — but that was several centuries ago.

His article, written in German, containing many words in Spanish and many in Indian dialects, had been printed in Quebec (in itself a document on the nature of science when wars leave it alone), and was clearly full of printer's errors. To make my disproof of his thesis waterproof I needed to have these errors cleared up, and I needed more Chorti.

In 1928 Doctor Carl Sapper was old and famous, he was President of Würzburg University, a mere list of his publications would fill several pages of this book. Everybody who could get hold of a copy carried his *Nördliche Mittelamerika* with him in the field and kept it handy to his desk at home. I was an unknown beginner, still lacking credits for my master's degree, holding a lowly post in a new, obscure, unproven institution, and had published one six-page article on certain Jacalteca ceremonies. So I wrote to him, in my best Spanish (which was not very good).

He answered promptly, beginning by expressing his delight that I had found the Morán Manuscript, continuing to correct the printer's errors in his article, and finally offering to send me all his manuscript field notes bearing on the subject, and ending with cordial good wishes. He addressed me as 'my dear colleague.' From then until the Nazis finally ended all such intercommunication, while he presided over Würzburg and after he had retired, we continued a delightful, sporadic correspondence and I still treasure the fan-letter he wrote me after he read the German translation of *Laughing Boy*.

This is the cream of science. Hooton of Harvard once remarked to me that scientists, or at least anthropologists, should not complain of the poor salaries they got; they should be grateful that the universities didn't charge them for the privilege of doing such enjoyable work. He wasn't far from right.

Even in describing the work itself this matter of one's colleagues and the half dozen men I mentioned earlier keeps creeping in. To understand that one must first understand the isolation of research, a factor which has profound effects upon the scientist's psyche.

The most obvious statement of this is in the public attitude and our folk-literature about 'professors.' (Folk-literature is a polite name for the work of lazy-minded, slack-souled writers who go through life exploiting the readily accepted stock characters of folklore without the curiosity or the integrity to seek out the truth.) The titles and subjects of Ph.D. theses have long been causes of a sort of exasperated humour among us, we are all familiar with the writer's device which ascribes to a professorial character an intense interest in some such matter as the development of the molars in pre-Aurignacian man or the religious sanctions of the Levirate in northeastern Australia, the writer's intention being that the reader shall say 'Oh God!', smile slightly, and pigeonhole the character. But what do you suppose is the effect of the quite natural public attitude behind these devices upon the man who is excitedly interested in pre-Aurignacian molars and who knows that, as a matter of fact, it is a study of key value in tracing the development of *Homo Sapiens*?

Occasionally some line of research is taken up and made clear, even fascinating, to the general public — De Kruif's writings, objectionable though they are in some ways, Zinsser's splendid *Rats, Lice, and History*. Usually, as in the cases cited, they deal with medicine or some other line of work directly resulting in findings of vital interest to the public. Then the ordinary man will consent to understand, if not the steps of the research itself, at least their importance, will grant their excitement, and honour the researcher. When we read Eve Curie's great biography of her parents our approach to it is coloured by our knowledge forty years later, of the importance of their discovery to every one of us. It would have been quite possible at the time for a malicious or merely ignorant writer to have presented that couple as archetypes of the 'professor,' performing incomprehensible acts of self-immolation in pursuit of an astronomically unimportant what's-it.

Diving to my own experience like a Stuka with a broken wing, I continue to take my examples from my rather shallow linguistic studies because, in its very nature, the kind of thing a linguist studies is so beautifully calculated to arouse the 'Oh God!' emotion. It happened that at the suggestion of my betters I embarked upon an ambitious, general comparative study of the whole Mayan Family. I found to my delight that I could get a lot of drawing into the work, having stumbled upon a way of representing the phonetic system of each language by a graph, and prepared a very fancy diagram showing the laws governing sound shifts within the stock. This released a never greatly suppressed desire to use three colours of ink on one page.

The further in I got the further there was to go and the more absorbed I became. Puzzle piled upon puzzle to be worked out and the solution used for getting after the next one, the beginning of order in chaos, the glimpse of understanding at the far end. Memory, reasoning faculties, realism, and imagination were all on the stretch, I was discovering the full reach of whatever mental powers I had. When I say that I became absorbed I mean absorbed; the only way to do such research is to roll in it, become soaked in it, live it, breathe it, have your system so thoroughly permeated with it that at the half glimpse of a fugitive possibility everything you have learned so far and everything you have been holding in suspension is in order and ready to prove or disprove that point. You do not only think about your subject while the documents are spread before you; everyone knows that some of our best reasoning is done when the surface of the mind is occupied with something else and the deep machinery of the brain is free to work unhampered.

One day I was getting aboard a trolley car on my way to the University. As I stepped up, I saw that if it were possible to prove that a prefixed *s-* could change into a prefixed *y-* a whole series of troublesome phenomena would fall into order. The transition must come through *u-* and, thought I with a sudden lift of excitement, there may be a breathing associated with *u-* and that may make the whole thing possible. As I paid the conductor I thought that the evidence I needed might exist in Totonac and Tarascan, non-Mayan languages with which I was not familiar. The possibilities were so tremendous that my heart pounded and I was so preoccupied that I nearly sat in the Jim Crow section. Speculation was useless until I could reach the University and dig out the books, so after a while I calmed myself and settled to my morning ration of Popeye, who was then a new discovery, too. As a matter of fact the idea was no good, but the incident is a perfect example of the 'professor mind.'

Of course, if as I stepped onto the car it had dawned upon me that the reason my girl's behaviour last evening had seemed odd was that she had fallen for the Englishman we met, the incident wouldn't seem so funny, although the nature of the absorption, subconscious thinking, and realization would be the same in both cases.

I lived for a month with the letter *k*. If we have three words in Quiché, one of the major Mayan languages, beginning with *k*, in Kanhobal we are likely to find that one of these begins with *ch*. Moving further west and north, in Tzeltal one is likely to begin with *k*, one with *ch*, and the one which began with *ch* in Kanhobal to begin with *ts*. In Husateca, at the extreme northwest, they begin with *k*, *ts*, and plain *s* respectively. Why don't they all change alike? Which is the original form? Which way do these changes run, or from which point do they run both ways? Until those questions can be answered we cannot even guess at the form of the mother tongue from which these languages diverged, and at that point all investigation halts. Are these *k*'s in Quiché pronounced even faintly unlike? I noticed no difference between the two in Kanhobal, but then I wasn't listening for it. I wished someone properly equipped would go and listen to the Quiché Indians, and wondered if I could talk the University into giving me money enough to do so.

This is enough to give some idea of the nature of my work, and its uselessness for general conversation. My colleagues at Tulane were archaeologists. Shortly after I got up steam they warned me frankly that I had to stop trying to tell them about the variability of *k*, the history of Puctun *ty* or any similar matter. If I produced any results that they could apply, I could tell them about it, but apart from that I could keep my damned sound-shifts and intransitive infixes to myself, I was driving them nuts. My other friends on the faculty were a philosopher and two English professors, I was pursuing two girls at the time but had not been drawn to either because of intellectual interests in common, my closest friends were two painters and a sculptor. The only person I could talk to was myself.

The cumulative effect of this non-communication was terrific. A strange, mute work, a thing crying aloud for discussion, emotional expression, the check and reassurance of another's point of view, turned in upon myself to boil and fume and throwing upon me the responsibility of being my own sole check, my own impersonal, external critic. When finally I came to New York on vacation, I went to see my Uncle John. He doesn't know Indian languages but he is a student of linguistics, and I shall never forget the relief, the revelling pleasure, of pouring my work out to him.

So at his greatest strength, at the vital point of his life-work, the scientist is cut off from communication with his fellow-men. Instead, he has the society of two, six, or twenty men and women who are working in his specialty (in my field I once was in correspondence with two at once), with whom he corresponds, whose letters he receives like a lover, with whom when he meets them he wallows in an orgy of talk, the keen pleasure of conclusions and findings compared, matched, checked against one another, the pure joy of being really understood.

The praise and understanding of those two or six becomes for him the equivalent of public recognition. Around these few close colleagues is the larger group of workers in the same general field. They do not share with one in the steps of one's research, but they can read the results, tell in a general way if they have been soundly reached, and profit by them. To them McGarnigle 'has shown' that there are traces of an ancient, dolichocephalic strain among the skeletal remains from Pusilhá, which is something they can use. Largely on the strength of his close colleagues' judgment of him, the word gets around that McGarnigle is a sound man. You can trust his work. He's the fellow you want to have analyze the material if you turn up an interesting bunch of skulls. All told, including men in allied fields who use his findings, some fifty scientists praise him; before them he has achieved international reputation. He will receive honours. It is even remotely possible that he might get a raise in salary.

McGarnigle disinters himself from a sort of fortress made of boxes full of skeletons in the cellar of Podunk University's Hall of Science, and emerges into the light of day to attend a Congress. At the Congress he delivers a paper entitled *Additional Evidence of Dolichocephaly among the Eighth Cycle Maya* before the Section on Physical Anthropology. In the audience are six archaeologists specializing in the Maya field, to whom these findings have a special importance, and twelve physical anthropologists including Gruenwald of Eastern California, who is the only other man working on Maya remains.

After McGarnigle's paper comes Gruenwald's turn. Three other physical anthropologists, engaged in the study of the Greenland Eskimo, the Coastal Chinese, and Pleistocene Man of Lake Mojave respectively, come in. They slipped out for a quick one while McGarnigle was speaking because his Maya work is not particularly useful to them and they can read the paper later; what is coming next, with its important bearing on method and theory, they would hate to miss.

Gruenwald is presenting a perfectly horrible algebraic formula and a diagram beyond Rube Goldberg's wildest dream, showing *A Formula for Approximating the Original Indices of Artificially Deformed Crania*. The archaeologists depart hastily to hear a paper in their own section on *Indications of an Early Quinary System at Uaxactún*.[1] The formula is intensely exciting to McGarnigle because it was the custom of the ancient Mayas to remodel the heads of their children into shapes which they (erroneously) deemed handsomer than nature's. He and Gruenwald have been corresponding about this, at one point Gruenwald will speak of his colleague's experience in testing the formula; he has been looking forward to this moment for months.

After the day's sessions are over will come something else he has been looking forward to. He and Gruenwald, who have not seen each other in two years, go out and get drunk together. It is not that they never get drunk at home, but that now when in their cups they can be uninhibited, they can talk their own, private, treble-esoteric shop. It is an orgy of release.

In the course of their drinking it is likely — if an archaeologist

---

[1] These titles are not mere parodies: they are entirely possible. There are faint evidences that the primitive Mayas may once have had a numeral system other than their present one; indications of it in the inscriptions of Uaxactún would be startling news. Doctor Shapiro *has* developed a formula for approximating . . .

or two from the area joins them it is certain — that the talk will veer from femoral pilasters and alveolar prognathism to personal experiences in remote sections of the Petén jungle. For in my science and a number of others there is yet another frustration. We go into the field and there we have interesting experiences. (The word 'adventure' is taboo and 'explore' is used very gingerly.) But the public mind has been poisoned by the outpourings of the LaVarres and Dyotts, it is laden with claptrap about big expeditions, dangers, hardships, hostile tribes, the lighting of red flares around the camp to keep the savages at bay, and God knows what rot. (I can speak freely about this because my own expeditions have been so unambitious and in such easy country that I don't come into the subject.) As a matter of fact it is generally true that *for a scientist on an expedition to have an adventure is evidence of a fault in his technique.* He's sent out to gather information, and he has no business getting into 'a brush with the natives.'

The red flare, into-the-unknown, hardship-and-danger boys, who manage to find a tribe of pink and green Indians, a lost city, or the original, hand-painted descendants of the royal Incas every time they go out, usually succeed in so riling the natives and local whites upon whom scientists must depend if they are to live in the country, as to make work in the zones they contaminate difficult for years afterwards. The business of their adventures and discoveries is sickening.

I have sat squirming through a lecture in which the lecturer told how he barely escaped with his life after desperate adventures among the Jivaro Indians of Peru, while (*a*) he showed excellently taken moving pictures of the said adventures, (*b*) I had recently finished cataloguing a very nice collection of their material brought us by a man who happened, quite casually, to pass through their territory, and (*c*) three of my friends, boys in their early twenties, were just back from spending their summer vacation among those friendly, kindly warriors.

I have read a thrilling account of an 'explorer's' hardships in fighting his way upriver in the jungle, the threat of disease, battles with lianas and thorny bushes, alligators, lions and jaguars on the banks, deadly snakes in the underbrush, and hostile natives peering menacingly from behind the trees. He embarked upon this wild adventure in order to find a lost city of which he had heard a rumour. The fact was that he heard his rumour from an archaeologist who had dug there and published on it twenty years earlier, maps of the city were already available and specimens from it were on exhibition at Harvard. It lies within one day's travel of the capital of British Honduras, the upriver trip takes four hours in a motor boat, and the few inhabitants of that section are peaceful Negroes who are proud of being British subjects.

The public, innocently, laps up the stuff, and so if one mentions work in the field one meets an expectation which requires that he lie like Munchausen or take a back seat. The men whom I honour myself by calling my colleagues go out alone or in pairs, sometimes in larger groups, not because 'there is a blank space on the map which must be filled in' or because 'the little we could learn about the Poopidoopi River and its dark inhabitants presented an irresistible challenge and a mystery,' but because the logic of their research calls for investigations in a given place, which may be five miles from a resort hotel or five hundred from the nearest human being. Year after year they go out, usually on a shoestring (I have been handed thirteen hundred dollars on which to buy all equipment, get myself from New York to Guatemala, live six months, and return), and they come back with *data*. They suffer from chronic tropical diseases, they occasionally encounter something vaguely resembling a romance, now and then they prevent 'a brush with the natives' from arising by mother-wit, tact, and a round of drinks, they carry out careful, exact work while malaria racks them, they suffer from hells of loneliness, and they experience peace and unflawed beauty.

These men by training express themselves in factual, 'extensional' terms, which doesn't make for good adventure stories. They understandably lean over backwards to avoid sounding even remotely like the frauds, the 'explorers.' And then, what they have seen and done lacks validity to them if it cannot be told in relation to the purpose and dominant emotion which sent them there. McGarnigle went among the independent Indians of Icaiché because he heard of a skull kept in one of their temples which, from a crude description, seemed to have certain important characteristics. All his risks and his manoeuvrings with those tough, explosive Indians centred around the problem of gaining access to that skull. When he tries to tell an attractive girl about his experiences he not only understates, but can't keep from stressing the significance of a skull with a healed, clover-leaf trepan. The girl gladly leaves him for the nearest broker.

The man is isolated all the way round. The snuffy fellow who gives a couple of unlikely courses in the Winter Semester leaves every midyears to spend the next six months in a fabulous wilderness where he is intensely happy. There he is a person of eminence and authority among wild, hardy people, he is a great man, well proven. He knows intimately a world so unlike ours that it seems almost as if he had left this planet when he enters it. There and at home he exercises his mental faculties triumphantly on matters which he knows are important. But he can't make any of this known to anyone outside his own guild. It is small wonder then that he develops a special attitude towards people in general and seems somewhat peculiar. In the face of the evidence, the remarkable thing is that I have found most of my colleagues in my own, small field to be delightful companions, gentlemen, and two-fisted drinkers.

It is too bad both for the scientists and the public that they are so cut off from each other. The world needs now, not the mere knowledges of science, but the way of thought and the discipline. It is the essence of what Hitler has set out to destroy, against it he has waged total war within his own domain. It is more than skepticism, the weighing of evidence, more even than the love of truth. It is the devotion of oneself to an end which is far more important than the individual, the certainty that that end is absolutely good, not only for oneself but for all mankind, and the character to set personal advantage, comfort, and glory aside in the devoted effort to make even a little progress towards that end.

CHAPTER 8

EVERYBODY'S BUSINESS

As A CRUDE generalization, people can be divided into those who have and those who have not a strong dash of the religious emotion in their make-ups. The religious emotion is that feeling, quite distinct from mere curiosity, which requires one to think deeply about religious subjects and to take the general question of religion seriously. It enforces a quest for understanding of what lies beyond our physical world, it is the expression of a spiritual need going beyond the common desire for 'the comforts of religion.'

Many men who are closely affiliated with regular churches, even many priests and ministers, are weak in this emotion. Lacking it they can be content with formalizations and routines of thought as well as of word and action. Lots of laymen who disapprove of my 'freethinking' attitude actually give infinitely less attention to religion than I do, and care less about it. That is one reason why they don't doubt the particular ritual in which they were brought up, but I can't see that it brings them appreciably nearer God. They have, not faith, but a comfortable acceptance.

There are a great many ways of attacking the established religions, as a whole or sect by sect, and almost all of them are irrelevant. If I wanted to, I could recite at length my observations among missionaries to the Indians in the Southwest, by cases and specific acts, and thereby I could prove that a most unhappily large percentage of the men entrusted with winning these people to Christianity of one form or another, or with keeping them Christian, are in themselves unaffected by the influence of Jesus Christ. By the same token I have known a group of Mayan priests in a tribe in Guatemala to commit a perfectly outrageous blasphemy in order to frame an innocent stranger for urgent reasons of self-interest.

This kind of thing is freely cited by shallow-minded atheists. It should be, and when proven I am sure it is, a source of far greater concern to genuine members of the religion or sect concerned than to anyone outside. Using it as an argument against religion is an obvious logical fallacy. If one is going to give any honest consideration at all to faith, one must begin by accepting the fact that numbers of people who *profess* any given faith are fundamentally irreligious persons who have no scruple about grossly betraying that to which they pay lip service, because as a matter of fact they completely fail to understand its nature.

Another common attack is that upon what are really non-essentials, the literal meaning of Genesis, the archaic provisions for the churching of women in the Episcopalian prayer-book and the unpleasant line of thought from which they derive, the importance of eating fish on Fridays, of not eating pork, of not crossing a rattlesnake's trail. This line of argument is valid for trying to free people from the idea that every detail of customary practice is equally important and essential to the religion they believe, but it does not touch the subject of religion at all. It does frequently bear upon the abuse of it.

This fallacy leads to the idea of the war between science and religion, assumed both by the churchmen and their opponents to centre around the scientific accumulation of factual knowledge. There really is no such war. Navajo medicine men co-operate with our doctors and willingly perform a blessing ceremony over a new hospital. The Catholic church shook for a while over the discovery that the earth was not the centre of the universe and again when it became apparent that man was descended from an animal of the primate family, but it quickly absorbed these facts and today there are Catholic priests who are outstanding anthropologists and astronomers.

Of course, when you turn from religion to the power of an organization, a conflict exists. If mankind could be returned to complete ignorance we should believe once more that failure to pay our contributions would result in our being struck by lightning, or suffering a disastrous drought, or what not, and the temporal power of our priests would be much greater. I've never seen a religious organization yet in which there was not some tendency, at least among individuals, to exploit ignorance. But that's human frailty, and none of it has anything to do with real religion.

Science and religion do run head on, only having done so, having entered into the really deep conflict, if one will stay with it he will find in the long run that it is not a conflict, but a unity. At least that has been my experience.

I have tried to describe, not the knowledges of science, but the discipline and the way of thought. The concept of this got through to me early in my time at Harvard, increasingly colouring all my outlook. It was inevitable that I should apply that way of thought to the rather formal religion, tempered by my mother's sincerity and independence of mind, which I learned at School.

As far as I can see there was no one at Groton, certainly no one in a commanding position, who had at any time entertained grave doubts of, for instance, the existence of God. Religion was taught upon a base of various assumptions which, it was further assumed, no one could question. It usually is. Now the average Groton boy's idea of science in my time was the same polite awareness of its existence that he had for his second cousin once removed in New Zealand, with whom he exchanged Christmas cards, or of somebody else's collection of postage stamps (provided that he did not collect stamps). He would, by requirement, take an elementary course of science at Harvard, but I've never known of any such course that attempted to teach the one thing worth teaching — the scientific outlook. Nine times out of ten, at a conservative estimate, he would move unscathed into the world of business without ever having had to think about the nature of the world he lived in, and he never would think about it. Most people don't. They never even attempt to conceive of eternity or infinity (two very unpleasant subjects of contemplation), the nature of geologic time, the operations of chance (or destiny or God), the very diverse and remarkably sound ways in which different groups of men have attempted to solve that great group of problems we call 'religion' and the variety of external, mundane factors which have controlled their thinking. In short, he has been equipped with what he believes to be a set of foundations and it has never occurred to him to examine them.

So long as he believes in them he, personally, is all right. His beliefs may lead him into erroneous thinking or evil actions, but being true beliefs, they won't give way under him when the time of pressure comes. He has the comforts of religion.

But once you start to examine them, you are in for trouble. The scientist who is not religious-minded can, like so many laymen, tuck his religious beliefs into a special drawer for reference only in time of difficulty and thus get by all right. But if he is religious-minded he can't do that. Then he is faced by difficult alternatives.

From childhood his religious instruction has centred around the concept of faith. As most religious instruction is given by people of ordinary intellectual calibre and no special philosophical equipment, faith is usually confused with will-to-believe. In any case, religion being speculation on the unknowable, in his formative years a deep groove is made in his mental-emotional system resulting in a strong predisposition not to intrude the self he has become into the belief which has been erected within him. The very heart of religious thinking is speculation upon the nature of God. To that all other subjects lead, from it all conclusions must eventually derive. He has, properly, been taught to approach that question with awe, but the awe has been developed to the point where instead of calling forth his very highest mental powers it tends to suspend them.

Add to this the purely emotional reactions built up around the subject and a man's natural reluctance to forego the comforts of religion, and you get a set of powerful urges towards rationalizations which beg the question. The ability of man to split his mind and his ego, and his ability to persuade (i.e. deceive) himself are fundamental factors of human conduct and perhaps the richest of all a writer's sources of material. In the case of many religious-minded scientists they result in the production of what might be called a set of religious euphemisms which enable them, by a sort of suspension of the faculties, to remain at home in more or less formal religion and to avoid a really distressing experience. In *Rats, Lice and History* Hans Zinsser dealt most amusingly and pungently with this tendency.

I wonder what happens to some of these men when the crisis comes. Having talked themselves into a set of beliefs which would not stand up under the pure scrutiny of their own discipline, when they desperately need these beliefs for sustenance do they stand up? Or do they break down like a rickety scaffolding?

That last was the fear which came to me as scientific thinking dawned. The idea of an undergraduate trying to grasp the absolutes of eternity and infinity and seeking to find what, if anything, he believed for any other reason than that it had been told to him and it was pleasant, may seem callow and even a little silly. It did not seem so to me. I had learned what amounted to a new concept of truth; it seemed, and still seems, inescapable that what I should believe about the greatest truth of all must be valid by that concept. I desperately wanted to believe in a purpose in life, in some importance in myself on an absolute scale, in life after death. Like everyone else I wanted and needed the comforts of religion.

The better one's education, the wider one's knowledge, the more he needs them. Primitive man lives in a man-centred world around which the sun and stars revolve. This world is eternal, that is to say, it has no end in sight. Judgment day in this sense is not an end, it is merely a change. As a matter of fact, he has no real conception of the meaning of 'eternal,' his entire time-conception is comfortingly small. If he should become godless he still lives in a small enough world to give himself some scale.

But the educated man is in a worse case. When I started examining my foundations to see if they were sound, I was conscious of geologic time, which was gratifyingly long. The foreknown, cold end of the world was too remote to concern me. But prying, I like an ass had to peep at eternity and infinity. I probably wasn't capable of really conceiving them, probably am not to this day, but I had a good shot at it. Then indeed I and my world and my miserable hope of seventy-five years dwindled into nothingness. Then indeed I had need of God, need of belief in something everlasting in myself, for seventy-five years, or a hundred, was so futile a speck in time that it was not even worthwhile to turn hedonist in it.

But I could find in my religion nothing in which I could feel secure unless I could honestly believe that at some point, somewhere along the line of myths and traditions and speculations, there had been a divine revelation. The only authority I could find for such a revelation were the statements of fallible men. The

Bible was its own authority for itself. This is true because I say it's true.

Suddenly, and it was quite sudden, I was out, stark naked on the barren rock of atheism with the icy winds of eternity and infinity blowing upon me. Believe me, it was no fun. I have known a few contented atheists (I except Communists, they have a religion of their own), and I have always wondered at them. They seem to belong to the division of mankind possessing but little of the religious emotion, for they are content with their small disproofs of religion, or rather of the accessory trappings of religion such as miracles, saints, and rites, and move happily in a man-centred world unaware of the terror of their own littleness.

I tried to take refuge in evasions. If I could not believe in any continuance of my ego after death, perhaps there was another sort of life in the continuance of my works and influences. Through such service as I might render mankind, through the effects I might let loose upon the world. . . . Suppose I made an important scientific discovery, or better yet, wrote a great book. There was immortality there. Was there? Homer is three or four thousand years old, a mere nothing, and in the periodic collapse of civilizations might be lost entirely. Even if he wasn't, in the end the world would die, there would be no more mankind. It was a long time till then but beyond that long time lay eternity. One couldn't get up even a fake comfort there.

All of this was going on in the head of Number Three on the Varsity one-hundred-and-fifty-pound crew. I am not exaggerating when I say that it was a terrible experience and that it took all my courage. Over and over again I shrank back from what I was facing, the loneliness, the humility, the futility, to a refuge in *belief*. But each time I had to face the fact that this was *not* faith, but will-to-believe, and I was out in the cold again. My crew usually rowed early in the afternoon that season, and when I returned my roommates would be out. I would sit for hours, contemplating, struggling, studying. I would arrange for dateless Sundays when I could have the place to myself and spend an entire day with it, for none of this could be thought through easily.

It all sounds young as hell, and it was, but looking back on it now I find it, though ill-informed and naïve, still valid as a process. I read in philosophy, but most of formal philosophy turns aside at the boundaries of the zone in which I was lost. Man has set up three disciplines, religion, philosophy, and science, the combined works of all three of which alone may serve to answer the riddle of the universe, then he has pried them apart and set them at war with one another.

Of course I looked up other religions and got my first ray of light from Buddhism and Brahmanism, for there, setting aside the folk-beliefs such as specific reincarnations, I first encountered a reasonably skeptical intellect seeking to pierce through to the nature of God. (I don't mean skeptical about God, but about man's inherited explanations.) It seemed to me that here, at least, was a good try. I got some comfort from it, but of a thin kind, and I was dubious about a system from which I had to discard so much before I was left with a credible remainder.

As a matter of fact I was still caught in the accessories of religion. I had not then grasped the anthropological doctrine of the *complex* (not the psychological, please), although I ought to have. Perhaps I understood it when I ran into it within my science, but like other scientists, I failed to apply it outside, at that time.

I think it's worth explaining in this connection, so here are two elementary examples of it. Many Indian tribes in the western United States make their arrows with a straight groove along one side, a zig-zag lightning-stripe along the other, and a crest of dark paint, black or blue, surrounded by red. Most of them agree that the zig-zag represents lightning, which adds to the arrow's power. Some say that the groove is to make the arrow fly straight, others that it's to draw blood more freely. Of course it does neither of these things. Some just say that that's the way one makes an arrow. As to the crest, one tribe explains that it's the arrow's eye, another that it's a way of identifying one's arrows and making them easier to find.

Save for the lightning symbol with its obvious magical value, none of these has any function at all. Some ancient tribe, bringing the bow and arrow to that part of the world — perhaps even earlier, the bringers of the thrown dart — made these marks for reasons of its own. Admiring neighbours, copying the missile, copied the marks. In time the explanations for them became blurred and changed, but the *complex* continued — that an arrow 'is not good,' 'will not fly well,' 'is not properly made' unless it has them. Over thousands of years it has been difficult for an arrow-maker to conceive of a finished arrow without them.

A friend of mine had an excellent Chinese cook. Wanting him to learn a certain receipt for making cake, she sent him to a friend's house to watch the process. The receipt called for six eggs and the friend broke them one by one into a bowl, putting each in turn into the batter. The fourth egg was bad, so she threw it away. A year or so later the cook, who had learned to make the cake to perfection, was asked to give the receipt to another friend. 'You take seven eggs,' he said. 'You put three into the batter, throw away one, then you put in three more.' This is a beautiful example of a complex. Our religions are full of them.

Now 'sacred studies' at Groton, insomuch as they weren't a rather interesting history of Christianity, were a training in the complex. I imagine that anything reaching further into the great mystery would have been lost on most if not all of us. But if, even, we had been made to have a real try at understanding such a concept as the Trinity, I would have had a lead into a type of thinking which I had to discover for myself. The European white man, as a matter of fact, is not very strong on grasping such things, and it has been my observation that the average white Christian may call himself a monotheist, but actually conceives of at least two gods, God and Christ, whom he doesn't really unite, and is distinctly vague about the Holy Ghost. The Catholic church is well aware of the tendency of its believers to transmute the saints and Our Lady into a pantheon, and where it is most conscientious fights constantly against it. Very few ordinary white men conceive of God in other than anthropomorphic terms, whatever phrases they may repeat.

The ignorant, illiterate Indians of Guatemala have shelved the Holy Ghost entirely, but they understand the nature of the Two-in-One of God and His Son, and assume that everyone else does — so much so that at first, in trying to record their beliefs, I became greatly confused. They also understand the impersonal, omnipresent nature of God, and never confuse Him with the white-whiskered old man of our mythology.

Having been trained chiefly in a collection of facts, procedures, and arguments concerning minor premises, the major premise having been already conceded, I had no preparation for what I was up against. In science, working from the known, one can project a hypothesis into the unknown by simple reasoning. There is a big difference between this and the use of rigourous self-discipline in a sincere quest for religious truth. And in approaching Christianity or Buddhism, although I began by rejecting the complexes surrounding the core of the belief, I didn't distinguish clearly enough between them. If the appurtenances were clearly mere folk-stuff, I was inclined to feel that the rest must be tainted.

Not being a Hindu mystic or a saint, I could not live permanently, hour by hour, with the frame of mind which non-belief induced. Having arrived at a devastating negative, healthy instinct made me set it to one side. My natural interest in the world and my sound, animal nature kept me enjoying life, but from time to time, left to myself, I had to face my emptiness.

Then I ran into a striking evidence of the correctness of the anthropological theory that the best preparation for understanding our own culture is the study of one quite unlike it, which can be approached without preconceptions. Among the Navajo Indians I encountered the concept of impersonal, omnipresent God in terms as lofty as Buddhism's, and with it an advanced religious philosophy including certain terms, such as *hozhoni*, of a technical, religio-philosophical nature, which are sadly lacking at least in a layman's English. The superstitious folk-stuff with which the core of Navajo religion is overlaid is very obvious to a white man, not being that in which he was reared, and in general being somewhat cruder. I was genuinely surprised to discover this other content behind it, also to discover the division (the fancy word is dichotomy) which the more thoughtful, advanced students among the Navajos recognized between the trappings and practices on the one hand and the heart of the religion on the other. What I encountered was a genuine sophistication stated in unusually clear terms, and all in a frame so unlike anything I had previously known that I could come to it without preconceptions. I was also, of course, encountering the exceptional genius of the American Indian, outpost of the Orient, for unconfused, evolved religious thinking.

I did not become a convert to the Navajo religion, but it showed me the way out of desolation. Incidentally, a year or so ago I spent an evening with an educated Navajo, educated in both white and Indian terms. He was interested in the doctrine implied in one of my novels, and as I might have expected, had penetrated a good distance beyond the symbolic statement made therein. We fell to discussing the nature of God and the soul. To do this, neither of us being trained in white philosophy, we had to establish a set of arbitrary definitions, and I was interested to learn that in his own language many of these terms already existed. He kept telling me that we could carry on our talk so much more easily if only I knew Navajo. This interview with a thoughtful, well-informed, devout Indian who was linguistically equipped to make himself understood to me more than confirmed everything I had suspected about the high nature of Navajo religious philosophy.

What my creed finally came to be is not important, it represents simply one individual's private groping for God. I doubt that I, Oliver La Farge, that inner essence of individuality, that spark distinct from all other sparks to which we cling so desperately and without which it is difficult even to imagine a universe in existence, that centre and self which we denote so aptly by the single, narrow, upright stroke of a capital I, will continue as such. The loss of that belief is the loss of one of the greatest of the comforts of religion, it makes it a little more difficult to face growing old and to contemplate death. The answer to it is to contemplate and become accustomed to the idea of the extinction of the ego, hand in hand with contemplating the nature of God. This can be done, although it does not come easy to a full-living, sinful white man.

I suspect that much of this chapter suggests the Swami, certainly these last paragraphs do. Fortunately, I have no desire to go about making converts. I see a lot of evil come out of the sects and complexes in which people believe, the prevention of birth-control where it is badly needed, the mulcting of the poor, the promotion of prejudice and suppression of knowledge, but I see just as much good. Pseudo-religion may make some ugly people smug and enable others to be bad while admiring themselves; religion sustains, comforts, and guides the internal lives of millions. Out of it comes individual and mass good. To many people, most I should say, my particular religion would seem cold and devoid of comfort. Personally I find the former untrue and the latter increasingly less true, but the point is that on the few occasions when I have tried to argue it (save with unusual thinkers like that Navajo) people draw back and feel uncomfortable. I'd have to work very hard to make a convert. And having denied to all other religions their automatic claim to the certainty of being right, why on earth should I think I am?

These observations have led me to think a certain amount about faith. We are all told to have faith, it is dinned into us that we must not doubt or question, but have faith. Taking the word on that level, faith would be a great force for evil in this world, for it is used to mean that one should turn off his mind and blindly follow self-appointed authority. On a little higher level the word is used for the will-to-believe, and here it represents one of the finer aspects of the universal practice of self-deception. But faith is a great deal more than that.

Take a sincere, uncorrupt believer in any given religious complex. At the heart of his belief is faith, that is, conviction. Real faith is not afraid of doubts and arguments, it does not fear that God will be lessened by the discovery that the earth revolves around the sun. It has no fear of any knowledge, knowing that two truths cannot be incompatible, and it recognizes instinctively that no scientific advance has ever been made which did not add to our ability to perceive the glory of God.

But outside this citadel are a series of superfluous outer works thrown up by will-to-believe, which is a mechanism created by the emotions in order to retain certain comforts. This is a familiar, purposive psychological mechanism, and like all such mechanisms it secretly recognizes its own weakness, wherefore it is constantly on guard. Will-to-believe springs into action when an attack is made or threatened against the most outlying parts of the complex. The arrow must have its 'lightning,' its 'path,' and its 'eye.' If the need for those be questioned, the next thing will be making one without a head, or no arrow at all. The reasoning is ridiculous, but its emotional basis is easy to understand. It runs all through life, it is constantly recurrent in the fields of politics and social reform, here in religion it amounts to a denial of faith.

CHAPTER 9

AMERICAN SPLINTER

P<small>EOPLE</small> brought up as I was have had the changing world practically slapped in their faces. To this they have responded in different ways. Some feel it to be a good thing and are changing with it, some are making a virtue of necessity. A sizeable part of the class to which I am supposed to belong is either fighting with all its might to stop the change — or at least to nullify its effects upon them — or is combining that effort in an odd way with an ostrich denial that such a thing is happening.

My kind, in my time, grew up to order, security and privilege of a degree which it is difficult for most Americans to grasp. Their world-view, ethics, and code of manners, all their mechanisms, were aimed at the perpetuation of that security. Now it is more than threatened, it is in the course of being destroyed. This is an old situation, recurring over and over again in the world's history, it is a situation which arouses unexpected viciousness in those whose way of life is threatened. The drab, deep emotions behind Chamberlain's Munich and the suicide of France, the exceptional bitterness both in serious talk and in jest, the violence of feeling levelled against President Roosevelt, have sprung from it in our time.

I was born to this security and I no longer have it. I find it curious now to look back and see what that lost world was like.

It was a world and it is still trying to be one. Some years ago there were published two maps, one showing a Bostonian's, one a New Yorker's view of America, amusing distortions of the surface and proportions of the country, the Atlantic Seaboard huge, the rest dwindled away, the centre of the country vaguely filled in with items of misinformation. They were entertaining maps and they were quite correct.

As far as America was concerned, we recognized a narrow zone running along the coast from a short distance north of Boston to the Mason and Dixon line. Within this zone was civilization, people who mattered (and an unfortunate intrusion of low persons of Irish, Italian, and other alien descents), this was what we meant when we said 'everybody,' or 'America,' or 'the country.' Across the Mason and Dixon line there was another tribe in Virginia which we recognized, and which also mattered, but with which one could not have close relations since it was almost impossible to persuade a Virginian that anyone from north of him could be a gentleman. On the California coast around San Francisco there was a sort of colony of our kind, and one had connections and knew people in Saint Louis, really quite a civilized place and not nearly as middle-western as one would think.

The rest of the country was what a Frenchman would have called 'the provinces.' It was strange, often ludicrous, and of no importance. We had absolutely no conception whatsoever of its scale, let alone its population. In one section there was a rather glamorous folk called 'Southerners,' genteel and faded. There was a lot of thinly populated desert country where cowboys and Indians roved. There were exotic sections worth visiting for play or sport. Then there was the Middle West, producer of objectionable things such as Babbit, Prohibition, and the La Follettes. People from the Middle West behaved stupidly when they went to Europe and made the French and English think we lacked culture. But they were not America, we were America.

In fact, of course, our numbers were infinitesimal, but we did not know that. We were so few that we were no more than a splinter of America. But included in our ranks, either by birth or by an established system of wise incorporation, were those who controlled the flow of money; that power added to our advantages of education and general distribution of wealth and our network of mutual help enabled us to make trouble away out of proportion to our numbers. We thought we were the country, we were in fact a splinter of it, but the splinter was firmly imbedded in America's thumb.

I find it hard now to believe what our view of America was. I remember that when I was an undergraduate, not only boys my age but our elders seriously stated, over and over again, that 'the country' did not want prohibition, it had been put over upon us by the Middle West. That by this they meant that an overwhelming majority of the American people had voted in favour of Prohibition, did not occur to them. Somehow all those citizens did not really count, they might swing election after election, but they were not 'the country.' We were.

It was an Englishman who first forced me to look my own concepts in the face. I had been several times to Arizona, I knew the look and breadth of the land, but I had not allowed that to penetrate my insularity. He was seeking knowledge of America, and various of us, his friends, invited him to come and sample this or that part of it. I wanted him to see the Indian country of the Southwest, a picturesque appendage to the nation of my conception. Others urged him to Bar Harbor and Charleston. He chose to take a job on the Kansas City *Star*, at which we all protested in horror.

'I don't understand you,' he told me. 'Almost every day I hear you and your friends damning the Middle West. It supported the Bull Moose Party, and you're worried now about La Follette's campaign. You say it hung Prohibition on you and won't let you get rid of it. It has produced the Farm Bloc and the Progressive Bloc, it controls your foreign policy. And yet all of you say it doesn't count and that there's no point in studying it. It seems to me it's the most important part of America and you'd all do well to go and take a look at it.'

He was quite right, but no such idea had occurred to me until then.

Part of this attitude was wishful thinking. One did not want to admit that the group which once did control the Union had lost most of its power. If one's own ancestors did not include senators, cabinet officers, governors, and so forth, at least these were sprinkled liberally among one's acquaintances'. Also fairly common was descent from men who had taken an important part in freeing and founding the Union. Those had been the good days, when the country wasn't full of foreigners and politics were clean and genteel. In our own time, we clung to individual resurgences — Theodore Roosevelt (distressingly radical, but still a gentleman in politics), Henry Cabot Lodge. Andrew Jackson had started a regrettable revolt of the masses which continued with ever-increasing strength, and it was comforting to dismiss these masses by pointing to their ignorance, provincialism, and naïveté, as if by so doing one could talk away the living facts of history.

The strength of this class lay, and lies, in its control of money. A person like myself, neither rich nor affiliated with a financial family, did not formulate this thought. But the great men of our kind were financiers, and they, realists to the core, knew that their power was stabler and more enduring than ever-shifting political power. In the long run money could outlast and wear down any popular movement, with a concession here and there.

That was the strength, or perhaps better, that was the trustworthy weapon which the strength wielded. Perhaps the strength in itself lay in an interlocking directorate just as important as the actual directorates of corporations which have been described so much. This was an interlock of friendships, loyalties, affections, relationships, a responsibility to one's kind which bound the whole group together, and out of which in turn the individual received the sense of security and order which would make him a loyal fighter for his kind.

To a young man growing up this created a situation which no one would find it easy to relinquish of his own free will. My family was not rich. My parents made severe sacrifices to put us through college, and even so we were hard up. In fact, we thought of ourselves as poor. This conception of poverty was not reached by contemplating the average per capita national income. It was a poverty which made a real effort to win scholarships, which regarded 'Final Club' dues as a necessary expense, which would not think of wearing a suit unless it had been made in England or bought at Brooks Brothers'. There was nothing to be afraid of in our lack of spare cash, merely an irritating disadvantage in entertaining girls, a mild amount of foregoing some of the fun the boys around us enjoyed. If anyone had suggested to me as an undergraduate that I consider my financial situation in terms of the average national income, I should have rejected the idea. In terms of my class I was poor, and no one could tell me differently.

Poor — but safe. There was an interlock of thousands of people, commanding infinite resources, to watch over me. When people of my kind were arrested, they didn't get the third degree. One was accustomed to courtesy everywhere, to ready credit, one was 'placed.' Hardly recognizing the existence of habitable land outside of our narrow, coastal province, one didn't have to give much thought to what might happen if one moved to Podunk not to visit but to live. In Europe, of course, one went armed with introductions and letters of credit, and was confident of adequate attention from consulates and embassies. If needed, there was almost no one to whom one could not have access.

So, too, being reared in New York, I not only took for granted my inherited acquaintance with a network of wealth and influence, but also the reception ready for me, through numerous relatives and parents' friends, in Philadelphia, and the always somewhat cooler but still definite acceptance awaiting me in Boston.

Here was a snug world full of friendliness, of real affections, and privilege. In that world one foresaw a clear course, which can be typified by the fact that, during the First World War, we completely took it for granted that if we got into the army it would be as officers—almost everyone we knew had a commission. The way was made straight for our kind.

In college it was time for me to think pretty seriously about my career. In my sophomore year I realized, definitely and for all time, that more than anything else in this world I loved writing, that a writer, pure and simple, was what I wanted to be. I was already started in anthropology. This new realization involved important decisions.

From my father I had acquired a distaste for people who fooled with the arts. Any art was a serious career which must support itself. I knew, too, the struggle my father and mother were making to send us through college. Unproven in writing, it was clear that I could not ask them to support me while I went through what would probably be the long process of learning my craft and developing it into a source of income. It did not, of course, occur to me that on graduating, or even before, I might simply go forth and live in real, not relative, poverty. It wasn't that I thought of this and lacked the courage to carry it out, I didn't think of it.

In order to stop being a burden to my parents as soon as possible, I must continue as a scientist with the expectation that shortly I could win scholarships and other aids. Writing I must pursue in my spare time until the day when I had sold enough to enable me to tell myself, my father, the world, that in fact I was a writer and could make a go of it.

All of this was realistic enough, the plan of a young man who expects to make his own living, a schedule of double work to which I stuck for eight long, discouraging years. But in this planning and the initial will to endure a period of drudgery there entered another element — the complete assurance that in time, by one means or another, drudgery would lighten and straitened circumstances be replaced by relative prosperity. The network of connections assured a young man of some kind of position with good prospects of advancement. Men who got into trouble or who failed badly were the subject of a good deal of consultation and head-shaking, but niches were found for them. Granted a reasonable amount of intelligence and industry one could be perfectly certain of a decent job of some sort, a gentleman's job. In due course there would be marriage to a girl of one's own kind and place. She might bring money with her, she would surely bring additional connections and aids. One would continue all through life to have plenty of use for a tuxedo and evening clothes, one would belong to a club or two, and one could look forward in time to seeing his son graduate from his own college, a member of the same Final Club as his father. Rich or poor, there would always be certain amenities, the gap between one member of the group and another would never become so great as to cut off social relations, there was, in short, the certainty that one would continue always in the general type of life into which one had been born.

The last war and its aftereffects struck a terrible blow at this group security. Events since then have continued hacking at its very roots. That is what has had the endowed classes all over the world so desperately up in arms. The wolf who has just made his pile and intends to hang onto it is one thing, nothing he feels can compare in intensity to the emotions of the men and women who have never known anything but security, who feel that security is theirs by right, and see it all going by the board. It is not just a matter of the crude feeling of safety; attached to it are a thousand graces of life, a certain kind of education for their children, riches of the mind and spirit that come with the possession of leisure and some means, the well-being of friends and relatives, the powerful feelings attached to an ancestral home, to a bit of countryside in which one grew up, to institutions, customs, manners. The cry that Mr. Roosevelt has betrayed his class is not an idiotic wail referring to the loss of certain extra profits, it is the expression of a genuine dismay and indignation at one born within the group, endowed with all its blessings, who has helped to undermine the entire structure. It refers to everything from the pleasure of owning many books to the children's future.

Not being a literary historian I cannot carry out an accurate comparison between the writings of those who were always secure, in the sense I have described, and of those who had to make their own way. Conning the matter in my mind, the odds seem heavily in favour of the latter. I have a feeling that one can see in some genuine talents of the protected group, such as Owen Wister, the recurrent, harmful effects of being too free, too far removed from need. If I have as much money and position as I need anyhow, it is not important to me, that is, not important in any real sense of the word, that my book sell more than moderately, although I should appreciate the gratification of wide sales. If in addition I am quite sure of my position in my own group and feel that mankind outside that group is less important, I am relatively impervious to the opinions of those who know and judge me only by my works. So Henry James can wander off into England and preciousness, so Wister, who is nonetheless the best writer on the West we have yet produced, can intrude an irritating set of stuffy reflections into the mastery of *The Virginian* and can perpetrate *Lady Baltimore* with entire serenity.

A snug world. If you are brought up entirely within it you are as innocent of its actual scale as you would be of the real meaning of 'mountain' had you never seen anything but the hill behind your house. In this I had a little luck. My parents were not perfect conformists. My misery at school gave me a little cynicism, a touch of detachment, largely vitiated by my emotional craving to align myself with the pattern which had rejected me. The habit of unpopularity and the offensive behaviour which arises from a roaring inferiority complex stayed with me at college. Success for my kind at Harvard depended more than anything else upon social honours, election to the Institute and to a Final Club. In my sophomore year I was elected to nothing. This God-sent year of disgrace enabled me to form strong friendships outside of my predestined group. When I did make the clubs I had not become emancipated, but a few ideas were rattling round inside my head. I was at least conscious of the mathematical fact that all the Final Clubs between them comprised not over a hundred men out of the eight hundred in my class, and that that was definitely not a majority. I knew and loved certain splendid men whom the clubs would not accept.

When I left Harvard for New Orleans there were no signs that I would learn to participate in the real America. I held to the habit of mind of the secure and privileged. I had begun to perceive dimly that forty-eight states actually meant forty-eight states full of human beings possessed of an equal right to say how the country should be run; there were some leaks in the dyke through which new thinking might come, that was all. With many good intentions towards my fellow men, and desires for social reform, I was nonetheless a little conservative, responding to the instinct which shies away from any threat to the enfolding structure.

CHAPTER 10

Completely New

Nobody knew me, that was the wonderful thought. Until yesterday there was no one in all this city who had ever even heard of Oliver La Farge, and no one knew anything at all about me.

I sat in the bottom of the truck, slightly tipsy and feeling the unaccustomed heat of the noon sun in February. I was wearing a sort of yellow smock which represented I never knew what, and a small, black mask. In the truck with me were four unusually pretty girls and five extremely likeable young men, all also costumed and masked. The neck of one of the bottles broke, and it seemed necessary to polish it off before the precious whiskey was wasted.

Ahead of us were other similar trucks decorated to a greater or lesser degree with streamers and ribbons. Further ahead loomed the high mass of the Mardi Gras floats themselves. Yesterday and last night I had seen the parade go by, a strange and wonderful sight, and I had felt intensely lonely finding myself a total stranger in New Orleans at the height of its celebrations. I had even tried to date the girl behind the counter in the steamship office. I suppose she was my first item of education in the character of the people among whom I was soon to live. I went about suggesting a date with the greatest hesitation, awkwardly, for in New England the attempt might be met with anger and injured virtue; it was received as a harmless compliment, not to be accepted, but nothing to be annoyed about. The girl was frankly sympathetic towards my plight and awfully nice about turning me down. I was in New Orleans, but I did not yet know what that meant.

Ahead of me lay Mexico, unknown, romantic, strange, and work in its remoter corners under a man whom I knew only slightly. I was eager to go and I was frankly afraid. Yesterday my loneness, my strangeness had been hard to bear. Reporting at the University I met the President for a formal word. The one member of the staff of my Department who was on deck had been rude, clearly anxious not to be bothered with me, resentful that I had been brought down to go on this expedition. Needless to say, he was not a New Orleanian.

Then everything changed. In the bright morning I was dumped in front of the house at which the people of the truck were to gather, left to walk in and introduce myself as the Yankee about whom they had been telephoned. I had been further encouraged by the information that this group was clannish and exclusive, having grown up together and running always together. Actually this exclusiveness came from no lack of ability to mix, but from a combination of deep affection and the security of celebrating special occasions among friends who would not misunderstand or misuse the liberty they wished to allow themselves.

I stood on the sidewalk feeling like a damn fool with the silly, yellow smock over my arm and the mask in my pocket. A bunch of teen-age kids were climbing into a truck. They all knew each other, and masking was familiar to them. I heard the flood of wisecracks which grow out of long acquaintance, the incomprehensible allusions, the laughter and the Southern voices. They made me feel entirely lost. Some people my own age were on the porch. I went towards them reluctantly, to tell them, 'I'm Oliver La Farge. Natalie Scott sent me,' and hope it would be all right.

It was all right. There was a brief period of polite mutual examination, then I was caught in the wave of their high spirits. By-and-by Ellis Moore, seeing that I was a trifle self-conscious about getting into costume, took me inside and gave me a drink of Benedictine. Then we climbed into the truck.

I was discovering the glory of a fresh start. The gang on the truck were delightful, *and they liked me.* On my merits only, coming out of nowhere as if dropped by the stork, they liked me. Harvard was nothing to them, Groton they had not heard of, there was no one anywhere around to whom I had to be grateful because he did not call me Bop. Something fell away which I had been dragging behind me ever since I was twelve years old. From form to form, from Groton to Harvard, to New York and even to Saunderstown, wherever I went the chain of the past continued unbroken, each phase of my being was lineally descended from Bop, everywhere there were people around me who knew what I had been, the rumor of my failure and inability seemed to me to be always muttering in my ears, rigidity and fear of rejection dogged me. That had ended. I felt deliriously light, I seemed to be someone I had never been. Nobody knew me. *Nobody knew anything about me.* They liked me, God had given me a chance to go ahead and prove myself.

My general impression of that day of days is hazy, for I got thoroughly drunk on the mixture of whiskey and elation, but certain details are very clear. They formed the beginning of my education in New Orleans.

I saw that this gang, whose members were most obviously ladies and gentlemen, was free-speaking and free-acting to a degree I had never before encountered. The conversation was frequently racy, high jincks were very much in order, and the girls drank, not too much, but as Boston girls would not have dared. But I had, thank God, also the sense to see that all this freedom went on within and was made possible by a set of rules which everyone understood. There were no passes or amourous gestures, and racy talk never slid over into crudity. I was encountering for the first time in my life a people who did not associate good behaviour with primness, the first hint that the Boston code with which, through Groton and Harvard, I was more familiar than I was with any other, enjoined lines of behaviour which were not functionally related, but merely a complex in the anthropological sense I have described before.

I worked out the broad lines of this perception that morning while I was still sober enough to think, and after some deliberation cast off the collegiate attitude which would have inclined one almost as a matter of duty to one's self to see which of these girls one could get to neck. All those standards had to be junked. It was a lucky thing for me that I had sense enough to see it, otherwise that gang would have unloaded me without a moment's hesitation.

As it was, they became the centre of my group of friends in

New Orleans. They were poor. The boys worked at hard, small jobs, most of the girls earned their own pocket-money if not their livings. Their futures were insecure. The tradition of poverty is old in the South; they turned it into an asset, developing to the highest degree the fine art of providing one's own fun out of one's own faculties. Our parties were generally held in my apartment, since as a bachelor in the French Quarter I had a place in which we could laugh and sing without causing parents to protest or scandalizing the neighbours. A bottle or so of absinthe, some sandwiches, some Saratoga chips were all we needed for a gathering which would last from nine o'clock to three the next morning. For the first year we didn't even have a phonograph.

They were poor and they understood the ways and needs of poverty. I hadn't realized until then what a burden it was to live habitually among people better off than myself. It was characteristic of them that they never came to my place empty-handed. The girls brought things — a pint of real whiskey (this was during Prohibition), something to eat, some contribution. In the course of the evening one of the boys would take me aside, and I would find that they had accurately estimated my outlay and chipped in their shares.

The parties would end well on into the morning. They would go, as they came, in a bunch, and I would turn back from the courtyard door to climb the spiral staircase to my single room. The quiet would buzz slightly in my ears, I would be tired, a little tight, the room would be both empty and messy. Over and over again I would find myself telling myself solemnly, 'Well, Oliver, you certainly have nice friends.' A weak, New England sort of understatement, but I meant it. Waking the mornings after those parties was different from most such wakenings. The sense of fun, the more important, deep happiness I derived from these friendships remained with me, I felt better than I had any right to expect, a good memory kept me company through the tiring day.

My mother told me that in her opinion, every young man should leave his native section for a year or two and go to live and work in a strange place where he was unknown. In a way she was thinking along the lines of the anthropological theory that, by the study of alien cultures to which we come with fresh perceptions and without preconceptions, we shall eventually acquire a new point of view which will enable us to analyze and understand our own. I found this true in New Orleans, for the culture there was strikingly different from my own, the people and their ways, like the countryside and the architecture, were far stranger to me than England had been.

That discovery by itself was instructive. For the first time I was encountering a purely *American* society. Regardless of the strong memories of France these people cherish, they are not Colonial. They have a self-assurance and self-sufficiency which protects them from looking to anyone save themselves for the stamp of genuineness on what they are.

That self-assurance is a gentle thing, neither obtrusive nor smug, yet underlying an important part of their behaviour. It makes possible the gaiety of Mardi Gras; I felt it that first day in a freedom of behaviour which arose from the fact that my friends guided their actions by standards instead of by the possible opinions of others — which means among other things, without self-consciousness. Living in the French Quarter and being in the process of evolving from a scientist into a writer, I naturally made close friendships in the art colony. These did not conflict in any way with my relations with the 'uptown' people, for your New Orleans débutante associates in entire simplicity with the artists on the elementary basis of likings and friendships between people of an age. The two communities were at home with each other. The same governing factor made this possible. More than anything else except the nature of their hospitality, this factor made me see why the South questions the existence of a true aristocracy in the North.

Any society develops to some degree the anthropological complex I mentioned before, the association together of requirements of one kind or another which have no functional relation whatsoever but which, by long association, have come to be taken as inseparable parts of a whole. This is likely to be particularly developed in a tightly organized society primarily concerned with holding firmly to what it already has, such as the Hopis of Arizona. A complex of this kind is made up of a multitude of taboos and required activities, worked out in narrow detail, which, however irrelevant in their original assemblage, have acquired a secondary functional relation of exerting a constant pressure upon the individual towards conformity. Where behaviour is rigidly controlled one can usually postulate the existence of fear — fear of hell-fire, of conquest, or poverty, or perhaps merely an uncertainty of social position which seeks to reassure itself by insisting upon minute details. Through the machinery of the established pattern the causing fear is reinforced by another — fear of public opinion.

The Late George Apley describes such a society with the selective clarity of caricature. The book has a definite anthropological value. To what it describes, the character of New Orleans contrasts strongly. Of course New Orleans, too, has its pattern, its complex, its taboos, compulsions and inhibitions, supported by sanctions of public opinion. This complex, happily, does not contain the element of the eternal scapegoat which gives an unpleasant cast to some Southern communities — the attitude of mind which keeps the Civil War and the Yankees ever alive and contemporary, the objects of a sort of ennobling hostility and of all blame for the failures, hard times, and decay of the past eighty years. In spite of the real economic insecurity which is a major factor in the lives, not merely of some groups, but of Orleanians as a whole, the patterns of the city's society, in The Social Register sense of the word, seem to be based on personal security, an aristocratic assurance that each one stands on his own feet, with the results I have already described. To this is added, and its effects are most important, a sincere and quite simple belief that everyone should have fun, that one of the major aims of life and work is the enjoyment of life. This applies not only to the bright young people; in the stiffest, elderly society, highly organized, formal, and in many ways quite severe, there is still this understanding and acceptance of fun.

Theoretically it is easy for a carefree, fortunate group to have fun and enjoyment, although in fact everyone is familiar with the lack of gaiety which is likely to characterize pleasure colonies. The New Orleans people are not such a group. They have a turbulent, up-and-down history and a difficult present. The French built their city in the teeth of great obstacles. Then they passed under Spanish rule, which they did not like, and just as they were rejoicing at being returned to France, discovered that they had been basely sold up the river to *Les Américains*. After they got used to that and began to absorb the northerners to whom they referred generically as Kentuckians, they had a period of roaring prosperity which ended in the disaster of the Civil War. The city was conquered and occupied by enemy troops under the notorious General Butler. After the war they found themselves under a black legislature guided by carpetbaggers as bad as any that we produced, elections were flagrantly stolen, basic civil rights destroyed, and they were caught in a grim poverty which rendered a meal of hominy grits and syrup a luxury. They remained gay, and won back their freedom by armed revolt. There was another period of high prosperity which dwindled away in recent times until, in the lush nineteen-twenties, New Orleans was already a depression city. After 1929 their condition became disastrous. Through all of these events they were gay, through them all they found the means of fun. The people who fought the ever-recurrent floods, who worked out a detailed plan for rescuing Napoleon from Saint Helena and were ready to carry it out, who sold their ancestral plate to raise funds for fighting Huey Long, are the same ones who drop everything for the Mardi Gras season; they are a strong, gay, determined people, hard for a Yankee to understand, hard even for the purely Anglo-Saxon sections of the South.

It is probably a factor that this society exists against a much gaudier background of the general population than can be found anywhere in the Northeast, perhaps anywhere else in the United States. I lived in the French Quarter when the present slight movement of well-to-do people back into the beautiful old houses had hardly begun. The Quarter was a decaying monument and a slum as rich as jambalaya or gumbo. The small art colony centering around Jackson Square was insignificant, although it didn't know it. The population included Negroes, Créoles, and Cajuns, an occasional Malay drifted in from the Barataria marshes, Italians, Greeks, Jews of both French and North European origin, and a great many Latin-Americans. There were sailors of all kinds, antique dealers, second-hand dealers, speakeasies galore, simple workmen, a fair variety of criminals, both white and coloured nuns, the survivors of a few aristocratic Créole families clinging to their ancestral homes, merchants of all sorts, and whole blocks of prostitutes. Except for part of Royal Street and a section around the Cathedral which had been brushed up and enjoyed the tourist trade, this was the real thing in slums.

Most of these assorted inhabitants were united by love of playing the ponies, by the pleasures of eating good red-beans-and-rice and gumbo and of connoisseurship of coffee, by liking their Quarter just as it was, and by pride in its peculiarities. In that climate the poor city-dweller's life is largely conducted at open windows, on the balconies, and on doorsteps, and thence flows into the street. There are never people lacking to advise you in any undertaking or to yell at a cop who is arresting a drunk. Start something that needs help or get into a fight, you'll soon have company. One time I set out to hoist a big packing case, which I wanted for a coal bin, up to my balcony. Pretty soon half the block was out, a better rope was found, poles were produced with which the thing could be pushed and guided from below, utter strangers were on my balcony testing its strength, and a fine, fat, slatternly woman took charge of the whole procedure.

The Quarter was ruled over, or rather kept in a state of mild irritation, by a splendidly corrupt police force. These cops were required to keep their records up by making a certain number of arrests per month, and this they did by picking up anyone who looked like easy game. Because of them all New Orleans dined early, since it was not safe for a coloured maid to walk home after the police began its night prowling. They, too, united the slums in hatred, contempt, and distrust.

Then, of course, there were the Negroes, not merely as a component of the Quarter but as a city-wide class by themselves. I believe that the New Orleans attitude towards Negroes, with its French elements, differs somewhat from that of the South as a whole. The city of the Octoroons and the aristocratic Free Mulattoes, of the armed militia 'Regiments of Free Men of Colour,' would have to be different from, say, a Georgia country town. However that may be, the sheer numbers of Negroes, their situation and way of life, are startling to a New Englander reared in the Abolitionist tradition and personally familiar up to then only with the very few Negroes of his own township and one or two in Boston.

It is intriguing to know that the French-speaking Free Mulattoes used to own slaves, but one sees almost nothing of that curious group, as they live mainly outside the city and keep themselves very much to themselves. The famous Octoroons have long since vanished. That many of the ordinary, slave-descended Negroes speak their own dialect of French, and that, infuriatingly, they can understand your French but you can't understand theirs, fits so naturally into the general picture that it soon ceases to make an impression. What bores in upon a Northerner is the broad, general Negro situation.

It seemed to me that it would be gratuitously ugly for me to flaunt my opinions or my anthropological theories in the faces of my new friends. Besides, the Southern Negro was so unlike the Yankee one that I felt as if I were encountering a new race and wondered whether indeed either my tradition or my science had any application.

Of course some question as to my ideas on the general, related subjects of the Civil War and Negroes was bound to come up. I have great contempt for those Northerners who, in the South, ape the Southern point of view as if thereby they thought they could ally themselves with the aristocracy, and who go about, in effect, apologizing because their side won the war. Too many of our people died much too sincerely for us to betray their cause or try for a cheap superiority through race prejudice.

When the question came up, I answered truthfully. I was a Yankee. My grandfather fought in the Union Army, I was reared in the Abolitionist tradition. Of course I was glad that the North had won the war. By the same token I was heartily sorry about the Reconstruction (like Margaret Mitchell, I ignored the matter of the Black Codes). As for the present, I wanted to learn. I certainly made no attempt to defend General Butler; on the other hand I did on one occasion stand up vigorously for Shaw, 'buried with his niggers.' I could hardly not have done that, and what I had to say was generously and understandingly received. I think the New Orleans people approved of my position. Many of my friends were frank, temperate, and thoughtful in helping me to understand their point of view, we discussed it freely, and never with rancour.

It seems to me that for a white man, born in the South and not specially trained, to think other than as they did would be remarkable. Every instinct of self-preservation and the deep urge to perpetuate and protect one's kind, operate to develop their point of view. The average American of any section, although he may grant the equality of this or that race, does believe that race inequalities are well proven. Knowing little or nothing of social science or genetics, most Americans readily accept the superstitions which have grown up around the Negro. If Northerners wish to reform the South, they should study first the practical, realistic factors governing the present relationship and then see if they can offer equally practical and real methods of change.

The Southerner is conditioned; so is the Yankee. My own conditioning could not have been more opposed to the Southern. In my part of Rhode Island there were a very few Negroes, as native to that soil as any white man. They lived, spoke, acted as we did. There was no Negro dialect. In race, they were brown rather than black, that is probably about half and half as the result of long-forgotten minglings. I called the older men 'Mister' as I did any others, they called me Oliver.

When such a man married a white woman, nobody thought much about it. If the children inherited the qualities of their parents, were industrious, skillful, and intelligent, hence respected, it was almost inevitable in a section where Negroes were so scarce that they, too, should marry whites. By the time one had reached the third generation the classification 'Negro,' which had referred primarily to a physical appearance, was pretty well forgotten.

Rural districts have long memories. Tom Shattuck's descent would be well known, but the thought would be not so much, 'Tom is one eighth Negro,' as, 'Tom is old Albert Shattuck's grandson.' Attention would focus upon the fact that Albert had been greatly respected, that is, Albert's remembered personality would dominate the question of his race. The chain of thought, then, would lead to whether or not Tom had inherited his grandfather's qualities.

So the Negroes or people of Negro descent whom I knew intimately were full, free participants in the common culture of Rhode Island. It did not take long to see that what I had learned of them was of no use to me in attempting to understand Southern Negroes, any more than what I knew of the inner life of a Boston girl could guide me in courting a Créole débutante. Southern Negroes are participants in a special sector of Southern culture which the surrounding whites understand and the New Englander finds as hard to grasp as it is for him to learn how Southerners express affection, their form of joking, their way of scolding — and vice versa.

What came out of this contrast was what, as an anthropologist, I should have expected: that with Negroes as with all other peoples the dominant factor is not race, but culture. There are so few places in the United States where the kind of equality I have described exists, that this cultural factor is disguised from us. White Americans on the whole treat the Negro wherever he appears in a special way because he is Negro, thus subjecting him to a uniform conditioning. But anyone well acquainted with the real New England product, be they simple farmers or intellectuals such as Doctor Dubois, cannot help noticing how purely they are the products of their environment, and that they are closer to a white man from their own part of the country than the white man is to a white Southerner.

These observations are inseparable from my picture of New Orleans and education there, for it was there that scientific abstractions and humanitarian theories came up against mass reality and the conflict had to be thought through. The thing which struck me more and more, and which I still feel, is that the Southern system is only a postponement, a makeshift. I think that when a thoughtful Southerner contemplates the very far future he perceives so insoluble a problem, so dark a picture, that thinking of it is intolerable, and as we all do, he quite humanly falls back on the present and the near future, which can be controlled.

As a result partly of my time in New Orleans, partly of work among Indians in the United States, Mexico, and Guatemala, I formed a theory which later, when it turned out to have broad ethnological applications, I called by the resounding name of the Theory of Constrained Cultural Adaptation. It's a nice mouthful. I believe that it contains the corrective to some of both the Abolitionist and the Southern errors.

Putting this theory in a simplified form, it falls into two parts. The first is that if restraints, restrictions and oppressions are forced upon a group from above, so that its life becomes constrained, the group will adapt to this. Under this constraint it will still seek and to a considerable degree find the satisfactions of life — causes for laughter, fun, gratifications and releases of various kinds. It will even form warm relationships with members of the dominant group.

Thus far the theory counteracts the New England error, for your New Englander, arguing from his own experience, expects to find in a group which has been subjugated for generations the same unrelaxing resistance and continuous resentment which would characterize him if he were suddenly put under such a yoke. The achievement of happiness he sees among such peoples bewilders him, and renders him an especially gullible sucker for such remarks as that Negroes are always laughing, happy and carefree. He does not understand laughter under oppression for he has never needed it.

The second part is equally important. No matter how well a people adapts itself under constraint, the consciousness of constraint will always exist and with it the desire to escape from it. The simplest comparison is to wearing tight shoes. One may have shoes on which hurt and nonetheless dance, laugh, have all kinds of fun *despite the pain*. For various reasons the wearer may put on those shoes day after day, seemingly of his own accord. But show him that shoes exist which meet all the requirements without hurting, and he will long for them. Let him obtain them, and he'll throw away the old ones. And even if he believes that these shoes and these only can be worn, he will enjoy exquisitely the times when he takes them off.

This is where the Southerner misses out, although he usually knows in a general way of the gatherings at which Negroes give themselves the relaxation of forgetting that white men exist, their care in addressing each other by the titles, 'Mister, Miss, Mrs.,' which white men will not accord them, the thousand small reliefs and easances they seek.

No human situation remains static. Education, ability to look after their own interests, and an increasingly sharp perception of what a free situation would be like are all spreading through the Negro world and will continue to spread. This isn't a matter of theory, it's a fact which some day may change the very face of America.

Meantime another law is operating. Any anthropologist knows that, remorselessly and inevitably, any two groups living side by side will mingle. If proof is needed, one can take a look at India and note how an iron caste system has failed to keep the light-skinned conquerors from absorbing quantities of the older, dark blood. We know, too, that our Negroes are constantly receiving more white blood. It is not a question of whether we like or are shocked by what is happening, it is that the facts which confront us have implications so serious that we cannot afford to blink them.

No reliable figures can be had on the number of 'white Negroes' who each year become white men and women; the best indications are that it runs to several thousand a year. Startling though that may be, it is actually less significant than the fact that Negroes as a special group are steadily becoming whiter, better educated, more competent.

This group numbers nearly ten per cent of the total population. And there is no way in which we can stop what is happening, no one has ever devised a manner in which millions of human beings could be kept segregated and in the dark. The process is very slow, the change in one generation is not great, but looking forward a few centuries one sees that somewhere along the road there will have to be a complete change or else an explosion. It seems only hard common sense to start building now towards stability by helping the oppressed group to achieve equality and freedom which will eliminate the constraints and the dangerous resentments. As a matter of fact, there would probably be less interbreeding of Negroes and whites if Negro women were economically and civically secure.

If those who are in power anywhere really want to remain safely in power and perpetuate their rule, it seems to me that they must make it their business to see to it that all the people are comfortable, otherwise in the long run the sufferers, the uncomfortable, will reach and reach again for a better life, and in the end will get it or else bring everything down with a crash. Conservatives, if only out of self-interest, should be ardent promoters of social reform. I ran into this idea in reverse during the election of 1940, when the Communists and their sympathizers wanted Roosevelt defeated because the New Deal, and particularly the various relief measures, made it impossible to hope for a revolution.

I don't want to overstress the Negro dilemma in describing my personal New Orleans. It was only one line of thought. Without conscious effort, completely without any urge to proselytize, the city and the people simply by being themselves offer a willing stranger a post-graduate education, new ways of thinking, new knowledges of the world and of himself.

One line of education was the experience of living as a relatively poor man among the poor. I have already described the New Orleans police force as it was in those days. I was no longer living in a world in which I could expect courtesy from them, or immunity from the third degree. I was just another of those damn artists, a folk whom the cops disliked. I witnessed some arrests that were utterly outrageous and knew a sense of sickening futility. I learned why the non-criminal poor fear and hate the police and shy away from municipal institutions in general. I acquired that fear myself, I would go out of my way to avoid a cop, the sight of them made me bristle.

I had occasion to see, too, the rough, casual treatment given to a poor man rushed, injured, to the Charity Hospital. Medically correct and efficient, but with the heartlessness of young internes who have been allowed to feel that charity patients don't count.

One bit of class security had rolled away from me, and along with it there went another. The real meaning of poverty was vivid around me. I was far from home and falling out of the habit of thinking in the snug terms of the protected. My excellent job was in danger; finally, after months of uncertainty I lost it under circumstances which were likely to make it difficult for me to get another. My poverty was of the genteel kind, but occasionally the hot breath of the real thing brushed me, periods of terrific contriving, the occasional missed meal, periods of serious worry. They were only samples, and mild ones at that, but they shook up my serenity.

With this, the concepts of Groton returned forcefully. I fully remembered the Ungroton Boy again, the boy who had failed in being, who might bluff the world for awhile but in the end was doomed to total failure. Being reoccupied by him, I doubted my friends, and so saw less of them. Bop had caught up with me in New Orleans at last. I clearly saw that after all, it was quite as possible for me to land in the street, homeless and broke, as it was for me to be picked up by a stray cop or suffer any other of the common ills of mankind. I looked forward into life, and saw that it was up to me alone to forestall a desperate old age, and I was not at all sure that I could do it. I was coming a little closer to reality, although I interpreted it in the unreal terms of my abiding nightmare (I still had The Dream often in those days), and I did not like it at all. Hampered as I was by that emotional certainty of eventual disaster, I found the real world too hard to take. I began seeking for ways to flee back into the past.

Laughing Boy provided it for me. That success, which should have ended the need for escape, became the means of it. The book was the culmination of years of hard work and stubbornness, it was something entirely mine, spun out of myself, an achievement as unspoiled as my quick friendship with the people on that truck. But most unfortunately I hurried from New Orleans back to my little nest in New York, back to where one could still believe that the old securities continued. I sloughed off almost everything that New Orleans and trouble had taught me and postponed the enjoyment of life by another decade. It's impossible to tell, of course, what would have happened to me if I had stayed away from home and allowed *Laughing Boy* to mean what it should have. I suspect, for one thing, that had I done so I should not now be as completely tagged as an escape-writer as I am. As it was, I was to go on running away from myself, or from the Ungroton Boy, for some time to come.

Then, too, I should have remained among artists and writers. I have been back among them for the last few years, and I not only find their company very pleasant, I find them an enormous stimulant to my own work and growth. The colony there was small; I once figured that it could not possibly number over fifty people, and it was lacking, except for Lyle Saxon and for a time when Sherwood Anderson was there, in older, established men. Among the unknowns was a considerable number who were eventually to have more or less success — Milburn, Faulkner, Bradford, O'Donnell, Basso, for example. But we, of course, lamented that we hadn't been there when the great gods still walked the earth, the men who had achieved fame. We didn't realize that they had seemed just as ordinary and unknown as we did, and that it had been just as impossible then as it was now to tell who would become famous and who would eventually give up and go into selling insurance.

I don't remember anyone cherishing the idea that he was an as yet unrecognized genius in our midst. All the ones I knew well had the same abiding ambition, and all seemed to feel that they would be lucky if they just managed to get by. The determination to continue writing or painting was not based on a conviction of coming success, but was an unreasoning one based on an inner necessity. When one of us achieved anything at all, however slight, the other workers were delighted, and I think everyone took new courage.

I specify 'the other workers.' In New Orleans, and I think in most art colonies, there is a sharp distinction to be drawn between workers who are there because it was a good place in which to carry on the struggle, where living is cheap and one has the stimulus of one's own kind, and those who are primarily interested in a slack, easy way of life. The young artist who really intends to get anywhere works like stink. Many of them show great courage in the face not only of every imaginable discouragement but of hunger and privation. Their road to success is extremely hard and they must be willing to travel on it without ever having any assurance that it will become smoother or that they can attain either recognizable success in the world's terms, or even the inner satisfaction of having done the kind of work they would like to do. Man after man gives up and turns aside; the ones who stay with it have guts. The workers in the colony were real people.

They were outnumbered by men and women who simply liked the life. Some of them had a little talent, some may have had large talent but for lack of character been unable to exploit it. Some had neither talent nor character. The milieu enabled them to indulge their sexual oddities, or to present the world with a *raison d'être* when in fact they had none. These were the people who bitterly attacked any worldly success. If an artist sold a picture, if a writer placed a story in a magazine that paid, he had commercialized himself. Lack of recognition was the only test of the real artist, at moments it even seemed as if complete incomprehensibility was the ultimate goal.

With envy in their souls and much too much time on their hands they devoted themselves to malice. I have seen them unite against a desperately hard-working, independent painter who kept himself to himself, in not merely the attack of tongues which gave him the name of a monster, but an attack against allowing his pictures to be shown, against every activity he undertook, underhanded and mean and violent.

The workers, the comrades-in-arms, taught me a lot. Poor, coming of all origins, with the slums all around them, they were bound to be fairly radical politically. Some had merely the irresponsible radicalism of the young man or woman who has no direct relationship to the economic and industrial world, others held opinions carefully thought through, well worth considering. In the aesthetic fields they ranged all along the line from right to left. I was conservative in art and politics, but slowly their ideas filtered into my mind. I accepted nothing whole, but I received yet another stimulus to real thinking.

There was one curious phenomenon which recurred from time to time and was to us an unexpected source of encouragement. The horse-racing and open gambling and the general high living and good fun brought to New Orleans from time to time writers who were selling steadily at top prices to the big, slick magazines, men who wrote race-track stories, westerns, or some other single class of tale year in and year out, twenty-five hundred dollars a story and ten or twelve stories a year, twenty-five thousand for a serial, and movie rights popping up all over the place. They were so rich that we couldn't take it in, they made lavish gestures such as turning up with a couple of bottles of real whiskey or taking a bunch of us to eat at one of the good restaurants, without even seeming to know that the act was lavish. Good God, they could blow ten dollars on a meal and think it ordinary!

They sought us out, particularly they used to turn up, as everyone did, at William Spratling's studio (the man who later founded the silver industry in Taxco). That was our main gathering place, and at first we were distinctly flattered by the attention these arrived men paid us although we had our fingers crossed about the stuff they wrote.

They were first-class craftsmen, as one must be to sell to the good slicks. They were masters of the colorful word and fresh phrase, masters of the art of narrative. They were really wonderful talkers, for in discussing ideas or telling of what they had seen their gifts could have full play without being vitiated by the trite plot or the taboos of their writing. They spread themselves for us — and they hung around. Then we saw that behind these fireworks there was a desire to impress us with their artistic ability, and behind that there was a certain wistfulness. We were still ferocious and undefeated, we had never yet toned down the truth or made use of what we knew to be inferior material for profit, we did not believe we ever would. We had in us the possibility of becoming artists. These men had had it once, and now they were craftsmen and forever would be. So they acted a part before us, craved our company, and gave us a new strength. It was a strange thing to see, and years afterwards the memory of it shaped vital decisions for me.

There was another bit of instruction, which began on that first day with a small incident, shortly after Ellis Moore gave me that encouraging drink of Benedictine and I got into my costume.

We were starting for the truck when out of a clear sky one of the girls said, 'I like you. I think you're nice.'

We don't do that in New England, rarely in New York. I was, of course, unable to make any answer, but I did see that this remark was being made in a totally new way, not flirtatious, not shallow, but a statement of an existing and agreeable fact. One simply didn't make that kind of statement, but I found it warming.

One can make the broad generalization that the English code of not expressing sentiment is actually a system for conveying extreme sentiment by understating and underacting, but that New Englanders are simply voiceless. In this I am thinking mainly of my own people, the country-folk of Rhode Island, but in a general way the same thing holds true for most of New England. Sections vary, and one must avoid the error of mistaking Boston for all six states. Boston is a section possessing its own peculiarities. Or rather, Boston is a section of Massachusetts, and Massachusetts is a part of the whole having entirely exaggerated notions of itself. History shows that the best minds and spirits that tried to settle in Massachusetts were driven out and usually landed in Rhode Island, endowing that state with unique advantages.

There is a great deal to be said for the pithy nature of New England speech and the effective formula of mingled directness and allusion by which ideas are often conveyed. It provides an enjoyable, tart humour with a high content of wit, and it causes common conversations to be unusually high in quotable remarks. But the language makes little provision for expressing the warmer emotions.

Of course 'language' is the wrong word, unless by it one means not only the vocabulary and grammar of speech, but all methods, customs, taboos, and devices affecting communication with others. The New Englander is deeply inhibited against the display of emotion, which in turn is bound to affect the emotions themselves. The man who controls his temper eventually has less temper to control. If I never 'make an exhibition of myself,' never 'slop over,' that means that my feelings never get the best of me, and from this it follows that the feelings themselves become disciplined, so that they may not be weaker but insofar as we are consciously affected by them they are weaker. And your New Englander does rather distrust strong emotion within himself, especially an emotion of the 'soft' variety. The potential is not one whit less than that of other peoples, and from this repression follow various conflicts.

In the field of affection New England lovers are equipped with a fair number of ejaculations which they use rather sparingly. In friendship they are mute, and compliments come very hard to them. These lacks relate to an acute, deep shyness which it is difficult ever to convey to a Southerner, especially as it is not at all apparent on the surface. It is also difficult if not impossible to explain to a Southerner how New Englanders do communicate or the extent to which they can convey to each other considerable depths of feeling, apparently by a kind of telepathy. They are experts at the art of reading between the lines and understanding the thing left unsaid. They achieve at moments a delicacy and penetration of communication possible for very few peoples.

The New Englander also believes, and in his experience among his own kind has seen, that those who profess friendship or love glibly and say nice things with ease are likely to be insincere. Like the Englishman, he believes that Latins are all talk and no heart. He is under the impression that strong, sincere emotions cannot be expressed, or — even more important — that if they can be, expressing them will cause them to evaporate. The girl he courts will mistrust him if his speeches are too pretty.

When I came to New Orleans I honestly believed that Southerners could hand out a very smooth line because they were insincere. That startling 'I like you, I think you're nice,' was my first glimpse of the existence of something else. Lord knows Southerners dish out mere sweet-talk in a remarkable manner, and just as a Yankee can understand what his fellows don't say, so the Southerners can tell the difference between a line of talk which is a rather artistic social form and the simple, direct expression of their warm hearts.

I lived in New Orleans about three years. In that time, chiefly among the members of that first day's gang but not entirely, I made more lasting friendships than I had made in the rest of my life. I mean friendships, not just people one knows and likes but the feeling which the Elizabethans were not afraid to call love. Again and again I received the new, deep pleasure of hearing fondness for me openly expressed, and I slowly learned that these expressions were real.

As we got to know each other intimately the girls got after me for being uncouth and ungracious. I never said anything nice, I never returned a compliment. True to my upbringing, if I thought a girl looked especially pretty on a given evening, I might tell her friends about it but to her I could hardly get beyond 'You're looking nice,' if that. These people were sensitive enough to see that I did love them, but even so they found my lack of demonstrated affection chilling.

With painful self-consciousness I forced the first warm remark past my jaws, something clipped and inadequate. Saying it gave me a glimpse of a new pleasure. I tried again. True affection, I found to my astonishment, was not dissipated but renewed in warmth by being expressed, and the expression of it was a source of happiness. Finally I said something either complimentary or affectionate with sufficient ease to draw amused applause. I was delighted with myself, and I could feel a physical sensation as if bands were being released about my heart.

It is not that I became, or could become an Orleanian. By descent I'm a pretty mixed sort of a Yankee; at first in the presence of the Créoles I thought that I should jettison every aspect of Yankeedom, but I learned better than that. One cannot falsify his inheritance, one need not pretend not to be what one fundamentally is because he has added to it new-found goodnesses and ways of growth. I was not remade but educated, above all in certain simple things touching the happiness and wealth people can give each other. Of all that I have seen and done and felt in New Orleans in those early days and since then, the most important, the most significant summation I can give, is that I came there totally unknown and was thrown by chance among certain people. They were within me before I had time to mistrust them, and so for the first time I can remember I met them without any guard and put my heart in their hands freely. They never let me feel anything but gratitude that I did.

I opened my last novel with the line, 'New Orleans was a mystery and a promise,' having in mind the French Quarter on a warm night. I condensed a lot of my feeling about the place into that line. Anything could happen there, in the blocks of houses too beautiful to be true, under balconies and in the shadows of the arches, and where the jangling, jerry-built shacks have fought their way in among the ancient bricks. The hot nights stirred you until you had a cat's longing to prowl, down streets turned utterly silent, past speakeasies, by doors that gave out snatches of music, and the blocks where the whispers and eyes of the whores behind the shutters made a false promise of romance. Anything could happen in a town where the signs on the trolleys along Canal Street showed that one line ran to Desire and one to Elysian Fields.

One time we were working nights up at the University. On the night I am describing I came home for supper, and to bathe and change, then walked up to Canal Street for the trolley. There was still a touch of dusk in the air, a blue-grey softness colouring the dark. At Canal Street I stood waiting, thinking that I was tired and not feeling in much of a mood for work. I had on a fresh linen suit, I had a little money in my pocket. I wished I were not going back to the University to labour in that foully hot office. I wished I had a date with a girl, that we could go somewhere and dance for a while, and then perhaps come back to my place and sit on the balcony with a cool drink, talking slowly and listening to the banana leaves rustling, and then perhaps . . . It was easy to get thinking that way on those nights.

A girl came up to the car-stop where I was standing, taking her position a few feet from me and more nearly under the street light. She didn't look directly at me, but I could feel that she was conscious of me. One has less hesitation about looking at a pretty girl down there; I was able to study her while we waited.

She would fit perfectly into any dream of tropic romance. French or Spanish, one would say, with heavy black hair coiled in a knot at the back of her head under a smart little hat, long eyes, and heavy lashes. Her nose was beautifully cut, high, fine-nostrilled, aristocratic, delicate. Her mouth was sensitive and full. The shape of her face was a fine oval, a frame for the features, the colour of her lips, the olive skin. She was small, slender, neatly made, with desirable legs and hands. Her whole dress was as smart as her hat, very simple and tailored. There was a quality of chic about her. Except for her lipstick she seemed to be wearing very little makeup.

She had a music roll under one arm. Something about her made me feel that she was probably a good deal of an artist. Her hands were fine. Had she moved into the French Quarter? If so, how had I not noticed her?

She was definitely aware of me. She glanced at me from time to time, quickly, and then looked away again and there was nothing in her expression to suggest that she could be spoken to. I wondered if there were not some way. Tell her, I am a stranger here, knowing few people, but I'm not such a bad guy. I want to know you, I don't plan any cheap stuff, I'm not taking you for a chicken just because you're beautiful. . . . Was there some way to speak to her, here in New Orleans where anything can happen? You hate to give offense, you hate to be slapped down, and still you feel that if you never try you'll never know.

The car came before I could make up my mind. She got on ahead of me, and paid her fare, which she had ready in her hand. I lost a moment fumbling, then paid mine.

The car was nearly empty. I saw her standing in the aisle ahead of me, then she turned and looked directly at me, a strange, wry, defiant look which I have never forgotten, and sat down in the Jim Crow seats.

There was nothing to do but go on by, there was absolutely nothing to do. There was no solution to that problem. I went to the forward end of the car and settled myself, intensely relieved when she got off, feeling strange and at odds with myself in the warm air, wondering.

CHAPTER II

Incident in a French Camp

ONE OF THE infuriating things about fiction is that it must always be more credible than fact. We live in a world of coincidences, *dei ex machinai*, odd happenings, and strange behaviour on the part of quite ordinary people, but the novelist must make everything seem reasonable and build up to each event, or the reader rejects him. In real life many a situation is completely resolved by a main character's being killed by an automobile, but if we use this device in a story the reader feels flatly cheated.

I had an experience in the French Quarter which involved very odd emotions and motivations, and hence behaviour, on the part of at least two people, myself being one. You could not use it in fiction without carefully building up to it and supplying explanations which are unknown to me. It fits the purpose of this book, and this book provides a God-sent chance to tell it.

There was a man in the French Quarter whom we can call Dumaine, who was a little more than my acquaintance, a little less than my friend. He was a good deal older than I. He was cultivated, an artist of some talent, and rather unhappy because of certain frustrations which external circumstances had caused him. He was at once reserved and complex, a man with whom it would be difficult to form a close friendship. At the same time he was a delightful companion. When he was in the mood there were few men who could give one a better evening. He had the quality of real intellectual stimulation.

Dumaine had a mistress, for whom Selma will do as a name. It is a common observation that American women are more readily adaptable to new social surroundings than are the men. Anyone who has been in any kind of business acquires a considerable respect for the American working girl, at least of the professional, white-collar, and secretarial classes. I don't know enough about the others to specify. The percentage of those who think for themselves, are quick to learn, and adventurous, is high. Any scion of an old-established family who is worried lest the stock may run out and the family name and estate disappear should marry his secretary.

Selma was of this kind, newly introduced to the French Quarter. She was pretty, smart as a whip, lively, extroverted, an habitual flirt, and very young. That last descriptive phrase is one I shouldn't have written at the time but springs from the sad passage of time over my head. She was young enough to be slightly dazzled by the fun, freedom, and general trappings of the eccentric community into which Dumaine had introduced her.

I think I first met her independently of him in a friend's studio, and was attracted to her without realizing that she was his girl. And it was part of Dumaine's complexity that when he saw which way the wind blew, and when we were all three together, he should go out of his way to keep me from knowing about it. I don't understand this, but then almost the whole of Dumaine's behaviour remains beyond my understanding. What I want to do is to report it, and mine.

Pretty, smart, flirtatious, enjoying and exploring a new world both of people and of the mind. I think that some of the things about Dumaine which most appealed to her, his real sophistication and his evolved mind, also at moments repelled her because they were a step or two ahead of her. My close French Quarter friends and I were younger, cruder, simpler in our pleasures, and we probably had livelier fun; she wanted that as well as what Dumaine could give her, and as a result she created a conflict, of which I was unaware, between us her contemporaries and this wiser man. He was aware of it, I realized later, probably frightened by it, for he was more than intelligent enough to know what strengths we had as well as to know his own, and he fought us in his own way. Possibly not allowing me to know that she was his mistress was part of it; I think some of his hospitality was, when he would open up with his most delightful qualities and outshine us.

I was at that time in the stage I have analyzed, when the matter of relations with women, of a girl of my own, was confused with the quest to prove myself as good as the next man and also with escape. If I hadn't been, things could not have happened the way they did. Selma looked good to me and I went for her. There had been a lot of flirting, sentimental passages and kissing, before I learned that she belonged to Dumaine and loved him.

That was that, then. I was rather angry at her, and crossed her off the possible list. For some time I saw her irregularly as a friend, and that was all.

But her attitude towards Dumaine became increasingly odd. She would analyze his character shrewdly and cruelly to me, rail at him, appear in open and final revolt against him — and then return to him. She began to give me the impression that he was a sort of Svengali against whose hold she was struggling. Then I was absent from New Orleans for a short time. We corresponded. The correspondence shortly became highly romantic with a strong element of pure slush, and her end of it finally came to the flat declaration that she loved me and was going to leave Dumaine for me.

That was all right with me, provided it was cleanly done. I insisted that she tell him, which she did. The man asked me up to his place on my return, gave me several drinks, made a rather sentimental speech including the phrase 'bless you, my children' repeated a number of times. It seemed to me he was taking it very decently.

There followed some curious weeks. Selma had dinner at my place as many nights as possible, she was as affectionate and delightful a companion as always, each evening started with every possible promise. But it would develop that she was tired, not well, her back ached, or her father was suspicious and she must go home. Night after night she left around eleven o'clock, each time with promises for the future, on certain nights she stayed but we did not make love. When even one who had confused the idea with the reality as badly as I was about at the end of his tether, then she did give me love and it was both good and convincing.

During these weeks she made a number of scattered remarks which I suppose I could have put together had I been more experienced or even in better relationship to life and myself, that she wished I were her brother, that she wished sex were not so important, and others along that line. But of Dumaine what little she had to say was caustic.

I had had affairs, the accidental, almost impersonal, brief relations that come along by chance, but never a stable relationship, and I longed for it. Around me were a certain number of linked names, Hal and Jenny, Paul and Marie, they might live together or they might not, but they were recognized as attached to each other, and to me they had seemed to promise great happiness and comfort as well as meeting the highest demands of the ideas, romantic and otherwise, which plagued me. I was not courting Selma, I was struggling through her to create a picture for which I had been longing, and having made up my mind that I could do it through her I projected love (part of the picture) upon her and I willfully refused to admit any evidence that it might not work. Yet the oddness of the situation was apparent, and I was far from happy in it.

I analyze my own attitudes and behaviour in this situation because those are the ones to which I have the key. The behaviour seems wormlike as one looks it over, yet I was not a worm by habit. Here is a study in the influences and self-deceptions which will cause a man to behave oddly.

One evening Dumaine asked me to come and see him. He began with general conversation, but his manner was rather jerky and he was restless. He gave me cocktails as fast as I would take them, and as his drinks were always good and made of materials I couldn't afford, I took several. That evening he introduced me to the writings of Robert Nathan, till then unknown, and also gave me some advice, as sincere as it was worthless, about my own writing. It was not until I was rather tight that he asked me how Selma and I were getting along. I told him, excellently.

He said that he suspected I might be having some difficulty, noticing perhaps a certain peculiarness in her behaviour.

This was true, but I said, no.

He thought he ought to warn me that there was another man in the picture. He liked me, he thought I was a promising, sensitive young artist, and so he wanted me to know. There was a third party, a newcomer, a man I did not know, a man who had never been on the scene at all. He mentioned various of my friends who had shown interest in the girl and specified that it was none of them, it was a stranger, and a dangerous stranger, a man of unusual capacity with whom I could not hope to deal.

He did not put it as briefly as this. He ran on and on about the stranger until I got thoroughly sick of it. When I tried to question him he evaded me, he suggested no line of action, he piled up his protestations of friendship until they revolted me, and rambled on. He was drinking glass for glass with me, and I imagine had had some before I came. Anyhow, feeling the liquor pretty strongly myself I decided that he was flatly tight. I could make no sense whatever out of his talk unless I assumed that there really was a total stranger on the scene, which I doubted because his manner was so fishy, or more likely that he was telling me a fairy story for the purpose of making trouble. The longer I listened the more I felt that that was the truth, and as a result I got angry. When I left I was barely civil.

The dragging situation acquired an increasing staleness and frustration, it could not have continued very long no matter how skillfully Selma handled herself. Then one night again we went to bed together without making love. A fair amount of beer in my system enabled me finally to sleep, to glide off into solitude and completeness, free for a time of strivings and strainings and internal arguments in deep, contented nonentity.

I was wakened by a light flashing in my face and a rough voice cursing foully. Into the cone of light protruded the muzzle of a revolver pointed at me. At the time it passed through my mind that I had always heard it was good psychology at the start of a hold-up to curse the victim and that that was true. The fierce 'Come on you god-damned son of a bitch put your hands up' was convincing of a will to kill with which one could not parley. I put them up, wondering what was behind the light and what would happen, trying to gather my wits in the face of the confusion of sleep and plain fright.

The cursing went on. It was a trifle too cultivated in tone, then I recognized the voice. He must be drunk, I thought, or else he's gone off his nut. The thing to do is to be ordinary and deflate his excitement.

I said, 'Hello, Dumaine,' in the most ordinary voice I could imagine and let my hands come down.

He said, still ferocious, 'Where's Selma?'

'Take it easy. Wait a minute till I make a little light, I can't think with that damn flashlight of yours in my face.'

I didn't know whether he'd let me turn on the light or no, and half expected a shot. He didn't stop me. As soon as the light was on I felt better. He pocketed his flashlight, but he was still acting rather like a madman, his eyes were dilated, his talk jerky, in general he did not seem the proper person to run around loose with a gun.

After a few more remarks he jumped across the bed, seized Selma by the shoulder (she was still asleep), and jerked her half out of it. I yelled at him to let her alone. She woke up with a start. He let go of her and stood by the far side of the bed, now cursing her furiously.

She was remarkably little upset, telling him in a nearly normal, cross voice to go away and stop bothering her, and then as he went on, saying 'Stop being a fool.'

At this point I realized fully and definitely that something was thoroughly wrong with the whole scene. It was not just a question of what I was observing, it was in myself. I was humiliated and angry over the position I was in, over being held up with a gun and having my girl pulled around, but I was neither furious nor much frightened. I felt that I owed it to myself to do something, but I had no real urge to action. It was solely out of a sense of duty that I jumped across the bed and grabbed Dumaine at a moment when his gun was hanging slackly in his hand.

The gun fell to the floor. I pulled him back onto the bed. He was a solid man, not weak, but neither he nor I was putting into this fight the desperation we should have. We were both doing something we ought to do. I yelled at Selma, 'Get his gun! Pick it up! Get his gun!'

She did absolutely nothing.

It was not at all real. Dumaine and I stopped struggling by mutual agreement, he picked up the gun and put it in his pocket. I said it was cold, closed the windows, put on my dressing gown, and turned on another light. Then I asked him what the hell this was all about anyway.

With a good deal of pomposity he explained that the other man of whom he had spoken was his new self, a changed Dumaine. He was no longer the man he had been. He elaborated on this thesis. He was in triumph.

Now I really disliked him and found his conceit intolerable. I should have liked then to have taken a poke at him, but the time for that was past. Everything had become low-key and drab and futile. Selma had been sleeping regularly with him, all those times she had had to go home to her father, it had been to come to him. He had, in fact, never lost her for more than a few hours. And then more about the new man. He remarked, calmly, that of course she was a lot of a bitch.

I said it seemed to me he'd taken a pretty complicated way of letting me know how things stood. I was thoroughly angry with myself by then, and secondarily angry with him, not for holding onto his girl, but for all the damn foolishness when five honest minutes would have done just as well. As for the girl, I was through. I could hardly even regret her. Also, I was still sick with disgust at having been held up, frightened, outdone.

Dumaine told her to get dressed, she was coming with him. That seemed reasonable. She said she couldn't strip in front of us (she was in pyjamas). Almost as one man we told her we'd both seen her naked, get on with it. So she did, and then they left. Just as he was going, to make things perfect, Dumaine showed me that his gun wasn't loaded.

I went out on my balcony for a moment to watch them go through the courtyard to the street. It occurred to me to wonder why on earth he should want her back. I was too young then to allow for youngness in her, much too far from calm thought to figure out double attractions which set her to trying to have two things at once without understanding how to place each relationship on the basis she wanted.

Then I realized the collapse of the structure I had worked so hard to set up and maintain — for that, not the girl, was my loss. Humiliation and anger and the sense of having been fooled and bitched swept over me and I was in a weak, violent, silly state of fury and despair. The place was cold, there was nothing to drink in the house. I put on a minimum of clothing and went to rout out my best friend, who gave me gin and sympathy. As I talked to him I found myself beginning to make a story of it. He was a good fellow and a patient one. An hour later we were involved in trying to analyze what made Dumaine tick.

CHAPTER 12

FIRMER THAN STONE

KIETH SAID, 'It's a swamp. The only hard ground around here is artificial, and you could hunt yourself blind trying to find a rock.'

I nodded. The remark was an old one which we never got completely away from, and besides, it was too hot for small talk. My water glass was sweating but the ice in it had already melted and its frosted appearance was fraudulent.

'The Créoles enjoy the heat,' I said after awhile. 'Last May Pierre was saying how glad he was it was getting warm again.'

The thought was too outrageous for comment. We were at the season when the heat has you worn down to your fibres. June piles up on May and July on June, now on top of them we had August, and ahead of us stretched September with the time when we could even hope for relief too distant to be believed in. I am a Rhode Islander. Kieth is a Scottish Australian, he lived for some time in Scotland and his ties to the northern land are close. It seemed strange to us both that we had become planted in New Orleans. We had to watch our talk of home. You could stir yourself into an unseemly display of homesickness.

Picking up the old remark, I said, 'At home they have to build stone walls so as to clear the fields.'

'Hence the Battle of Concord.'

'Yes.'

'Do you suppose they really used cotton bales in the Battle of New Orleans?'

'I don't know. I'd think they'd catch fire. But they didn't have much else.'

'If you tried to dig a trench you'd hit water.'

I said, 'That happened in France, didn't it?'

'That was rain water. Here the level's right under the grass, the trenches would fill and you couldn't pump them out.'

We thought that over. The electric fan droned. The shade in the room had the look of coolness but through it ran a dry, hot pressure from outside. Through the shutters you could see the sunlight beyond the balcony as a golden fire.

I asked, 'Where are we going?'

You're better off in the heat if you go outside and move around. On Sundays we usually went somewhere in his car, with sketching as a purpose.

'Let's go out to Chalmette. They're working on the levee there and there might be some good sketches in it. We can take a look at the battlefield.'

On the way out Kieth talked about what one picked up on revisiting the battlefields of France, and the buttons and things he had found at Vicksburg.

'We might find some buttons from Packenham's men,' he said. 'Even down here the buttons would last although everything else would rot. I think he had some Highland regiments with him.' After a little thought he said, 'That must have been a hell of a place for a Scotsman. Wading through the swamps for Dominique You to shoot at.' He drove on for awhile, then he said, 'There are twelve yards of wool in a proper kilt. And the red coats. Impractical with the mosquitoes, too. A real Scotsman wears nothing underneath, you know.'

'Yes.'

The old battle became less of a set-piece. You thought, not of 'The British,' but of men from the heather and gorse country in dismay under the cypresses, the ground wet as a sponge under them when they fell.

We left the car near the Chalmette Monument. Hunting would be poor in the long, wet grass, but outside the levee where the high water had recently been scouring the banquette you might find something. That way, too, was the easiest to come at where they were working. The levee there is a good twenty feet high, a mod-

erately steep slope running up to a crest as wide as an ordinary
road. At the foot of the far side the banquette was a yellow-brown
beach of dried, sandy mud reaching down to the river. It was too
hot to do anything industriously. We ambled along, scouting
vaguely for relics of war. We had a desire, too, to throw a stone
into the water, and we kept an eye out for one.

Ahead of us a piece of old levee stood like a high, narrow island
in the river. There the ramparts had been forced to give ground,
at some time there had been a break-through, and the line of defense curved gently inland. The island was covered with high
brush.

'Old Man River pushed them back,' Kieth said. 'The drainage
of thirty-six states.'

I nodded. The river seemed lazy, its level well below the foot of
the levee, brown and heavy. Here and there reflected sunlight
burned on it with the colour of steel. The water came out of the
nation: thinking of its sources I longed for those colder, harder
places. Water from the high New Mexico country and the Spanish
villages, from Colorado along the side of Pike's Peak, from the
Sioux country of the Dakotas and all the Missouri drainage, from
Pennsylvania, Ohio, and Illinois, from almost to the edge of New
England, and all the states below.

The river had all the time in the world. No commander-in-chief
ever had such resources for a siege. It could rise and fall and go
down and rise again for centuries, forever. It rose up, smashed at
one place, poured over the top of another, bored through underneath another. The men fought it back. Sometimes they couldn't
and it broke through to cover a hundred miles or so of rich land,
sugar, cotton, rice, cattle, villages. It reached forever towards the
city. These were raids, no more. What it waited for was the day
when men would fail and the united waters could reach out on both
sides to occupy all the land.

You can hardly resist personalizing Old Man River, but when
you do you underrate it. The river does not grow tired, any more
than it has an ambition or a purpose. Men have those, and so
they must keep going in spite of being tired, against the waters of
the north and the west and the middle pouring down aimlessly. If
they let go, the blind force of gravity will spread the water over
thousands of miles of fertile land. In flood-time the rich farms will

be lake-bottoms, in the dry season there will be islands of dry ground surrounded by a paradise for birds. On a small scale it was that way when the French came here, but now the river bed is higher and the floods come in infinitely greater volume. Against that the people near the mouth of the river may never stop fighting. They can take time out to curse the northern freshets, and pile on more sandbags.

We went on past the island without finding any relics nor any stone to throw. Ahead of us we heard work going on, men shouting at the mules, the drag of scrapers.

'Sundays and all,' Kieth said. 'The levee nearly broke here. If it had, you'd have gone swimming off your balcony.'

Each scraper was pulled by two big mules and guided by a magnificent Negro. The men's shoulders and arms were beautiful with the swell and smooth shift of muscles under their dark skins. They handled their mules by voice and line, swung their scrapers, picking up dirt from the banquette, dragging it into place, dumping, down again, in a curving sweep with a slow, marked rhythm. Up with effort, dump, turn, go down holding back, dig in, and up again.

We watched for long enough to smoke a cigarette slowly.

'We must be behind where the British lines were,' I said. 'Maybe if we go back of the levee we can find something, if there's a clear field there.'

We went over the rampart at a place where the work had been finished. The raw earth was damp under a light coat of dust. At the top we stopped, looking down.

The acres beyond were neatly tended, covered with clipped grass, the trees standing in order. There were some straight-ruled, gravelled roads. At some distance stood a small, formal building and by it an American flag stirred sleepily at the top of a high pole.

'Military cemetery,' Kieth said at once.

The little markers stood in straight, oppressively long lines, broken here and there by larger ones. You knew the thought was stale and banal, but you couldn't help thinking that the men were still in ranks, a sort of extended order in platoon fronts.

'Do you suppose they gathered them all in?' I asked. 'Or are these just the Americans?'

'It looks like an awful lot of them. Let's go look.'

The regulation stones were about ten inches high and a foot

wide. On each was a number. They were arranged in divisions on each side of the roads, each division about ten graves deep. We looked at the first marker we came to, right against the levee. The lowest number was 714. Across the road, owing to the system of numbering, it began much higher. We looked at the levee.

'Under there,' Kieth said.

The gravelled road was solid enough. When we stepped on the turf we squeezed up moisture.

Kieth said, 'What a swamp.'

Some of the graves, perhaps one in twenty-five, had been provided with less anonymous headstones, by relatives, one supposed. The usual form was the simple, traditional gravestone shape, about two feet high. We read the nearest one. A John Adams of Quincy, Massachusetts, of the 14th Massachusetts Infantry, killed in action in 1864.

I said, 'My God. John Adams of Quincy.'

We went on, hunting out the named stones. Adams, Clark, Gould, Eldridge.

'I knew a slue of Goulds around Saunderstown,' I said. And then, 'I went to school with a boy called Eldridge. Boston.' Then I stopped talking.

Pearse, Hancock, Gardner, Gardiner, Palmer, Bradford, Tew, Weeden, Saltonstall, Brown, Langdon, Greene — 14th Massachusetts, 10th Rhode Island, Vermont, New Hampshire, Maine, New York, Pennsylvania, Ohio, Illinois, Massachusetts, New Hampshire, Rhode Island, the rocky states, the places of the hard winters and the twanging speech. Josiah Eldred of Wakefield, Rhode Island. Wakefield's a market town with a pretty little harbour and lots of elms.

Kieth said, 'The names. They're all old English.'

'Yes,' I said. 'That's the way it was up there.'

There was a monument rather larger than the rest, simply decorated. It was in memory of Jonathan Hartshorn of Newburyport, Able Seaman, aged seventeen years, killed in the attack on Fort Saint George. It had been erected by the officers and men of his ship.

Seventeen, with his parents' consent and prayers, no doubt. What a name, Jonathan Hartshorn. What did this kid have that the officers and men built him a monument? Newburyport.

Not far from there another stone seemed to complete the statement that began with Hartshorn. It had been set over the grave of David Starbuck, also a seaman, fifty-six years old, 'native of Prince Edward Island.'

I said, 'Prince Edward Island's north of Nova Scotia. I knew a girl from Nova Scotia once. In the winter she used to drive to school in a dog-sled. She spoke Gaelic at home.'

Kieth nodded. 'He was old. Why do you suppose he enlisted?'

'Starbuck's a Nantucket name. He may have had convictions.'

Of course his schooner might have tied up in Boston or Newport and he might have got drunk with Navy men. I thought it more likely that he had convictions.

Kieth said, 'Hell of a place for a Prince Edward Islander to wind up.'

'Did you know this cemetery was here?' I asked.

'No. I never heard of it.'

'Neither did I.'

To the South, the thirtieth of May is an enforced holiday and somewhat of an insult. Confederate Memorial Day, when the old flags are hung out and their dead are honoured, comes earlier. In the end of May a detachment of soldiers would come here and fire a volley, there would be some stiff, military forms. In two years no friend had mentioned to me that thousands of Yankees lay buried just outside the city. I don't think most of them know.

There was another tall marker. 'Here lie the bodies of three hundred and fifty-two Union soldiers.'

At the beginning, when the Northern ships came up the river and the forts still held out, they were killed in action. Then they died. 1865, 1866, 'died of fever,' 'died of yellow fever,' 'died.' These were Butler's men. They were not responsible for his stupidity or his notorious General Order 57. They had not chosen this assignment. These were the men at whom the ladies spat in the streets and on whom the slops were dumped. They had enlisted in a burst of excitement, because they were bored, without knowing quite why, and because of deep beliefs. To free the slaves and save the Union. Before they left they prayed with their parents and the Bible was read aloud. They were going to fight in resounding battles, win victories, and come home.

Lee surrendered. Why in hell don't they send us home? What

in tarnation are they keeping us here for? If I could be discharged now I'd be in time for the shad running, in time to plant, in time to keep that son of a bitch Thomson from marrying my girl. The war's over, when in hell do we go home? I got a bucket of slops down the back of my neck yesterday when I was patrolling Chartres Street. This country ain't nothing but a damned marsh, in all the time I been here I ain't seen a rock big enough to throw. Have ye seen the ticks on the caows? Enough to turn your stomach. When do we go home? I feel kind of feverish.

These were Butler's men. They came from the sources of the waters, and beyond, clear to Prince Edward Island where a fisherman keeps an eye out for icebergs. Died of fever.

We were back at our starting place, looking at the first stones at the foot of the levee. We had found stone, all right.

Kieth said, 'And so they just dig them up and pile them in.'

I felt angry about it myself, and then to my surprise I said, 'No, that's all right. That's what they came here for.'

Seven hundred of them here, the same number across the road, and then again beyond. The earth of two thousand or more Union men had gone into the dyke to guard the alien sugar and rice and cotton and the city that hated them so. Only it is not alien. Even this strange, wet, stoneless land is theirs. It is part of their country. They fought, among other things, to hold the country together, although it's doubtful if they had worked out a detailed philosophy of what that meant, or remembered their purpose all the time, when they were bored or drunk or good and mad at the Rebels. Most of them went home at last with strange tales of Octoroons and absinthe, of the balconied city in the mud, and the power of Créole hatred. The others died, pointlessly to their minds. There were no stones to strengthen this soil. Their own American earth united with it and stood guard again, holding this part of the Union. It was strange but it was right. One nation. You wouldn't hesitate now to brigade a Rhode Island and a Louisiana regiment together.

I said, 'If we go back by this road, won't we reach the car quicker than the way we came?'

Kieth said, 'Yes. Let's be getting back.' He sounded rather relieved.

I was grateful to him for his understanding and the amount of silence he had given me, which was what I should have expected from him. We walked almost briskly to the car. When we got home it would be time for a drink, which was a happy thought. Once the car was well under way we became absorbed in talk about some familiar matter of interest.

In the back of my mind I was still thinking, yes, it's right. But it would be good if on Decoration Day someone, some woman of the South, would go there and put a bunch of flowers on the side of the levee.

CHAPTER 13

INDIANS

THE FIRST Indians I ever saw were purple. It would be reasonable, too, to say that I was thoroughly green. We had come by car over the San Francisco Mountains and down in a staggering sweep to Deadman's Wash and then across the Painted Desert to the little, tin-roofed trading post at Cameron on the edge of the Navajo Reservation. All that in a few hours was too much. The country repelled me, its emptiness, its gaudiness and its sheer size all proclaimed 'not for human consumption.' We were dazed physically by the fierce, colour-killing sunlight and emotionally by the mass effect of this sudden presentation.

The trading post was a real one in those days, a windmill, a hitching-rack for horses, a small, rectangular stone building with a rusty, tin roof, a couple of trees, nothing more. Inside it was dreadfully hot but at least it was shady. One's eyes had a chance. We looked around at the strangeness of it, the familiar aspects of a general store all slightly twisted awry — the extra-high, wide counters, the emphasis on saddles and brilliant blankets, the trader's unlikeness to a storekeeper.

Three Indians came in. We couldn't have believed it if someone had explained to us that this was part of the sophisticated edge of the Navajo Country, close to civilization. We thought we had just discovered the meaning of the word 'remote.' These men must be the real article, the savages of the hinterland. They wore ragged work-clothes, two of them had battered hats, the third a dark, dirty headband. Their hair was done in a knot behind, I remember the contrast of the bright turquoise in their ears, but nothing else was picturesque about them, they were merely shabby and surprisingly dark. I had had an idea that Indians were a rather light, bronze colour. These men seemed purple. I found their faces expressionless and stupid. I was, as a matter of fact, rather prepared to dislike them in advance, and this first impression of shabbiness and heavy, dull expressions was not unexpected but nonetheless depressing.

Our first camp was in Tsegi Canyon, a great, harsh, beautiful, wild wound in the earth running for miles between its painted cliffs. We covered the last few miles on horseback. The horses looked fit only to boil down into soap, the western saddles seemed grotesquely oversized contraptions, built up like the poop and forecastle of a Spanish galleon, hung about with a mess of dangling strings. I could see that there would be no problem here of keeping control of the traditional, fiery mustang, hardly even any pleasure in riding. I mounted without enthusiasm.

The two Westerners — good fellows as a matter of fact — who were guiding us assumed that none of us had the faintest idea about riding. I had ridden and handled horses since I was a child, but I could see it would be useless to tell them that. I did remark that I was in the cavalry (National Guard), which was a waste of breath. Their elementary instruction, their cautious advice which was always clearly intended to prevent an incompetent from committing suicide, were constant irritants continuing until through pure luck I had a chance to demonstrate that in fact I could ride. I was nineteen, and I had no conception then of the nature of a dude-wrangler's experience. Later I learned what utter sheep dudes are, the absolute necessity of assuming the worst until something better is proven, the infinite patience, vigilance, and tact by which the wranglers succeed in bringing the most unlikely persons unscathed and oblivious through difficult country and moments of danger.

We rode at the deadly packtrain pace, a walk alleviated by occasional, brief moments of fox-trotting. There is nothing duller or more wearying. Tsegi Canyon oppressed and repelled me just as the southern part of the desert country had done. Its mile-wide floor was arid, useless. Its cliffs were too aggressive, the spruce and fir high up in the crannies were a cheat. The heat danced on the flats and echoed off the walls. The damn country was a howling ash-heap, and this kind of riding was a pain in the neck.

The going included the bits of narrow trail above a drop, the steep descents through sand or rubble, the scrambling climbs one finds in all eroded, desert country. The boys expected us to be alarmed, in fact, humanly, they desired expressions of surprise and fished for them, partly by (to me) superfluous warnings. They were also generous with prophecies of the stiff muscles and sore tails we were going to have. Between times they pointed out to each other and to us things I could not for the life of me make out — a cliff-dwelling perched on a high ledge, a Navajo camp in a corner behind a dune, readings of the trail from which they deduced things that seemed fantastic such as, to parody, that someone had gone by wearing a red headband.

I had been rowing all spring, and riding before I took the train west. My tail was solid leather. I could decipher no details in this jumbled landscape. So this was Arizona. The hell with it.

These boys were on their own ground where they possessed the key — not unlike the adjusted members of a school in relation to newcomers — and they were beginning to try us out. With such people I was conditioned to expect failure, an expectation which warred violently with the bumptiousness of a boy who has just become a SOPHOMORE and achieved a few minor distinctions in college. I was shaping up rapidly to take the typical refuge of developing a private interest at a tangent to the group's.

The obvious interest was the Navajos, not a very pronounced diversion since everyone was interested in them to some degree. A man with a sense of inferiority seeks exotic occupations. He believes deep within himself that his failures are not due to inability to accomplish the ordinary things to which he sets his hand, but to an obstacle which is created by the presence of others — and in this he is correct at least in part. So he seeks for the unusual field, one in which he can work alone, one which by being different from the occupations around him will, he feels, give a special scope to the abilities he is convinced he possesses and at the same time exempt him from rubbing elbows with others. Everybody around me had some interest in the Navajos, but I determined to really find out about them, to know more and understand more deeply than any of them.

I had come West reluctantly, essentially because I had been challenged. Doctor Tozzer, the wise director of the Division of Anthropology, had told me that a season at the labourer's end of excavating would give me a chance to find out if I really wanted to be an archaeologist. Behind that I sensed a second meaning, that the hard, dull work would show whether I had any real determination. So I went unwillingly, full of sophomoric sophistication and impressed with myself as a budding scientist. I was not going to be fooled; the West of Owen Wister was dead, cowboys existed no longer, Indians were ragged pensioners of the Government, Navajo blankets were woven in Chicago and shipped to the reservation for the Indians to sell. I vigorously denied in advance all the romance at which I had played as a little boy. Dime-novel stuff. That was my surface.

Everything else ran counter to it. My father was a great outdoors man, a wilderness man, with an unusual gift for getting on with Indians. He knew them from the Abenaki of eastern Canada to the Hopis of Arizona, and I had a secret desire to emulate him in that as well as an avowed one to emulate him in the outdoors generally. He had given me a little advice about getting on with Indians — go slow, be absolutely polite, observe every rule of good breeding, don't force talk, don't jabber, don't push yourself at them, never show surprise or lose your temper. All excellently true, and this, too, hinted at a challenge, at something difficult to do, perhaps requiring a special talent. My father thought so, and today I do, too.

Then he brought me a message from Doctor Parsons, worded in mild scorn of archaeology and hoping that I would become an ethnologist. With this she sent me reprints of some of her articles on this area. Her interest derived from the belief that I might have some of my father's qualities, in itself a compliment, and here was a little secret to have by myself, the suggestion that my official occupation was not the very highest one and that I could privately prepare myself for a higher.

We had spent one night at Kayenta. No one could be even that short a time in the Wetherills' house, hearing them talk, seeing the beautiful things hanging on their walls, without catching some sense of the riches to be found among the Navajos and being stimulated to some desire to learn for himself.

These Indians in the northern part of the reservation were quite different from the ones I saw at Cameron. As a matter of fact I've never seen those purple ones again, they seem to have appeared out of nowhere that first day, a different race, to disappear again forever. Cameron, I soon learned, was close to civilization when one measured by the fantastic scale of that country, the Indians were sophisticated, their ways had changed. Around Kayenta we saw the last of the old times, the men still in velveteen shirts, calico leggings, moccasins, almost all long-haired and wearing the headband, carrying bows and arrows on their saddles; we had a glimpse of what the tribe had looked like in simpler days. Here was colour that was bound to attract anyone, and very soon I began to feel qualities in the Navajos who were around our camp. These were people, a strange people, impenetrable to all appearance, yet behind the mask of race there lay a humanity one longed to explore. All the denied romance was flooding back in me, strengthened with a powerful urge of curiosity.

And then there was the country and the life it required. Our camp was on a sandy knoll in the shade of some Maxfield Parrish piñón trees under a Maxfield Parrish sky. Across from us a great headland, buff, dull orange, iron-brown, thrust forward from the canyon wall, around it and beyond the dry sand lay in sun-dazzled, aggressive silence to the far wall. The place came at one, the place attacked. One looked and rejected. Then, trying to cope with this thing, unexpectedly I saw the sea, I remembered the quality of being out of sight of land in a small boat, I remembered barrenness, monotony, hostility, and beauty. What I was seeing was of the same order, man in the same infinitesimal scale to it. I began to see the country with a rush and to know that it was beautiful and that I loved it.

To go about in that country meant real camping and some hardihood (not until nine years later did I ever sleep in a tent), the horse was the means of transportation and a good one could be had, there were skills as great as any woodsman's to be acquired. In that country, living that way, in a new pattern and land having no visible connection with anything I had ever known before, one was surrounded by an equally strange, new people who might unfold unimaginable riches and (this was always present) the distinction of having become one of those rare white men who really understands the Indians.

There was a fine old man called Black Goat who lived near us.

He was an old friend of our Director, Sam Guernsey, and visited us often. I think I gave him some cigarettes the first day and amused him by trying to pronounce a Navajo word. One morning when I woke I saw his moccasins and leggings just behind my head and realized, first with a start of fright, that he was standing over me. Remembering my father's precepts and certain of his tales, I sat up without looking behind me, pulled on my boots, and then said what I believed to be the correct Navajo greeting, 'Hala hastiin.'

He laughed. I gave him a cigarette. A little later he said something complimentary about me, I forget what, to Guernsey. It was a triumph which provided the last weight needed to tip the scales. The men of the Old Stone Age in France disappeared from mind, archaeology was a comparatively dull occupation, Doctor Parsons was right and in the end I should become an ethnologist — specializing, of course, in the Navajo Indians. There would come a day, at the end of a great number of utterly delightful days of desert camping and horseback, when I should sit at ease in their hogaans, speaking the language, wearing the costume, accepted, perhaps adopted into the tribe. . . . The Indians had got me.

There are some people, such as traders and government officials, whose acquaintance with Indians and resultant fondness for them is solidly founded on the realities of life. Most of the rest of us, scientists (it's highly noticeable in them), serious amateurs, and the broad group that is known in the West as 'yearners,' are escapists. How escapism operated in my case is clear by now, I think. As one goes deeper in after having succumbed to the initial attraction and the well-established glamour, the appeals to the escapist become ever stronger. As a result Indians are surrounded by a cult with a series of degrees of initiation, elaborated and maintained by people with an instinct for avoiding reality.

Apart from their picturesqueness and the fact that being one who 'knows the Indians' has been elevated into a distinction like a sort of Ph.D. which one partly awards to one's self, partly receives by acclamation from one's friends, about the most powerful abiding pull they exert lies in the simplicity of their native way of life.

This simplicity is real. I am not talking about idylls. I can clear the decks here by stating that Indians are not idyllic, any more than I am. They are also not superior to us. They are just as stupid and just as intelligent as we are, just as noble and just as mean, just as good and just as bad. They produce some of the most astute, devious, and unscrupulous politicians I have ever encountered as well as civic leaders whole-heartedly and intelligently devoted to the public welfare, they produce heroes and villains. They are different from us, strong in some things where we are weak, weak where we are strong (just as white men are stronger than Indians in the hands and arms but weaker in the back), but averaged all together neither better nor worse.

Their life is in many ways that of a very poor farmer or sheepherder, or the struggling cattleman with a tiny bunch of cows, deprived of most of the comforts and amenities to which we are accustomed. If most of us tried to live by doing just what an average, hard-working Navajo, Apache, Maya, or Pueblo Indian does, we'd soon play out. It's a tough life, a life in which unattractive dirtiness and raggedness is often enforced by circumstance, and it has also the primitive rewards which appeal to us so much (just as Indians love the movies).

But in its original state, or where it approximates that, it has great simplicity. At the present time we are thinking hard about the creation of a better earth, thinking hard and a trifle wearily. We think in terms of the whole, round globe, we struggle to find the place at which to begin unsnarling a complexity which we still do not understand and of which we are more than a little frightened, although we know that we have created it ourselves. Most of us, when we try to formulate a plan at all, fall back on a more or less openly admitted conclusion that we hope (dear Lord, how earnestly we hope) that our leaders and their counsellors and experts will be able to find the way out.

The Indians, too, seek a better earth. Who does not? But save among the most sophisticated, this desire takes such simple forms: more rain, less sickness (and prayer is effective for both of these), a little more land perhaps, good hunting in the fall, peace within the community, peace all around, not to be pushed around by white people, above all peace and continuity. Thanks to the white man these last, most important wishes are difficult to obtain, but even the white man is focussed and simplified, as far as concerns his major pressures and influences upon them, into an organized government with which one can reason, which one can from time to time persuade. At the present time our Indians realize that Hitler menaces their safety, their world has begun to grow larger and to admit some of our misery. Their young men have joined up by the thousands in the hope of doing bodily harm to the Japanese or whomever else they may be sent against, the women are flocking to the Red Cross centres, they are digging into their little boxes and hiding places for change to buy Defense Bond Stamps. (I've never been able to figure out why our Indians are so very loyal.) But still their view is restfully simple. It's just a question of all Americans getting together, sacrificing together, and whipping these assorted mad people once and for all, and that will be that. Then we can go back to the important things such as settling whether that water-hole belongs to the reservation or to the rancher beyond, and we have perfect confidence in the fairness of the Supreme Court.

This world-view is most refreshing. Deep within the Indian country, surrounded by the people, cut off from one's friends and the papers, one can half accept it, perhaps more than half accept it, and in giving way to a real nostalgia fool one's self that it is in fact the truth. To his lovers the Indian is in no small part a mechanism for forgetting the things which make them walk in fear.

Of course the Indian-seeker who is still in the early stages of the cult believes in the idyll. He believes in Hiawatha. He thinks that if the Indians were only left alone they would be perfectly happy, and in his most naïve form he wants to see Indians kept as a sort of museum exhibit, uncontaminated by contact with whites, living their old life, wearing their beautiful costumes (he has never seen really dirty buckskin), preserved and protected under some dispensation which will not bar himself from going among them. Why should he be barred? He understands them.

Those who have taken a few more degrees are a bit more reasonable. Some of them exercise a valuable influence towards keeping alive those elements of Indian culture which have survival value in our world even while the Indians grow modern. Many of them work hard to right specific wrongs or correct abuses. But because of the personal angle of approach, the fundamental quest for a satisfaction within themselves, there is always likely to be distortion in their view, and when the test comes one can never be sure just who will think purely in terms of what will help the Indian.

They have the gratification of the approach from above downwards, and the dangerous weapons of Lady Bountiful. These white men and women, many of them, feel that they come among the Indians with superior wisdom, and this feeling, which is in part a sense of cultural, perhaps even racial, superiority, does not conflict with their worshipful reverence for Indian wisdom and the beauties of Indian culture. In fact, it makes that reverence safe, freeing it from any dangerous tendency to put them in an inferior position. They bring, too, comparatively tremendous wealth. It's the easiest thing in the world, and one of the commonest tricks in advancing themselves with Indians, to shower them with presents. The gifts are well received, of course, and the Indian code being strict in this regard, they produce return gifts of native articles which can be taken home like so many scalps and shown as evidence of one's close relations with the mystic people. When an Indian gives you a present out of hand, neither in return for nor in anticipation of your munificence, you may have begun to get somewhere.

Gift-showering is increased in response to the monopolistic urge. In its mildest form this urge is merely competitive: the seeker would like to know Indians, or his particular Indians, better than anyone else, and he feels rather jealous when he encounters someone who demonstrates superior knowledge. In this game, of course, the Indian Service is ruled *hors concours* and dismissed from consideration, while the traders, those extraordinary men, are treated rather as if they were king-pieces, a warm friendship with an outstanding trader being equivalent to two friendships with run-of-the-mill Indians. I suffer from the competitive feeling myself, but I have never been among any Indians without finding some white man who knew them very much better, indeed, than I, usually some inconspicuous, local white man; I find it impossible to rule the Indian Service out of bounds; and I know no trader who has not other friends older and more intimate than I. So when I feel the competitive jealousy coming over me I do my best to slap myself down.

At its strongest this urge is for true monopoly. One runs into both individuals and groups who absolutely refuse to consider that anyone else can know a given tribe, or Indians in general, better than they. This can take the form of ugly resentment; I have seen the welfare of the Indians jettisoned because working for it would have involved admitting the superior knowledge of an outsider. Monopolism also enables the seeker to reject ideas about the Indians which would force him to alter the concept in which he has become snugly nested. In fact, I have come to think that one of the prime tests of your real friend of the Indians as against those who are merely using Indians as a sort of ointment for the soul, is his willingness to admit superior information and to be corrected.

The best of the amateur seekers do form a band of defenders of whom the Indians stand greatly in need, and under sane guidance have done a world of good. Sometimes, especially if they have made themselves really useful, they proceed to develop the most advanced form of monopolism, the messiah complex. This is a desire to be recognized by some group of Indians as their one saviour, leader, and true friend. There is a little of this complex in almost everyone who has worked with Indians but most of us try to repress it. Where it is given free rein it is a vicious thing, driving off badly needed help, turning devious in order to keep important in the Indians' eyes, fighting their simple well-being in order that no help shall come save from the messiah. Thank God, few white people ever get strong enough to be able to implement this craze, but it has happened, and to at least one fine tribe of my acquaintance it has done irreparable harm.

Towards this maze of mixed intentions and results I was now headed, diving deeper and deeper as the Navajos became for me a surer refuge from my troubles than any dream world could ever become. The Navajo tribe, numbering close to forty thousand at that time, was a trifle too big for a young man's messiah complex and I was clearly aware that I should have to go a long distance before I should know anything like as much about them as did many white people I encountered, let alone more. These two factors kept me on the rails. The scientific idea I have described had already begun to govern my mind, and I really wanted to *know*. So I became an endless questioner, annoying those who were familiar with the Navajos not by a competitive attitude, but by pestiferous curiosity.

The more I saw of them, and the more I studied their culture in the material available in the Peabody Museum, the more they grew on me. I have told about what their religion did for me; there was no escapism in that, it was a solid reality. My sense of the depth and richness of their culture increased steadily. Above all I was hit where I lived by their remarkable literature. The people themselves I liked ever more and more, and I got on with them better than, up to then, I had ever gotten on with any group.

Most traders to the Navajos and their cousins the Apaches are inordinately attached to them. I have often asked traders in remote posts which are completely isolated in winter, if they did not find it lonely. They answer, sincerely and simply, 'No, there are always Indians around.'

Even in the unregenerate Indian Service of the nineteen-twenties with its load of ignorant, stupid, time-serving employees endowed with strong, defensive racial and cultural arrogance, when Indians were constantly subject to the ministrations of their social and intellectual inferiors, one heard over and over again how the Navajos, or the Apaches as the case might be, were the best Indians the employee had ever known. Every tribe has its virtues and its fans, but these people appeal exceptionally strongly.

Not so very long before Columbus a number of savages began drifting down through Kansas and Eastern Colorado to the edges of the Southwest. They were a crude people, possessed of few arts, rather simple ceremonies, little property. They told good stories and told them well. They were a democratic people, the nearest thing they had to organization being something on the lines of a mediaeval university — a good leader attracted followers until a strong band was built up; when a better appeared or the leader fell off, one drifted away from him. It wasn't quite as simple as that but it was along those lines, and behind it was a true, Jeffersonian sense of the equality of man. They were a thin scattering of little groups over the face of unpromising prairie country, not strong for war, not very strong in anything save the habit of freedom.

I have tried often to imagine them, visualizing a score or so of men, women and children on the move, their hair hanging long over their backs and shoulders and in need of combing, controlled somewhat by a headband of hide or pounded bark. The men wear breech-clouts and moccasins, the women rather simply made skirts of buckskin and probably blouses. The children are mostly naked. On their backs and on the two poles dragging behind their dogs are piled simple possessions, tents, some crude pottery, baskets, bundles of sacred objects which would seem childish if we could open one with nobody to explain the virtues of its contents.

They are strongly made, broad-shouldered, wiry, with broad, heavy faces which bespeak the far north. Their features and the mustaches, some thin and falling in points on either side of the mouth, some fairly heavy, which a good many of the older men favour, have a reminiscence of Asia and the Mongols. One or two of the women are beautiful although they need tidying up. They are a dusty, drab group, but there is strength in their faces, and in their talk together there flashes unexpected, happy humour and answering, clear laughter.

They have come out of the western, short-grass prairie country into the mountains for a bit of good hunting. Just ahead of them lies a fabled country which is the northern border of the civilized world. In it are the wonderful people who build thick-walled, permanent, warm houses well arranged in towns, who magically create pure white materials and others wonderfully decorated out of cotton, pottery of many colours and shapes, jewelry of turquoise, shell, bright red stone and polished anthracite, the people who make tall corn and lavish stores of other crops grow under irrigation, whose ceremonies and dances beggar description. The wanderers will go among them humbly to trade and learn a little, they are one of innumerable groups that are drifting in, over the mountains, to settle near civilization and spread out over the unwanted, harsh country where the water does not flow in ditches. Behind them in the plains into which they had originally gone as water enters a vacuum, highly organized, aggressive tribes are pushing at the edges of their country. They will come across the mountains more and more frequently.

It must have been something like that. The Pueblo Indians received these ignorant savages with some contempt and found them useful for trade, cornmeal and cotton for meat and hides.

There is no such thing as a people without culture, but these were as little burdened with anything to slow their advancement as was possible. They used their eyes and their minds and took over whatever things seemed desirable to them. They increased in numbers, little by little they settled into half a dozen or so groups which the white men, when they came, could recognize as tribes, naming them all 'Apache.'

It is characteristic of Indians when not under overwhelming pressure that they never lose sight of the great, fundamental question: *What makes life worth living?* This is one of the factors which makes white men find them exasperating to deal with, for our theory of profit is extremely simple and so deeply rooted that we cannot understand a man who decides that under the circumstances the money offered is not worth the sacrifices or efforts demanded for it. The Apaches understand this very well and they, above all the Apaches of Navajo, selected from what they saw around them only what suited their intentions.

Farming is dull work. Most of the Apache tribes learned something of it, but when one can get on just as well otherwise, why plant corn? Anyone who has ever hilled or cleaned a sizeable cornfield can understand. The greater part of the Apaches stuck primarily to hunting until the time came when with increasing strength, with the enormous advantages that came from having learned to live well in the ash-heap parts of the desert which no one else wanted, and under the growing irritation of the white man's incursions, warfare became profitable. They proceeded to make themselves masters and specialists in the art of war as few other peoples have ever been.

The Navajos were the ones who really studied the Pueblos. What they proceeded to do illustrates most clearly the quality of all these immigrants. The Pueblo Indian is a farmer, closely resembling the mediaeval European farmer going out from a defensible village to his fields. He has the virtues — stubbornness (both virtue and vice), tenaciousness, a sense of order, organization, co-operation, courage, industry, and in addition he is no slight artist, so that his farmer's life is embroidered with creative sidelines and an almost spectacularly beautiful religious ritual. With this go the faults. For several thousand years he has been an owner of possessions at the extreme northern boundary of civilization, holding onto them against the have-nots, he is like every farmer a worrier. He must watch the weather and the sky. No sooner are this year's crops in than he must worry about next year. If there is brilliant, sunny weather in February he looks anxiously at the mountains and fears there will not be enough snow, if the winter is hard and the snowfall heavy he begins to think about late frosts after planting. Anxiety, and the retention of possessions. In the fall the crops come in. One may feast, but one must keep enough to last till the next harvest, and it is well to hold a little over in case of a bad year. ...

Such a man wants everybody to do his full part in the common effort. He lives more comfortably than the wild tribes, warmer in winter, better clad, better and more steadily fed, more secure, but at the same time he is involved in an endless struggle with nature, and when the corn is ripe the wild tribes may come down. Some men in each Pueblo are fine hunters and sportsmen, in the old days they went often to the Plains to hunt buffalo in the teeth of the warriors out there, but the heart of life was in the close-assembled, defensible town and the fields around it. To these people war could never have anything but negatively beneficial results — driving off the enemy, removing a nuisance — chance on the whole was undesirable, the effort of life was for certainty. To achieve certainty one needed subordination, so the individual was closely and smoothly fitted into his place in the community and his course of life laid out for him. Nobody starved, nobody was quite free. Even today there are Pueblos in which it is possible for a man or a woman to be tortured, not merely punished but tortured and possibly killed, for stepping out of line.

This was no life for an Apache, for men and women who liked to gamble, to shoot the whole nickel at once, to feast well when feasting was possible even if you had to tighten your belt afterwards, who did not so much think that generosity was a virtue as that restriction of it was an impossible meanness of character. They were Jeffersonian democrats and it would go hard with any leader who thought he could order a free man beaten into submission or, for instance, forbid a man to go off on any trip he jolly well chose to make. So the Navajo branch picked and chose what it thought was good.

A clan system which gave form and better channels to the habit of generosity and mutual aid, weaving — among Pueblos a man's work, but in their eyes more of an occupation for women who had to stay home anyhow — the making of jewelry to give a man a creative outlet and to adorn his person. Those impressive ceremonies — yes, by all means, but grafted onto the Navajo religion and adapted to the needs of a people who were damned if they'd live in villages under everybody's supervision, and with this an interchange of legends in which the Navajos on the whole were on the giving end but from which they caught, and exploited magnificently, the idea of the heroic cycle. They took whatever could be used by a people who wished to remain mobile, nothing save farming which would anchor them to one spot, and that only ties one down for a year at a time. When the Spaniard came, his horse, his sheep and cattle, metal-working, and some of his decorative ideas in clothing were also good. The horse, of course, was simply splendid, and interesting, too, were new ways of gambling with painted cards.

Farming was useful and dependable, but it anchored one to tomorrow and it was awfully dull. One would not like, they still do not like, the thought of being tied for life to the yearly round and worries of crops. Sheep and cattle were better, but with the horse and with increasing numbers, raiding was better yet. When meat was short on the Scottish Border the lady of the manor served up for dinner a plate with nothing on it but a pair of spurs, and the Blue Bonnets went over the border. The Navajos said that they allowed the Pueblos and the Spaniards to survive so that they could raise sheep for them. It was a life which certainly had farming beat all hollow, it was a life in which a man could lose everything he owned in the world in one night of gambling and the next day set out to restock, needing only courage and a warrior's training.

Until the power of the United States broke them after the Civil War, they were the laughing, singing, deadly scourge of their part of the Southwest. During these centuries of war, they did not drop, but maintained and elaborated their arts until everything they had borrowed became peculiarly and distinctively Navajo.

By the time they had become a peaceful people established upon a reservation their character was well formed. It has not greatly changed, it sticks out all over them today. I know of no visual image which more perfectly expresses the inner qualities of a free people than the sight of a Navajo woman walking, her queenly carriage and her free stride. They, and the other Apaches, respect the fact that they were defeated in war and have a realistic understanding of what that means, but they also know that white men never did, probably never could, defeat them man for man on equal terms and they have the bearing which goes with that.

All Indians have a good sense of humour. The Navajos and

Apaches are unusually free in using it, a people completely unafraid of laughter, which is one of the things which makes it possible for a visitor to last through their all-night ceremonies. They would tell the President to his face that he was wrong if they thought he was; they have a reasonable respect for office and achievement, but no idea that any man is better than one's self. They are quick to sports and fun, and very good sports. I have raced horses against them many times, have both won and lost, and done this when my opponent and I were all alone in empty desert as well as before many people with Indians judging. There have always been bets. I have never known a loser to question that he lost or delay payment, I have never seen a raw decision. They are constant fun to be with, when they are angry they are really alarming, and God save me from the wrath of their women.

This is one group of tribes, the first I knew, the ones I still love best, though in that my allegiance has swayed somewhat from the Navajos to those we still call Apaches. To try to describe more groups would be to write another book; they are no more alike than are the nations of the white men, and they have the same, deceptive, general similarity. These must do as a sample.

What I've written may sound a little hard on the Pueblos; I do not wish to be, having a great liking for them, but as it was their opposite numbers I set out to describe, inevitably I played them for contrast. I could write the same account the other way round with the reverse effect.

I am not sure if in all this I have described a kind of Indian and a quality, or merely proven that, if the Indians got me in 1921, in 1945 their grip still holds.

CHAPTER 14

THE PERFECT CIRCLE

Y͏OU COULD LOSE yourself in the great spaces of the Navajo country. You could do this literally and die of thirst, or spiritually and forget that the white world existed, like water backed too high against a levee, all around the reservation. The life of the Indians seemed little changed except in surface matters of materials for clothing, wagons, some tools; the white man dwindled to a merchant from whom at rare intervals the people secured these goods; here in the canyons and mountains the Navajo way was immutable, secure, a complete refuge.

Bart Hayes and I were young, curious, and unwashed. I rode a skinny little black mare with more fire in her than one had any right to expect. His horse was various bright shades of pink, it was oddly constructed, and at one glance an observer could satisfy himself that the animal had all his ribs. Our outfit — cooking equipment, bedding, grub, grain, the other shirt — was wrapped in a canvas wagon-cover and tied with a squaw hitch onto an albino pack horse with blue eyes. Lorenzo Hubbell, the great trader of Oraibi, had lent us thirty dollars on our faces, but there was nothing to buy. When we ran short on grub we ran short on grub and that was that. We didn't need to buy as a matter of fact because there were plenty of Indians around. We had discovered why the traders did not get lonely.

At one camp they told us that there was to be a dance, so we stayed, eating out of the local stew-pots, to see more Navajos riding in than we had ever seen together before. Our hostess warned us to put our stuff inside the hogaan as newcomers, not knowing we were friends, might steal something.

At one end of the dance area, close enough to the bonfire to be comfortably warm after the night had taken on an edge, there was a big log. I sat on the end of it next to a middle-aged, grim-looking Indian, a man with the broad cheekbones, strong nose, and firm mouth of the true Apache type. You would say he was a formidable customer. Beyond him his wife was all but faceless in her blanket, watching the dance. The man had something under his blanket at which he looked from time to time. By and by he spoke to another, elderly Indian standing near him. The second Indian bent down to look, they both spoke softly and smiled. Then he spoke to a man behind him and the process was repeated. At length, after eyeing me a couple of times, pride was too much for him and he turned to me.

'Shoh,' he said, 'look how it sleeps.'

He opened the blanket enough to let me see a baby, screwed up tight in sleep.

'It sleeps,' he said, 'very much it sleeps.'

'Yes, very much it sleeps.'

It was small and pink with a brown overcast, its features were more neatly cut, it was more attractive than white babies.

'How many its returning snows?' I asked.

'Nine moons.'

'A boy? A girl?'

'A girl.'

The man's smile was lovely. The Navajo behind us leaned forward to join our admiring. The father repeated softly, 'Very much it sleeps,' and touched its face gently with one finger. I did the same. We smiled at each other. The baby half-woke and let out a trial cry. Its mother turned, spoke sharply, the man closed his blanket and settled to watch the dance looking like any husband caught off base, the other Indian and I felt sheepish.

Hastiin Asola said we should camp at his niece's place. He had not seen her in some time. Hastiin Asola was a friendly old man with a taste for small, rather dirty jokes. He found us diverting. He was grey-haired, impressive, and had the back, waist, and arms of a boy. We rode up to the hogaan near sundown. Navajo-style, the old man did not speak but sat leaning over his saddle, at first with his face gravely neutral although there was humour visible behind it, then with his smile slowly breaking through. The woman followed much the same procedure, and then there was that brief pause which is one of the pleasantest things about Indian politeness. Whether one loves or hates, one's spirit must always adjust to the impact of another person's presence, wherefore simple considerateness dictates that one pause a moment to let adjustment take place.

She rose with a cry of pleasure and they shook hands beaming. There was a brief greeting, then she said, 'Don't dismount, save yourselves trouble.' She handed us two water-bottles and a small keg and told us where to find the spring, remarking that it was a long haul on foot but easy for horsemen. It was an informal reception.

She took us for granted after that; her husband when he came was amused that she had sent white men on her errand and he was entertained by us. The atmosphere was such that the children, two little girls, were not afraid of our strangeness and for the first time we had the same relationship with them we might have had with nicely brought up little girls at home.

Bart and I slept near where the sheep were bedded down. We aroused their eternal curiosity, and waking in the night we would see their foolish, grave, white faces ringing us all around in the moonlight. It didn't bother us much. We were heartily tired, we had only a vague idea of where we were, we didn't care. We had achieved something close to total immersion.

My second expedition outside the United States, in 1927, was to the Jacalteco Indians of the Cuchumatán Highlands in Guatemala. With me went Douglas Byers, now head of the Andover Museum. Byers had been with me in Arizona, he was an ideal companion for a long, difficult assignment, he seemed about to become a banker, and I was in hopes of seducing him back into anthropology.

Casual information which Frans Blom and I had picked up when we passed through Jacaltenango in 1925 proved to us that here in secret there was a rich and rare survival of the ancient Mayan religion. To learn about that I came back with Byers.

The Highland Maya of Guatemala live in what can best be called townships, using the word in a New England sense. The townships are areas with legally determined boundaries, often secured to the tribe by royal grants of considerable age. (Jacaltenango holds its territories from Ferdinand VII.) Within the township is a village which is the seat of government, with the Town Hall, jail, church, market and other institutions. Two *alcaldes* and a number of *regidores*, or councilmen, democratically elected at least in theory, form the local government under the supervision of one or more officials representing the federal government. The Jacalteco tribe numbers about seven thousand, of whom the greater part lives all year or for part of the year in the village of Jacaltenango, leaving it at intervals to cultivate their fields in the outlying sections. Within the township they enjoy a measure of self-government, freedom to follow their customs, free enterprise, freedom in the small things of everyday life, which has been extended only recently to our Indians. Here for the first time I came to know a tribe of Indians whose future was not inevitable, steadily approaching ruin and disaster. The native culture had changed, was changing, and would continue to change until at long last it merged with the general Latin-American pattern but there would be no destruction, only adaptation and absorption proceeding gently. Although the Guatemalan Indian was a conquered man, meek before his conquerors, socially despised, subject to a special and unequal justice, exploited in many ways, and full of hatred, I felt that were I a native of one of our own tribes I would sooner move down here and face all the difficulties and humiliations than remain to await the deadly end prescribed for me. Here at least I could share in the American dream, that my son might become President. Here it had happened.

One descended upon the village from the high backbone of the Cuchumatanes, firs, pines, and tall cedars above on the crest, more great evergreens across the gorge a couple of miles away, alongside the trail manifold patches of corn and wheat on slopes so steep that falling would be a genuine hazard of farming. The houses, hundreds of them, sprawled over the delta-like hanging valley, straw-thatched huts scattered higgeldy-piggeldy with the big, white church and municipal buildings at the centre, here and there the deep green of coffee groves or the yellower colour of bananas. The valley was open to the west, falling off at the edge of the village in a cliff, then below the cliff the land dropped away, ridged and rugged, a thousand feet and another thousand and another, down to the Mexican border ten leagues away. Far beyond the Sierra Madre rose again, a jumbled, blue formation over which the red sunsets formed. Late afternoon light came yellow over the houses, in its bath the smoke seeped through the thatched roofs so that each house carried a trailing, sunshot nimbus. There were wild, white roses along the trail; in the village, hibiscus by the doorways.

Here were seven thousand people of whom I knew virtually nothing. I had done a little work among related tribes the other side of the border. I had heard tales that, pressed hard enough, the men of these tribes will kill to protect their gods. I knew what one could see in passing through. The men were slender, small, golden-skinned, neatly made. They wore a heavy, black wool tunic over white cotton shirts and trousers, kept their hair short, occasionally carried blowguns. The women were handsome, they too were slender, their long skirts of green cotton with an all-over blue and white design wrapped in a narrow sheath, showed that, unlike our Indians, they did not spread as they grew older. They wound their dark hair in a crown around their heads with wide ribbons of native weave, rich and lustrous in colour.

As one looked down over the steep edge of the trail one could see in front of the church the great cross, seventy-two feet high, slender, grey-weathered, skeletal. Its base I knew was a crude, square altar containing a number of fire pits. In the dusk I had seen a file of some six men go to that altar. Instead of the ordinary tunics they wore long ponchos of black wool, on their heads and also over their shoulders like stoles were kerchiefs with a striped design, predominantly dark red. They carried long staves. They had gone quickly and quietly to the base of the cross and prayed there while the clouds of *copal* incense billowed up from the fires they kindled. The dull flames of the pitchwood licked into the base of the rising smoke. Then they had risen and moved on to another part of the village, quiet, intense, oblivious.

These things I knew. We were riding down to face a strange personality and attempt the ridiculous task of persuading it that two young men, unknown to it, alien in race, should be accepted by it to the inner limits of confidence. This was my big chance, this if it succeeded would wipe out past failures, it would forestall the drudgery of getting a Ph.D. It would say something important to me about myself. The tales one had heard of that personality were strange and streaked with violence. The horses continued moving steadily, mechanically, down upon the village. I felt the gun under my leg and wondered if I should need it, I speculated upon failure.

The religion of Jacaltenango existed upon four levels. There was, first, formal Christianity, public and shared with the Ladinos — the small group of Spanish-speaking people who had settled in the village. Then there were Mayan practices so publicly carried on that it would be absurd to attempt to conceal them. These were *practices*: clearly observable, external performances and little more. Then there was that part of the old religion which was known to every Indian but jealously guarded from white men. This included the major myths and most of what a man had to know in ordinary times in order to ensure the well-being of himself and his family, but even in the course of an ordinary year a layman would not be able to fulfill all his religious needs unaided. Lastly, there was the completely esoteric part known only to the priests, without which no prayer could be offered for the community as a whole, no major ceremonies conducted, no serious personal crisis met. Penetration of this fourth sector was made more difficult by the fact that it was divided into specialties according to the divine gifts or the training of the practitioners, so that there was no one man who knew everything, although there were a few who understood the whole structure and had a general grasp of the specialties they themselves could not practice, as was necessary if the whole pattern of ritual and prayer was to be co-ordinated.

A few local white men had from time to time picked up scattered information concerning the fourth level. Many of them, from living side by side with the Indians, from daily contact and observation, and the casual talk of friends, had a sketchy, general idea of the layman's practices. But complete initiation of a white man was unthinkable. Items might leak out so that in the course of thirty or forty years one had learned a good deal, but no Indian would sit down and deliberately give a white man a coherent account of his beliefs. In fact, white men *were not capable* of receiving such knowledge, just as only certain Indians were capable, by innate gift, of induction into the esoteric part.

Further, the Indians did not like the Ladinos. And the Ladinos, with their sense of racial superiority, from time to time did things which violated the native religion, sometimes obliviously, sometimes out of mere curiosity or in a mood of idle, coarse humor. We rated, of course, as Ladinos, and the idea of telling us anything secret was so unheard of that it would be necessary to open new channels in the Indians' brains before such a thing could be contemplated.

I suppose ethnologists work in many different ways. I know, for instance, that most are in the habit of hiring informants. I have always suspected this method except where one finds, as among the Navajos, a positive desire to have the secret things recorded in books. Then it is fair enough to compensate a man for sitting down with you and working hard to achieve something you both desire.

I have very seldom paid an informant except for the making of linguistic lists. My method has been to hire men for normal, unsurprising work and then lead them into telling me what they know as a friendly matter undertaken almost without realizing it. This is not easy to do but the results are more trustworthy and in the end one gets much further. Of course one pays medicine-men the fees they would expect from other Indians, and even allows oneself to be grossly overcharged — ten cents for a service ordinarily worth a nickel.

The process is heartbreakingly slow; in other ways, too, it is close to heartbreaking, close to intolerable. First, to stick to this case which is typical, we had to establish ourselves in the minds of the Jacaltecos as something entirely outside of their previous experience and therefore of their established rules. We had to open their minds to the previously unthinkable. It was no use playing Indian. Byers was blond, tall, humourous — the last a characteristic to which they responded eagerly. I may be dark-haired and my skin tan deeply, but among these little Mongoloids there was no hope of my becoming an Indian. No, we had to be Ladinos. Then, we had to be a kind of Ladino they had never met before, we had to be utterly and totally new.

The main means of this is sincere democracy, a genuine belief in the brotherhood of man, and an unsurprised respect for all the tribe's customs, prejudices, and manners. Courtesy comes automatically out of this. If you really believe that these people are your full equals, after a long period of doubt, of suspicion, of watching for the fraud or the ulterior motive behind your attitude, will come a surprised, grateful, warm response and solid loyalty.

But it's a long period, during which your delicate tentatives meet nothing but rebuff — or, if you're skillful, the signs that if you pushed further you would meet rebuff. Nothing happens, nothing opens up, and all this time the secret, inner men, who are nobody's fools, are thinking and worrying about you and hardening their hearts against you.

He has asked questions of the young men. Yesterday Shuwan heard Kash Pelip, who works for him, telling him part of the story of How the Sun Rose. What is he after? Why has he come all the way from New York, a country which they say is even further than Germany, to disturb us here? What evil does he portend? We see him look at us as we go to pray at the altars of the guardians, what is he trying to do with his looking? He is a strange, new kind of a man and we are afraid of him, and it might be well to send him a message that he must not try to enter the House of the Prayermakers, he must not ask questions of the Prayermakers. Let us pray about him, let us ask the gods a question what we should do about him.

The unease runs through the village. The Prayermakers, seeing you at a distance as they go on their rounds, turn to look at you, speak to each other, and then pass on. A Knower, seeing you on the road, turns aside and detours to avoid passing you.

You let another rumour go out. Not only did Kash tell the man about How the Sun Rose, but the man already knew the story, a little different, but he had heard of it. Perhaps he knows something, perhaps he has some power. He is not like other Ladinos at all. Perhaps he has knowledge.

Week after week and nothing happening. In all this time you cannot be yourself. You cannot make enemies. You may know that a certain old man is a moocher and a fraud, but he has his position in the community and you cannot throw him out on his ear as you would wish. You are feeling in the dark along a blank wall, looking for a crevice, you may never stop feeling even for an instant, and you have no idea in what place, at what moment, the crevice will appear.

Therefore you can have no normal relation with anyone. This is irritating with casual acquaintances and people you dislike. The requirement to be everybody's friend, always a good fellow, a complete politician, builds up in you a deep longing to root an Indian, any Indian, violently in the tail. But it is much worse with your friends. You like these men and they have learned to like you. They are trusting you increasingly. Everything they say, their most casual remarks, their actions, must always be sifted in your mind. God only knows where the lead may be. You prostitute your friendships, and that is a nightmare. Throw in a touch or two of malaria, a few attacks of dysentery, but do not allow them to deflect your constant, steady attention to business. Why in God's name does anyone want to be an ethnologist?

When the pressure gets too heavy you have, in that country, the relief of saddling up and going to visit some small ruin you have been told of. The travel is refreshing, and no diplomacy is needed to clear away brush and draw a plan. A spell of skilled work with the inanimate is delightful. And then, of course, the men you have brought with you become more closely allied to you, you camp and eat together, sit over the fire, there is some legend about this place, and away from the village tongues are loosened. By golly, you have brought your torment right along with you.

Luck enters into every enterprise. What you are trying to do is to be ready for the break that must come sometime, but the waiting is dreadfully long. In the end, not through your skill but by an accident, you find the crevice. Then, to shift metaphors, the dam breaks. Then, if you have handled yourself rightly, you and a number of Indians become allied in the enterprise of putting the heart of their life down on paper. If your malaria gets bad at that time it's tough luck. Eat quinine till your ears ring, have a stiff drink, but don't let the process drop.

All of this is fairly directly contrary to escapism. You have made a major escape from the problems of your own world to those of an alien and somewhat simpler one, but now escape has been so perfected that it begins to become endowed with many of the drawbacks of reality. You have been robbed of sentimentalization; you have to make hard, accurate judgments of your men, you have to consider all factors, economy, relation to white men, good and ugly customs, stupidities, meannesses, nobilities, for just exactly what they are. You may bathe yourself in this Indian world, but you cannot go on pretending about it. Every factor which forms or malforms its character must be directly and fully faced.

In return you acquire a form of power as you achieve a fair degree of knowledge while retaining a perception which is impossible for the people themselves. For instance: one of the cornerstones of the esoteric religion is the process of divination or soothsaying, carried on by specialists called Knowers. The most important Knower is called The Shower of the Road. He is one of two or three key men in the entire hierarchy. He does not merely 'answer questions,' through his deep knowledge of ritual and communication with the gods he dictates major religious and, I believe, civic policies, prescribes prayers and rites, determines whether or not a man is fit to receive or retain priestly office. I had a natural desire to meet this man, and I discovered a Ladino who was on fairly friendly terms with him and to whom he had once let fall a few items of information — nothing much, for The Shower of the Road's knowledge is as esoteric as Hell.

I arranged to go to him to ask a question about a lost object, which gave me a chance to observe the process of soothsaying. It was thrilling to discover that what he was doing was the ancient, priestly process which the first Spanish conquerors had described in an incomplete way and which archaeologists had partly reconstructed, not entirely correctly. From what I saw and heard in those few minutes I knew that in fact there did exist here a survival of the ancient lore such as had never before been found. Here was antiquity still alive and functioning, archaeology on the hoof. I wanted more of this man.

He thought otherwise. After I left he became frightened and fled me. The door slammed shut again.

Putting together everything I had picked up from laymen, what I had seen, and what archaeology knew, I had a fair idea of how a divination worked. I can't exactly reconstruct that incomplete idea now because later, in another village, I became a qualified Knower myself, but I can describe the general system as far as it relates to this story. There are twenty powerful gods who rule the days in turn, much as if on Monday we worshipped the moon and it ruled us, on Tuesday, Tue, on Wednesday, Wodin, and so forth. Archaeologists refer to these characters as 'day-names'; they are not, they are gods. This gives a 'week' of twenty days. In addition, days are counted by numbers up to thirteen, the two systems revolving as do our weeks and days of the month only in reverse proportion. Thus if we start with a day ruled by Imish, god of the soil, it also has the number one. The numbers go on to thirteen then start at one again, so that when we come to the end of the list with Ahau ruling (he has too many powers to list here), the number is seven, then comes Imish with eight to start over again. At the end of two hundred and sixty days Imish will come in conjunction with one again.

Each of these gods has his own character, some good, some bad. The numbers also have their qualities. The soothsayer takes a number of seeds at random from a pile and throws them on a cloth. Then, starting with the god and number of the current day (that combination is the true day-name), he counts forward according to the number of seeds. Their arrangement will indicate that certain names and numbers reached on the way are important, others unimportant.

He may make one cast, one count, and give an answer, or he may cast over and over again, either because the answer is unclear or because he hopes for a pleasanter one.

I suspected then what I know now, that there was wide range for interpretation in this system. You seldom get a simple case of the ace of spades meaning death. You are more likely to get a bad god, say Chabin, who relates to death, with a pretty good number like four, and then have Cheh of the animals turn up with a neutral number, which can mean death or sickness to an animal or death or accident because of an animal, or might be overbalanced by Watan, the farmer's friend and one of the strongest gods coming along with a very good number such as thirteen. The soothsayer's predisposition is most important.

For various reasons it became increasingly important for me to get through to The Shower of the Road. I had begun to acquire the reputation of being 'one who knows something,' which means someone initiated in some part of the esoteric knowledge, and hence 'a man of clear heart,' which is a person innately qualified to receive knowledge and therefore possessing some power. And fortunately the Ladino who was my link with The Shower had a deep belief in the reality of all forms of Indian magic, however little he might think of their religion. So I tried a gamble.

I told my Ladino friend in the most impressive way I could that he was to take a message to The Shower and to use my exact words. He was to tell The Shower to bring out his seeds, to make his prayer, and to ask his question of the gods. I, of my knowledge, would tell him in advance what the answer would be. I knew that the gods would not lie, I was perfectly confident of the gods. They would tell him to receive me and tell me what I wanted to know. They would tell him that I was a man of clear heart, and that I ought to know these things.

The Ladino was astounded. He believed me. It had been a good act. And it worked. Since then I've pulled the trick twice more, once in rather a serious crisis, and it's worked each time. I've done it with a little more confidence since I learned to use the native phrases and to have the message conveyed so that it sounded like one priest sending word to another; still, I hope I don't have to try it too often.

The old man received me with the Ladino interpreting. He was a nice, sincere old man with a fine, wrinkled face. He was deeply interested in his lore, he had an alert mind and had done some speculating about the mathematical laws governing the calendar and other such things. He was prepared to talk now, and his confidence increased as he saw that I was not entirely ignorant and that my attitude was reverent. Now we met a new obstacle. The Ladino was a hopelessly incompetent interpreter. Not only was his grasp of Jacalteca extremely limited, but he was one of those dummies whom no amount of explanation can cure of rendering five minutes of careful explanation as 'He says, "Yes."' Also, his presence was a deterrent in itself, since I might be a man of clear heart, but he was just an amiable alien.

Antel, The Shower, had no Spanish. I had the kind of Jacalteca one might be expected to pick up in three months during which I had made some effort to learn. We were treating of serious matters which it was blasphemous to convey incorrectly, we both became interested. And between us this dope destroyed rather than aided communication.

I worded a rather long, careful question. I heard the interpreter render it in four words. I cut in and stated the question again, begging him to translate it in full. He pretty nearly did. The answer was nearly as long, and was returned to me as 'No.' We tried that again, and failed. The trouble was that the man didn't understand the full of what Antel had said. I think I understood as much as he did.

Digging into my brain for all the Jacalteca I could summon, I asked the next question for myself. Antel hesitated. Then a lovely look of relief came over his face in the candlelight, and he answered me *in halting Spanish*. The interpreter was astonished, so was I. It was a beautiful tribute, the laying aside of a shield, an advantage he had guarded for years. We worked together from there on, helping each other, piecing the two languages together in co-operation in order to deal fitly with sacred things. Of all my work among Indians, this remains the highest moment.

By the time I got through with these Indians I neither loved nor hated them. Culturally and linguistically I could think of them in the mass, but emotionally they had become many people; the sense of separation which enables one to generalize freely had grown dim and they were a number of human beings, some of whom I liked, some of whom I didn't. This experience and its attendant assorted knowledges covering everything from the extent to which they had an effective vote to the prevalence of unnecessary disease among a people served only by medicine men, coincided with my education in New Orleans. It was around these Indians, as I prepared to write at some length about their relation to the whole social structure of Guatemala, that I did my first broad social thinking, it was from them that I derived the theory of social conditions which one accepts perforce but which never cease to irritate, which I later applied to Negroes and which led me on to new political and social concepts.

The curious fact was that I was slowly, unwittingly turning into a liberal. It was all still rather remote. It is significant that the only novel I have written with a clear liberal slant is *Sparks Fly Upward*, which is safely laid not only in Latin America but in the past. If at the time I wrote it I had been asked to apply those same doctrines fully to my own United States, I should have been startled.

I had left the Navajo country after that long ride with Bart Hayes having come to one more conclusion. The Indian story had to end in tragedy. It was hopeless to dream that the Indian Bureau with its powerful church backing could be reformed, or that the children would cease to suffer. The culture must die away under hostile pressure and there was no sign of anything to replace it save hopelessness and sloth. Disease would continue, the death rate go on mounting. There had once been three-quarters of a million Indians in the United States, now the population was estimated at one quarter. They would go ever faster. Even so it would be a slow, heartbreaking process before the last Indian died — one comfort was that when that happened, a lot of bureaucrats would be suddenly out of a job.

I was angry, but I couldn't see that I could do anything about it. At any rate, it would be a long time before the full pressure of disaster reached the Navajos; I could still study and enjoy them. Perhaps they would last out my time. I met John Collier at Kayenta and, disliking him, made no attempt to find out what he and his Indian Defense Association were up to. I went my own way, was angry, and lamented.

Laughing Boy expressed the point which I had reached. I saw our own Indians as inexorably doomed, I saw that they must come increasingly into contact with our so-called civilization, and that (I then thought inevitably) contact meant conflict and disaster. I put this idea into the book, along with anger at certain evil things that I had seen, and then I let myself out by sending my hero, after the final tragedy, back into my own dreamland, the untouched, undisturbed Navajo country where the white man was not a factor and would not become one within my time. The whole treatment was specific, personal to the characters involved. It might prove good publicity for the Navajos, but it could lead to no reforms.

Laughing Boy catapulted me into the spotlight. Suddenly I was somebody, and prosperous to boot. I knew vaguely that there existed some societies for helping and protecting the Indians, and I thought I ought to join one. I subscribed in a small way to the first I came across, planning to read its publications and see what I thought of it.

With headquarters in New York was the Eastern Association on Indian Affairs, a small group with a good record of accomplishment. One of its officers remarked, correctly, that Oliver La Farge had a good name but knew nothing and it would be well to get him before John Collier did. Collier, now Commissioner of Indian Affairs and beyond all comparison the best Commissioner we have ever had, was then executive secretary of the Indian Defense Association. I did not know it, but the two organizations were deadly enemies. Out of the blue I was notified of my election as a director of the Eastern Association. I accepted the honour with some amusement at the method, and then, slowly at first, my troubles began.

I was free now to go where I chose. I was free to return to the Southwest, to stay among the Navajos, to roll in Indians. My position in the Association gave me a sort of status; with it came the first idea that perhaps something hopeful could be done. I tried one trip in the Navajo country for pure pleasure, and never having travelled before without a purpose, found that super-freedom rather flat. Ethnology should be a useful as well as an informative tool. I would see if I could give my pleasure a purpose.

Among the Association's achievements was that, acting in concert with various other groups, it had persuaded President Hoover to remove the commissionership of Indian Affairs from politics by making his appointments from a list to be submitted by those groups. He did better than this, he took the first two names on the list, Charles J. Rhoads as Commissioner, Henry Scattergood as Assistant Commissioner. They were good, sincere men, politically conservative, by no means ignorant of Indian affairs, taking office at considerable personal sacrifice. The first I knew of them was that they were already beginning to put an end to the torture, starvation, and slow murder of the children in the schools. So there was hope, so perhaps something could be done.

I went down to Washington and introduced myself. I thought I knew quite a lot about Indians — in one sense I did, I knew what can be seen by anyone visiting among them, I knew a good deal about their ethnology. I was as competent as most scientists to reconstruct their past, pure state, and to live in that mentally, which is what anthropologists tend so lamentably to do. In another sense I knew nothing. I had a narrow perception of the Jacaltecos as citizens of Guatemala, but of our Indians as citizens and wards of North America and the vast network of problems which we call the administration of Indian affairs, I knew as much as if I saw a few tips of twigs over the top of a wall and not only had never seen the main branches, trunk, roots, or the soil in which the tree grew, but had no idea even whether it was a tree, a bush, or a number of tall plants. It is impossible to understand our Indians today or to see anything but a sort of disconnected surrealism in what is happening to them, without a fair perception of that tree.

Mr. Rhoads evidently thought I was educable. He did me a great favour — or played me a very dirty trick, I am not sure which. On several occasions he made me sit beside his desk throughout an entire day, simply watching what went over it, listening to his conversations and conferences. I heard long, intimate discussions of tribes whose very names had been unknown to me, I watched the steady, unmanageable flood of questions of broad policy and minute details which poured across that desk. Here was every aspect of government except coinage, foreign relations and a military establishment, affecting over two hundred administrative units scattered from the Arctic Circle to Florida. The status of the natives of Alaska is somewhat different from that of Indians within the United States. The Pueblos of New Mexico possess special rights handed down from Mexico and Spain which place them in a favourable position and amounts to a separate body of law. The six thousand Indians of New York State are also in a different status, covered by treaties antedating our Union, the Indians of Oklahoma are covered by a number of unique laws, mostly vicious, some affecting the whole state, others only certain areas. Treaty rights vary from tribe to tribe. Here is a lawyer's field-day, an administrator's headache.

In the far North, Indian Service ships fly the flag of the Department of the Interior. A special arrangement has been negotiated with Russia whereby the Indian Bureau issues a sort of informal passport so that Eskimos can continue their ancient traffic with their relatives across the Behring Straits. The Papagos want to maintain their freedom to visit back and forth across the Mexican border, the Seminoles in Florida need help in getting jobs as guides, the Blackfeet are faced with starvation, the Navajo jewelry trade is being depressed by machine-made imitations, the principal of a school in Arizona is reported to be still using forbidden, physical punishments, there is a problem of delinquency among Indian girls employed as servants in Los Angeles, the farming program in Wyoming has broken down because some idiot tried to introduce the wrong crops for the country, the San Carlos Apaches want a herd of registered heifers so that they can breed their own bulls and the cattlemen's organizations will raise hell if this is allowed. , . .

It all goes over the Commissioner's desk, and the delegations of Indians, of friends of the Indians, and those who intend to take something away from the Indians come in, and back of all of it is the survival, the advancement, or the destruction of thousands of human beings. I sat and watched it, I returned to the Indian country with my eyes opened to things I had never seen before, I went back to Washington. My naïve days were being rapidly brought to an end.

I sat in the Senate Indian Affairs Committee Room. Soon, tomorrow or in a day or so, I should be up for a grilling. I had been subpoenaed. Meantime I watched the others take it. The cross-examiner, with all the wonderful advantages a senator enjoys, was Senator Wheeler. He seems to me to be a natural prosecuting attorney. His mind is quick. He knows just how far to go with invective for the record and sees readily where invective will work and where it won't. His voice is rather harsh yet not unpleasant. His profile has something of the hawk to it. His eyeglasses glitter. He uses his hands beautifully, although the effect of his gestures is often spoiled because a chewed-up cigar is wedged between his fingers. In Indian Affairs he is frequently just as wrong as he was recently in foreign policy but you would have a devil of a time proving it before him; also he is frequently right.

Looking back on that particular fight now, after twelve years, I think he was half right and my side was half right. I watched officers of my Association and Bureau officials whom I had regarded as all-wise go down before him in agony, partly because he was ruthless and sometimes unbelievably rude, partly because he knew his stuff and they didn't. Or rather, John Collier sitting near him knew and brought the most amazing quantity of unbelievably appropriate documents out of an overstuffed brief-case. The more I heard the sicker and angrier I felt. I think any American will get angry, regardless of which side he is on, when a senator starts working over a perfectly sincere witness. And this was coming to me soon. My stomach got worse and worse. At the same time I was learning. Why were we unable to answer so many important questions even on matters where we were certainly in the right? Why could none of us testify as to the geologist's reports on the Rattlesnake Dome? Good Lord, they were in the Indian Office files. Why didn't any of us know how the Lee's Ferry Bridge had been financed, what claim the Santa Fe railroad had to land on the Walapai Reservation (and just where was the Walapai Reservation?), the basis for assessing the value of improvement within the New Mexico Indian grants? We had helped appoint a Commissioner, we had helped defeat vicious legislation and secure the passage of good, we had improved the medical service, we were successfully developing a more saleable type of Navajo blanket, but we seemed to have overlooked a lot of bets.

The less said of my session under Senator Wheeler the better. I was taken beautifully to pieces. At breakfast before I was due to take the stand I was so frightened I could not even drink coffee. Not even love ever did that to me. As the hearing went on I grew less frightened, by the end of it I had myself in hand. I have had a bad time before the committee since then, but I have not been frightened. But as a witness I had helped no more than the rest of them.

I knew now why my side hated Collier and Wheeler so bitterly. But I had lost another segment of my innocence and there entered my mind a horrible idea that to some extent the other side had been right. At any rate, there had been altogether too many questions to which we did not know the answers. If one wished to serve the Indians one could not merely concentrate on that which was interesting — their arts, the improvement of the health service, the protection of their religious rights — it was necessary to study their situation as one would that of a corrupt municipality one intended to reform.

Certain ideas which Hooton of Harvard had started in my mind long ago were sprouting in my mind. Some of Hooton's theories as recently published may be a trifle wild, but he is an unusual teacher and one of the few anthropologists I know who has never been prevented from seeing the woods by the trees. He gave me the idea that eventually anthropology and its related social sciences would have an application to man in the mass similar to that which medicine and psychology have to the individual. In the long run science would be useful. I began increasingly to feel that there was a need in the Indian problem for a wedding between ethnology and politics, an idea which terrified my scientific colleagues. When I put it to the Commissioner, I also succeeded in startling him, partly because I presented it stupidly. I suggested that an alliance be formed between the Bureau of Ethnology and the Bureau of Indian Affairs, 'like what the Mexicans are doing.' That last remark was an error. It was not possible at that time to persuade the average

American that Mexico could be far ahead of us in a job of science-guided, practical administration, although that was the fact.

I had my doubts that Collier could be as black as he was painted, although I knew that certain of his ideas were cockeyed. In the heat of a political row one is inclined to become emotionally partisan and to reduce everything to terms of black and white, especially if in that field one is as utterly unspotted from the world as I was. Roosevelt was elected. Collier's appointment loomed over us. I rolled up my sleeves and began to fight.

Just before election time, when it was clear that Hoover was licked, there occurred a curious, hurried meeting of those directors of the Association who could be got together. Present were the few, wealthy people whose generosity had been our mainstay. Several propositions were put forth:

That dreadful man Roosevelt was going to be elected and God knew what would happen to the country.

Already things were so bad that incomes were curtailed, taxes were due to increase, and our benefactors stated that they could no longer support the Association in the style to which it was accustomed.

If Roosevelt were elected, that even more dreadful man Collier would become Commissioner, or else some creature of his like Ickes, president of his Chicago branch.

Such a Commissioner would certainly be bad and impossible to deal with. The doom of the Indians was sealed.

For all these reasons, therefore, we should disband the Association.

I was sincerely shocked. So, I think, were some of the others there, but they were also appalled by the prospect of trying, in those desperate times, to maintain income if our benefactors quit on us. My reasoning was simple. The worse Commissioner we have, the more the Association is needed. If the new Commissioner really turns out to be a stinker, we can create scandal and get lots of contributions. Anyhow, there must be at least two thousand people in the United States who will contribute an average of five dollars a year to give the Indians a decent break, and on that we could operate. And if, indeed, Collier and his associates were such holy terrors, it was our bounden duty to try to prevent their appointment and at least go down fighting.

I was just past thirty years old, *Laughing Boy* had sold to the movies, my second book was doing well, and I was beginning to hit the *Saturday Evening Post*. I had been undergoing a series of revelations concerning Indian affairs, I was sincere, brash, and young. So I expressed my ideas in a polite way, and as a result found myself president of an Association with eighteen paid-up members and nothing in the treasury, and a whale of a fight on my hands.

I may state now that I have been proved wrong about the two thousand people, a fact which puzzles me. On the one hand the country is full of people who have met the Indians and have an uncrystallized desire to help them; on the other what is now the American Association on Indian Affairs has done and is doing work which should win their support even, or perhaps especially, in war-time, but somehow it doesn't happen. It may be because we've never known how to make ourselves known, or it may be because so much of the interest in Indians is of the yearner type, which can be hit for a single contribution by a sentimental appeal but becomes bored with steady support of an organization which tries to be unsentimental and realistic.

This sudden promotion, which was more or less equivalent to finding someone dopey enough to be willing to hold a dying baby, put me right into the fight to prevent Collier's appointment. I fought, organized, conferred, learned a lot more about politics. The longer this went on, the more worked up I became. In the spring of 1933 I had lost all sense of proportion and I knew that we were licked. I wrote a bitter letter to an Indian friend of mine, in which I all but called my opponent a son of a bitch. Like an utter fool I wrote this letter, essentially personal in two senses, on Association stationery. The Indian showed it to another Indian, who showed it to a white busybody, who sent it to Mr. Collier. He received it the same day that he received my telegram congratulating him on his appointment and offering our co-operation. In return, he sent me two missives, dealing with these two communications as if he had been two separate persons.

With this happy background I went to Washington to meet the new Commissioner. I felt pretty sick as I walked into his office. Until I reached his desk and we had shaken hands I had no idea what I was going to say. I wondered just what was coming to me.

There were some generalities, a bit of a pause, then I was inspired and I plunged in, saying exactly what I felt. It was, in effect, that as far as we were concerned he had no existence prior to his appointment as Commissioner, that all the bitter feeling and opposition and disagreements which we both knew so well ended with that appointment. As Commissioner of Indian Affairs he was the man of all men upon whom the Indians depended. That was all we knew and all we cared to know. The rest lay in the future. If he worked to help the Indians we should be with him wholeheartedly, if we thought him wrong we should tell him so, if he persisted in what we thought were harmful policies, of course we should oppose him.

He said that that was his feeling, too. In three minutes we were planning joint action, in ten I had undertaken to make some investigations for him. He did not speak of that letter then, nor has he ever referred to it since.

Of course that was an inspiring experience for a young man and in itself a lifetime's education in the meaning of sincerity. I count that meeting, too, as marking the end of Indians as an escape for me. I had entered into my escape so well that it assumed the perfection of a circle and now I was on my way back. First there was a constructed world, perfectly integrated, charged with problems which were a product of the construction, and such problems are always this side of the border of that from which one is fleeing. Then this world began to absorb reality into itself until I was back in everybody's world again.

I was educable, and so was the new Commissioner. I don't think I played much part in his education in office, but I think he himself will grant that I did a little. Now I was into Indian affairs in a big way, and Indian affairs to my astonishment broadened before my eyes and within my mind until they could not be distinguished from liberal politics and liberal social thinking. Since I left Harvard I have steadily become less conservative, reversing the usual process. I don't believe in Socialism, I have no use at all for Communism, but if, using the word within the American scheme of things, you want to call me radical and say it pleasantly I'll hesitate to deny it. This the Indians have done to me.

I referred earlier to the powerful church backing which the old Indian Bureau had. Some of the reforms to be brought about in

Indian Affairs were simply returns to basic American principles, and one of these was the severance of Church and State. When I was first in the Indian country there were missionaries who boasted that no Superintendent could remain on their reservations if they were opposed to him. The influence was powerful in every aspect of the work of the Bureau, and I heartily favoured ending it, on grounds of Americanism as well as for the Indians' welfare.

I have gathered from various quarters, directly and indirectly, that as a result of the position I have taken there is hostility towards me in certain mission circles, and that there is a general impression that I am opposed to the existence of missions and to Christianity. This is a good place to say what I do think.

There are tribes, such as the Cœur d'Alènes, which are entirely Christian and have profited by it. There are tribes among which certain missions, over generations, have been real saviours and have made large numbers of true and loyal converts. In some cases, where the old faith has collapsed with the end of the old way of life, Christianity is the only thing that can fill a ruinous spiritual void. There is a great work to be done by men of God among the Indians. I can name missionaries, both Catholic and Protestant, whom I deeply admire and regard as true Christians.

Unfortunately, *so far as my observation goes*, these fine men and organizations have been in the minority. My first information on a missionary at work was a case which is notorious in the Indian Service. I learned on good authority that this man sold to the Indians for reasonable sums the candies and other good things which his supporters in the outside world had sent him to distribute at Christmas. It seemed a singularly small, mean thing to do. More important, he had achieved for himself a priceless spot of fertile land in the desert, and got the title sewed up so that the Indians, who greatly needed it, could not recapture it. He clung to that land like grim death and sold his crops for an excellent price.

There was another man who obtained a priceless possession, irrigated land at the head of a stream, the only stream for hundreds of miles which flowed steadily with enough water for irrigation. The right to a share of that water went with the land, of course. Downstream lay the fields of the Indians among whom he was supposed to work. Secure in his political power — for missionaries had great power in the days when hardly anyone but the churches paid attention to the Indians — he diverted onto his land many times his share of the precious water and the crops of his charges were accordingly diminished. When, after many warnings, a courageous superintendent under an honest Commissioner of Indian Affairs put a locked meter on his water-gate he went into a fury, claiming that the government had blasphemously metered the waters of the Lord. He, too, made a nice thing out of his farm — and few converts.

I have seen too much of this kind of thing. I believe that an Indian has a constitutional right to worship as he pleases, and by the same token, that white men have a constitutional right to try to *persuade* him to change his religion. I italicize *persuade*. Insofar as the loss of the old religions means the loss of an important esthetic, music, dance, costume, design, and literature, I regret it, or rather, I hope and seek for means to enable the esthetic values to continue without the old sanctions if that be possible. I resent the missionaries who fight all native arts because their designs and associations relate to the native religion and because seeing that the work of their parents is admired by white men, children may be led to think a little less harshly about their heritage.

When I see publications issued by irresponsible church groups stating that ceremonies, some of which I have happily attended and even taken part in, are the occasion of incredible orgies, filthy, drunken, and cruel practices, the issuance of flat, foul lies in order to promote 'Christianity,' I want to fight. When I see a mission organization publish a document stating, or hear, as I have heard, a high mission official state, that our Constitution guarantees religious liberty *only within the Christian faith* and that it is the government's duty to force Indians to become Christian, I want to fight and feel it my duty as an American to do so.

Although the wording of the regulations disguised it, the fact is that up to 1933 Christianity was compulsory in all Indian schools, though they are maintained by the federal government. Every child was assigned to a sect (the quarrellings among missionaries had grown so violent that some time before I saw any of this the government negotiated a sort of treaty by which it was agreed that only two sects could be represented at one school), he received instruction in that sect, he attended divine service in its church, and there was absolutely nothing he or his parents could do about it. As a result, a good many Indians were weakened in attachment to their own faith and some did become converts.

I had a part in preparation of the Order on Respect for Indian Culture and Religious Freedom, which although it is still disobeyed in some places, on the whole has given the Indian children freedom of worship. My part was a very small, consultative one, but I am proud and grateful to have had even that. The main credit goes to the present Commissioner of Indian Affairs, John Collier. It took courage, for it brought down on him the massed anger, not of all churches, but of many of them. Yet it is a very reasonable order, if anything still trespassing on the edge of constitutional violation, allowing time when children who volunteer may be let out of classes for religious instruction, and the use of classrooms or other facilities for the purpose.

I have heard a missionary praise the order, claiming that it returned the question of conversion to a Christian basis. But I have seen whole organizations bitterly fighting non-religious policies of vital importance to the very survival of tribes, merely because they emanated from the man who issued it. These people seem to have become confused as to the nature of their mission.

Indian religions, like all others, contain two archaic factors. One is a mythology compiled long ago to explain the physical world. An educated man can no more believe the physical facts stated in the Navajo Origin Myth than he can those in Genesis. The second is a belief that by the use of certain formulae, ranging from simple prayer to the most elaborate ceremonies, God can be moved to intervene in human affairs or that if these are omitted, material harm will follow. This belief, too, an educated man cannot but reject. The first item is a leftover from more ignorant times, a fossil from man's first gropings towards science; the second is of the same vintage but has, of course, a high persuasive value.

The stories, rites, and customs have been handed along and worked over for thousands of years by truly religious men of high thought, and as a result they have been charged with a second, spiritual content which remains valid and unshaken by any extension of our material knowledge. In large measure Christianity has recognized this change and asks its followers to be faithful, not because of material advantages or belief in the external course of a narrative, but because of these much greater significances. For this kind of religion to be vigorous and to fill the place it should in our present world, its leaders and expounders must be spiritual men, not mere hacks, and above all not mere seekers after power.

Many Indian religions are capable of making the same transition, but it is doubtful if they will do so. The break between generations is too violent. The old men, the priests and philosophers, have had little of our education, perhaps the majority of them speak no English even today. They think in terms of naïve belief, they are fundamentalists, urging the young men to dance lest the crops fail, to believe that mankind was literally created out of an ear of corn. Unlike some of our own fundamentalists they cannot prevent the young men from receiving elementary scientific instruction. Under the program which certain mission groups are fighting so bitterly for the reason I have given, increasing numbers of young Indians are getting an excellent high-school education, and as a result they are faced with an irreconcilable conflict between what they know and the external, material aspects of their native faith.

It may happen, particularly among the Navajos, that the step will be taken from belief in the narrative to belief in the spiritual significance of the myths, from ceremonies to secure a material end to ceremonies for the benefit of the soul. I think this unlikely. The Indian religions, or most of them, are doomed.

From this will come, is coming already, the ruinous spiritual void I mentioned before. Here is the call for Christianity, for the real article. But the water-thieves, the graspers for power, the time-servers, the men who will sacrifice the Indians themselves in attempting to preserve an un-American union between church and state, the non-Christians (regardless of what they profess), *the men whom the Indians hate*, cannot fill this need. What they are really doing is building up a resistance which would make it difficult for Saint Paul himself to get a hearing if he should come among the Indians.

I have no use for these people, and I see no reason why one should be soft-spoken about them merely because they, like the Communists, make use of a special invective against their opponents.

The tide of Indian survival was turned in the early nineteen-twenties with the reform of the medical service. There are more than three hundred and fifty thousand of them now, increasing at a rate which promises close to a million by the end of the century. They have become to me a part of America, their problem, for all its special aspects, one with the general problem of all our depressed areas, our rural communities, our half-ruined land. I do still love the old colour, I do still find that my interior relaxes and my innards are refreshed when I am free to spend a time among a group of these people and there is no problem in the wind, above all when I am allowed in their ceremonies. I love their colour, their humour, their music, and the way their minds work. But I can never again separate them from their fellow-citizens. I care more now to see an Indian repairing a diesel engine than I do to see one handle a bow and arrow.

This, too, I have tried to set forth in writing; a sort of antithesis of *Laughing Boy*. I don't see why a young Navajo adjusting to a changing world which involves Hitler, soil erosion, and the conquest of ignorance and poverty, isn't just as valid a subject of American writing as, say, a Georgia sharecropper or a young Okie. There are just as many Indians as there are Okies. And the white boy and the Indian are likely today to be found operating the same tank or flying in the same bomber, for the hopeless Indian picture I first saw has been turned upside down.

But if I write of such a boy, the people who thronged to buy *Laughing Boy* stay away in large numbers, because they like their Indians long-haired, beautiful, and 'unspoiled.' And the people who will throng to read about the social problems of any other section of the country despise the book because all writing about Indians is *ipso facto* escapist. Similarly, one could raise a good deal of money with sentimental appeals to keep our Hiawathas beaded, feathered, and pure, but when one talks of soil conservation, advanced education and sustained-yield forestry the yearners drift away and the supporters of liberal causes show their frank disdain. Indians are not a liberal cause but a sentiment; now the Firestone plantations in Liberia . . .

I can never again be exclusively interested in Indians, because I can never again believe that the Indians' interests are exclusive. Nor can I ever entirely escape. I still don't 'know Indians,' but unfortunately for me I know a good deal about them, they have become part of my discovery of America, and simple Americanism makes it impossible to refuse to help where one sees clearly that one can.

It's a strange chain of events, surely, out of a book read at Groton, out of the empty, horseback days and the singing and the exotic quest, to American politics and an acute sense, non-existent in me twenty years ago, of the threat to us all wherever in this nation democracy is betrayed.

CHAPTER 15

SECOND PAPERS

'BACK AGAIN,' I told myself bitterly, 'right back where you started from.'

In the back of the closet in the large, dark bathroom I had hung two malacca canes and a black one for evening wear. On the shelf above was, among other junk, a paper package containing a number of pairs of spats. I am still open to any reasonable offer on slightly used spats of various shades, all of the best quality.

The bathroom was part of what once must have been a bedroom, partitioned with a cheap wall of beaded planks. The linoleum was worn through in several places, the tub pitted and grimed beyond the help of cleaning powders. There was a curious, non-skid feeling to its bottom. It was a place which nothing could make look clean, but the lack of light took care of that. The paint job was unbelievably bad, it was so throughout the apartment. I have done better myself.

The small living-room contained the blessing of a fireplace. It had a two-burner stove on top of a refrigerator which made a noise like a coffee-grinder, a cabinet for dishes, a table, two straight chairs, a couch, a lamp. There was also a bedroom, five feet by twelve, with a bed. At one glance I could restore the original layout of the whole house, for I had grown up in one of these, and this apartment roughly corresponded to our nursery. It all could have been fitted into our nursery, but cut up as it was there would hardly be room to lay out the tracks we once had owned.

I moved my own stuff in. A big desk, a small table, a straight chair, an armchair, a filing cabinet, some Indian and Mexican things, some pictures, my bookshelves and books. I certainly had accumulated books, and there was none which did not say something to me. I have the practice of going over the shelves each year and eliminating the ones which have died.

With these things in the place it became snug, a trifle overloaded, and the pacing which is with me an occupational disease of writing was turned into a difficult figure-eight business around and behind desk, armchair, table, and couch. I had arranged certain things almost automatically in a way which was deeply familiar although it was a long time since I had arranged them so: the two pewter steins I got at Harvard on the mantelpiece, a Navajo blanket of which I was especially fond hung on the wall once more, the whole arrangement of the room dominated by the requirement of putting the desk in the best light regardless of other considerations, and the windows stripped of drapes.

I had brought with me, besides the canes and spats, some other trailing clouds of my vanished glory, nearly a case of excellent sherry, a bottle of madeira, some claret, the correct glasses for drinking these, a burdensome pile of white vests and white ties, a ream of expensive typewriter paper which crackled slightly when handled, a thin, carefully tended mustache.

The glory was over. The well-served dinners of eight, apartment houses with doormen, Irish whiskey and imported wines had vanished along with the necessity of changing for dinner, not to ape the British, of course, but because one felt so sticky if one did not. Dinner hereafter would be at the counter of the Greek restaurant across the way. I had hit the jackpot the first time I put in a nickel, and outside of true gambling it *is* a law of this world that for a while after hitting the big jackpot, at least medium-sized ones follow. Magazines are eager for successful writers' stories, the novel after a big success is bound to have some sale, the people one meets, editors, moving-picture men, publishers, look over one's prosperity with the thought that they might wish to add to it. In short stories I had hit a formula which brought down a thousand dollars at a crack. Pleased and purring I had entered at last the way of life and the milieu to which any good Groton boy aspires, the way which is his by right.

Well, it certainly seemed to be over. The flow of money had stopped like water in an irrigation ditch when the gate is shut. I knew where the next month's rent was coming from but I was not at all sure about the month after. On the desk were the outline of a novel and the opening chapters. Back again where I had started from, only then I was twenty-eight — no, twenty-seven, and now I was thirty-six. Well, it was my own fault, in no small measure by my own choice. That last was a certain comfort, although when I made my choice I had not quite seen how far it would lead.

I finished fixing the books and was relaxed by communication with them. It was dusk. I poured sherry, not into the correct glass but into one intended for claret, which had more capacity. From this place I could see a lot of sky, the wonderful, deep before-dark purple which is one of New York's greatest beauties. Sherry is a comforting drink with its rich smell and its colour. I supposed I could be a lot worse off. New feelings were stirring in me. No, they were old ones. Familiarity. More than that, stronger. There was a definite physical sensation in my interior of a great many tightly rolled up threads uncurling, reaching out. If a man who was almost completely paralyzed were restored by a slow-working, gentle miracle it might feel something like that.

The threads were uncurling. They were restoring life and feelings and they were uniting — from behind the years New Orleans leaped up vivid and alive, there was someone I had begun to be and then I had cut him off with a cleaver, ended the threads, the strands, the spinal cord of my life to hang for nearly a decade in suspended animation. Now by God's grace the spinal cord was being spliced and life was beginning again. Perhaps at last I should know myself. I had wasted a lot of time, but here I was on my own and poor again.

Poor? I had observed poverty, and I knew I had never been poor. This room was heavy with possessions, its texture snug and rich. How would I stand up if I did have to face real poverty, the bare, wretched, repellent room precariously clung to, the recurrent grip of hunger, the hovering fear? Maybe I was going to find out. Things were getting interesting.

An awful lot of years to have wasted. I had forgotten New Orleans, but it came flooding back now, the deadened nerves were coming delightfully to life, blocked channels in the brain were opening almost painfully to a flood of thoughts. Behaviours and points of view I had forgotten came back freshly reasonable and restraints and a whole number of things one believed necessary were vanishing. I knew now why, when I had to spend a hot, summer night in New York, I used to wake to the sticky weight of the morning and in half waking be in New Orleans, then remember where I was. The realization, the pleasant bedroom, and the well-appointed tray coming in the door never brought me any pleasure. I understood that now, as I did certain violent reactions towards the French Quarter I occasionally had when I was drunk, and why during recent years my regular drinking had grown so much heavier — not getting drunk, constant nipping. That seemed no longer necessary, although of course one does not shake off all at once the habit of making one's self muzzy before dinner.

I checked over the writers and artists whose work I admired. There were a few who stayed in the money without betrayal of themselves, but they were few. Most of them toiled like dogs and contrived endlessly in order to get by, they had their occasional windfalls but their lives were firmly based on the assumption of narrow means and insecurity. I remembered Sherwood Anderson long ago in New Orleans saying that a writer was doing well if he could count on three thousand a year, and I also remembered that that was about six times the average annual per capita income for the nation. Well, I was one of the boys now. On the whole it felt rather good. It was also going to be tough, for I had softened a lot. It's not everyone who has a chance to go back and pick up again the man he used to be. It seemed to me that something ought to be done to mark the occasion. Having downed the sherry I went into the bathroom and shaved off that carefully tended mustache.

Even then I saw that the intervening years had not been entirely wasted. I had acquired a lot of miscellaneous information of value. I had done one or two difficult things such as helping the Hopi Indians to organize a system of self-government, of which I could be sincerely proud. Some of my writing was all right. I might be a lot older than when, in similar financial condition, I was writing *Laughing Boy*, but I had the enormous leverage of reputation. I had grown skillful, that I knew. And at least, sincerely alarmed by the channel into which my writing had fallen, I had deliberately diverted it, and with that cut off the ready income. I still didn't know in what new directions my work would flow, as a matter of fact, that's not definite yet and I am beginning to hope that it never will be. If an artist doesn't change he deteriorates, there is no such thing as remaining at a fixed level.

There was more than that, although I could not see it then. A symptom of it was in the fact that this time I compared my situation to that of the average American instead of to that of my class. A miscellany of observations and perceptions had filtered into my system, everything that working in Indian affairs had taught me was lying there unco-ordinated along with a much wider first-hand knowledge of the United States, places such as Kansas, California, Chicago, which my East ignores, and the great instruction a North American receives from Latin Americans if he will give himself the chance. Dry farmers on the high, unfarmable prairie, migratory workers, sharecroppers had become real to me, I actually knew what they meant in human terms, and I had already been baffled and frustrated by the impossibility of telling most of my own people what it was the government was not only trying to do, but for our very salvation had to do in the West.

Listing things like this reduces them to insignificance. No one of these carries great weight, and in fact these larger perceptions which one can call quickly to mind and readily cite are important only if they are a part of a whole texture of new ways of seeing which can penetrate all of a citizen's fibre and make an American out of him.

Big things and small things change within one, it's difficult to say which is the most significant. During my correct years I had from time to time gone dashing off along the lines of my true desires only to come walking back like a good dog on the end of a leash. In my sallies I had come to know some people in and around Greenwich Village who corresponded in a general way to my fellows in New Orleans. They were writers, painters, musicians, dancers, poor as church mice and struggling hard. The girls were attractive, which was, of course, a real consideration, but more than that I felt their integrity, the vividness with which they saw the world, the trueness of their responses, and their utter independence. In my snug, placid life that independence seemed remarkable. I had forgotten that I once almost had it. I got a keen, wistful pleasure from being among them, and I tried hard to prove that I was to some extent one of them and that I, too, was brave. I did not see the deadly parallel to the big-money writers who hung around us starvelings in New Orleans, and at least there was the difference that these people thought well of some of my writings.

For a year or more I had seen nothing of them, because I had found it quite impossible to mix them with the gentry with whom I habitually associated. I wanted to be among them again under the new dispensation and I called one up rather hesitantly, conscious of my own snobbish betrayal and nearly able to see just what my former rôle had been. I was surprised at the warmth of invitation I got in response and deeply grateful for it. I returned to that milieu with a sense of homecoming. It occurred to me that for the past eight years I had had remarkably little to do with artists of any kind. In fact, I had from time to time declared that the whole business of artist colonies was a lot of bunk and Bohemianism nothing but sloppiness and self-indulgence. How readily we lie, how deep and false and vehement are those lies when they are primarily directed at ourselves!

As I detached myself more and more from uptown New York and my centre of social gravity moved toward Greenwich Village and Santa Fe, my contact with people who were also engaged in a constant struggle to pay the rent through the arts in order to be free to practice the arts steadily increased. The feeling that came with it was one of having been long dessicated and then put back into water. I was beginning to discover where I belonged.

People with good minds, stimulating talkers and thinkers, are always a source of strength. It is a bankrupt society, and a rare one, which does not provide a few people from whom one's own mind strikes off sparks, a few contacts which enrich and strengthen one's own work. But if I had to pick out the occupational groups from which I receive the most today, I should say with a good deal of certainty that they were fellow-artists, preferably not too stable financially, and the best of the top men in government service. Both groups challenge not only my specific ideas on this or that side of a common interest, but my entire *Weltanschauung*, both are a constant test of my own sincerity in two fundamentals of life—the practice of my calling and my relation to my country. To these, if I had my full pick, I should add newspapermen and those scientists who have retained some realism and sense of humour, and beyond them it would be a matter of individuals.

I could hardly be expected to have settled all this in that first evening in my hide-out. It takes a long time to shake off habits of manners and thought. One has flashes of complete perception and violent set-backs, one progresses finely in one sector while another remains unchanged. I was to know lots of self-pity and lamentation.

It takes a little time to become completely adjusted to a fundamental change in one's world. When I was growing up, for all that the First World War cracked our foundations, the general course of one's life seemed clear enough and pretty safe. Even when choosing to be a writer, one did not imagine that one's career was not definitely intended to serve as a means of continuing along that course. In part the reality of my choice had caught up with me. The kind of writer I intended to be simply could not be financially secure nor could he flourish in that environment unless he were a rare exception. Certainly this specimen couldn't. Perhaps this was so urgently true in part because not only my own, but all the world had changed and the old securities were no longer there. When one first looks this situation in the eye he is bound to become frightened, and even now I admit that I wish there were some way that writers could attach themselves to Social Security. We need it as badly as do mechanics; in fact, in view of the difficulty with which we practice thrift we probably need it worse.

A man who wants to do what I want to do and live as I want to live had better make up his mind that he is in for the kind of life in which the only woman who will stay married to him is one who likes to do her own housework. He'd better chuck his illusions of luxury to be won, and become an American. He was born with his first papers, now he has a chance to become completely naturalized. Most artists don't need to be told this; they were native-born. It's people like me who have to learn it, and there are many who started off about where I did who will fight to the death to keep from having to learn it.

You get a lot in return. There is the monthly triumph of paying the rent. There is the blow-out when you sell a story. There is the wonderful occasion when your wife can shoot the works on a really up-to-date evening gown, in which you participate as you never knew you could participate in a matter of women's clothes. More than this, there is a new liveliness and changeability in life and a new willingness for change. The momentary sense of loneliness and lack of enclosure which comes from having stepped outside of a snug, closed society is replaced by the much greater warmth which the mass of the American nation radiates to everyone who shares its daily problems and desires. It is a grand thing to be ready, both mentally and in lightness of material bonds, for uprooting and unexpected changes. In this time when we are smack up against the greatest insecurity of all it is a solid advantage to be even partly accustomed to the condition. More than anything else, it is wonderful to be united with yourself, to like what you naturally like and be frankly bored with what naturally bores you and not give a damn about what your preferences are supposed to be.

CHAPTER 16

MAIN LINE

For a writer there is no pleasure comparable to writing. It is also hard, fatiguing work but that is a minor matter. There simply is nothing else like it, none of the other things in its genre — an eight-oared race, the long days on horseback, getting drunk, the diverse absorbing pleasures which lift you completely out of yourself — contains what writing does for him. Making love is equal to it but unfortunately that does not last long enough.

There is, first, anxiety and anticipation in the search for a new, good idea. Some writers get these easily, for me they're hard to come by. I fool with situation after situation and find no story in it, or at least nothing that makes me feel that I can write it. Then an idea comes and with it the first lift of excitement. You consider the idea, hardly more at first than a brief statement of some situation and a sequence running out of it, and in figuring out whether there really is a story there you suddenly see the story, sequence, events, treatment, a whole complex of ideas which it would take several hours to express fully grasped in a moment of time. Then you go over it, testing it. Sometimes it just bogs down, you have a disagreeable, empty feeling, and that's that. Start again. If it stands up, as you work it over and test it excitement mounts steadily, for in going over it you see treatments in detail, passages on which you can cut loose, sections you long to get at and handle, others where you will have to use every item of skill that you possess. Your faculties organize themselves and you know you are going to need them all.

Now you enter upon a life rather than an occupation, especially if you have an idea for a novel, which is to me the king of them all. Everything else will revolve about this for six months or more; you will eat, breathe, and sleep it, think of it at odd times, and find all other interests completely dominated by the idea of the completed job — and wonder what the completed job will be like. The story changes as it grows, you constantly surprise yourself.

On a different plane you are expanding yourself as completely as in rowing or in football, none of your faculties is left out. You are also working like a dog. If you really are doing your best you are thoroughly tired at the end of each session. You do not merely let your soul flow, you use discipline. You are judging each sentence, phrase, word, as you set it down and judging them all over again in retrospect. All the parts must fit each other to form a closely locked, clear logic; characters and events must arise from each other, above all your characters must do and say and be always just what their natures, not as you have imagined but as you have shown them, would in fact dictate. You cannot merely state that A is a likeable fellow with a good sense of humour and B is an international scut; you must demonstrate these things so that the reader states them to himself. In nothing can you merely *will* that it be so. Although you are the omnipotent and omnipresent god of this your creation, you must see to it that every slightest thing is proven to the satisfaction of the utter strangers who are going to read it. All of this to be done without halting the run of your story, all to be handled so easily and smoothly and interestingly that the reader will never feel that you are pointing anything out to him. This does not mean that all must be action; if you are as great a writer as Thomas Mann you can indulge in almost interminable static passages which a very considerable audience will find fascinating. I shall not be one of them.

What you write comes out of yourself. Even though any given scene be purest imagination its ultimate source is in realities that you have seen, the ideas behind the action are your ideas. Therefore they are all clear and interesting to you. One does not find writers working on passages which bore them. A writer interested only in suiting himself would put into a story innumerable passages which for reasons of association or intellectual content meant a great deal to him but which conveyed nothing to the stranger, or which, good in themselves perhaps, did not fit the story, did not belong, and slowed up the action — in short, were dull in their context. Leaving them in a story is sheer self-indulgence. You are also tempted to include certain passages merely because they offer you a chance to strut your stuff. There are certain situations which give a wonderful outlet for purple writing. If you yield to self-indulgence and leave them in, again you damage or even ruin your story, and besides, the passage which you thought so hot usually turns out to be banal and heavy, even bathetic. A dreadful example of this is the death of Slim Girl in *Laughing Boy*. Because I was young and emotionally excited when I wrote this, and my own emotion over my climax craved an outlet, I made her as long and vocal in dying as Aïda and at its high point my book turns ridiculous. I am still hoping to talk my publishers into making the new plates which will enable me to cut this passage.

You are, then, constantly at war with yourself to check self-indulgence. In this present book that has been a hideous problem, and I fear that it has not been successfully conquered for the very nature of this account is self-indulgent. Even so, the number of things of great interest to myself which I did not put in and the number of excuses for purple writing which I omitted is truly large and cost me a lot of agony.

You must discipline yourself in all these things because their result is dullness. No matter how brilliant, profound, and true a book may be, if it is dull it is a bad book. Many pseudo-intellectuals confuse dullness and lack of clarity with significance. There is even a cult of books which are difficult to read, a sort of pygmy quest of the esoteric, but no sensible person will be fooled.

You may, as you work or when your book is about finished, call in various critics. A writer's wife usually gets it in the neck. Your critics may be wise or foolish. You have to know how to accept or discard their opinions, and in the long run all they can do is arouse criticism in yourself. You have to be your own critic. You have to set up within yourself the nearest thing you can create to an absolute measuring stick. This is a hard thing to do, it calls for all the character you've got. If you are going to get anywhere at all you must have the character to be remorseless with yourself, including the willingness to work endlessly on the grind of revision. These are councils of perfection. I know I don't live up to them — I know, too, that I'd be a better writer if I did.

Writing is not self-expression. No art is, in the sense that self-expression usually conveys. Most writers start with that in their callow youth, as one can see by reading any school magazine, but they get over it. Art is the expression of something one has seen which is bigger than one's self. I don't think there is any individual alive whose mere ego is sufficiently interesting for the expression of it to be a book, although someone else's analysis of it might be. I hear a distant sound of razzberries at the man who states this in the text of a book which is on the face of it nothing but self-expression. Part of the experiment of this book is to see if I can handle the material within myself as if it were about someone else to whose innards God had miraculously given me complete access.

The thing seen is bigger than the man and the intention to communicate it is more important than himself. The result is that the artist becomes, if he be indeed an artist, bigger than himself and his work far outshines his own, small, fallible being. So we come back again to character, in this case the ability to devote one's self to something sincerely felt to be more important than one's self.

The escapist partially fails in this great requirement by a weakness in his character. Escape writing is not a question of setting; if merely laying a story in a remote part of the world or in ancient times were escape, then all books written more than a generation ago as well as everything not dealing with the reader's own environment would fall into that classification as far as the reader was concerned. Escape lies in a desire on the writer's part to avoid or get away from the hard facts of all men's lives, or to enable his readers to do so. A tissue of fundamental lies like Gene Stratton-Porter's debilitating works, the greater part of the stories in the slick-paper magazines, *Anthony Adverse*, and *Ivanhoe* are all equally escapist. I don't think there is any such thing as a great escape book although there are plenty of good ones, for one of the elements of greatness is that quality of universality which makes *War and Peace* or *Alice in Wonderland* continue to be living documents on humanity.

Much of this book has been devoted to tracing the evolution of an escapist. As far as I can make out, the creative urge of writing or story-telling was there first, then it became absorbed in the refuge of day-dreams, but it still existed. Like so many other adolescents, the beginning of writing was in part imitative, in part arose from the discovery that writing compositions was a pleasure at times when I was able to handle the kind of subject I liked. My writing at school was imitative of many authors, mainly those with a flowery style, the subjects were as remote and imaginative as possible. When I got altogether too lush my father, who took all attempts at art seriously, toned me down. I wrote largely about pirates, vikings and Elizabethan seafaring, with some wistful stuff about Rhode Island and some attempts at fantasy à la Dunsany. It was kid stuff, just about like all the rest.

Then the Indians came into my life and my whole urge to flight found its direction. From the point of view of writing I think this was a lucky thing for at least it set me to trying to tell the truth, as far as I could learn it, about actual people. It also had the same appearance of reality that my whole study of Indians had, and a purposefulness which was real in fact. This enabled me entirely to disguise from myself the nature of what I was doing.

At school I spent a great deal of time in inventing and elaborating a set of imaginary nations, worked out their geography, government, and customs, even made up a language which at one time I spoke fairly fluently, and evolved a complete biography for myself including an unhappy love affair and a romantic death. This kind of thing, fairly common among children, was a wasteful diversion of creative energy. It contained a good deal of satisfaction in itself, but it was a thing which one had to keep secret, and art is communication.

Every artist knows this intuitively, although many will quite sincerely deny it, believing that they write or paint or dance primarily to please themselves and that an audience is entirely a subordinate matter. Of course some people are quite happy talking to themselves, and so, too, there are exceptional cases like Emily Dickinson, but even in such cases I think you will always find an imagined, perhaps unavowed, audience.

Writing, as against day-dreaming, held the possibility of communication by being published. Even unpublished it did give the satisfaction of having created something, which a day-dream never did. I was a really prolific writer in school and college and for some years afterwards, whereas today ideas come hard and it's a good year in which I can think up a dozen usable ones. I flatter myself that this is because now I am more critical, but it may be merely that I have a lot less juice in me. At any rate I poured out stories and the more I wrote the more I loved doing it. As I evolved from the Fourth Former's inevitable sketch to constantly longer and more satisfying constructions, the organized day-dream faded away. But day-dreaming is not writing; nor does writing fill the need for it where that exists, it merely exhausts the creative energy which would enable one to maintain long, elaborate dreams, so that they are reduced to detached, self-contained fantasies.

When circumstances removed me from the Southwest to Central America, the subject of my love, the Navajos, became less real. The Navajo country, out of reach, became even more the promised land than it had been when I could go to it. I kept on studying the subject on the side, and compiled a pretty good thesis on it. I also kept on writing about it.

In the course of my study I had to read as much of the mythology of about forty tribes as I could unearth, which was a lot. I remember particularly the work of a Franciscan, Father Pettitot, who translated the rather drab legends of half a dozen northern Athabascan tribes word for word into French. It made remarkably hard sledding, but from time to time one ran across nuggets of pure gold. There was one passage describing how a Chippewyan stole back his wife, whom the Crees had captured, after she had been enslaved for more than a year.

'All that night,' the story ran, 'he moved back and forth on top of her. Yes, all night long he was marching on her. Why not?'

Much of the material I read was in literal translation, more than one might have hoped for in the free translations had been done by men with enough literary gift to render the character of the original. These texts interested me deeply, above all I was struck by the clarity, economy, and emphasis of the literal wording. Up to then I had been a great user of the periodic sentence, an addict of the flowery passage. When I started to write *Laughing Boy* I was soaked in Indian literature and deeply affected by the Navajo and Apache particularly. Very shortly after I started I translated a number of myths from the Jacalteca. As I got going in the novel I found to my astonishment that all my sentences came out short. My construction looked monotonous to me when I studied it, I was seriously worried, and believed that I had fallen victim to a vice of style which would ruin the job. But still I rather liked the writing when I read it unanalytically, and besides, I found it impossible to write in any other way. I was well started in the story when Hemingway and Faulkner together burst upon me like my first view of the sun. Hemingway comforted me a good deal on the question of short sentences. The curious fact is that, to whatever extent my style in that book is modern of its period, the Indians did it.

Laughing Boy was written for myself alone as nearly as that is possible in an attempt at a work of art. All my friends were agreed that no book about Indians could ever be sold. It was a rare bit of luck that enabled me to place one Indian short story in *The Dial*. (I wish someone would endow such a magazine today, there is a great need for it, which *Story* definitely does not fill.) Negroes one could write about, Latin America perhaps, but Indians, absolutely not. I was pretty well persuaded of this. But I had the idea, and once conceived the idea carried with it the necessity that it be written. With that, too, was the emotion of longing and farewell to a beloved country which I might never see again. In this book I should pour out all my love. Self-expression? Perhaps, but indirectly through the expression of a beauty seen.

I worked on it in my spare time. In my spare time I wrote things that I hoped would sell, the indulgence of the novel was for afterwards. Having, in the course of some eight years, three times determined that I had thoroughly proven to myself that I could never be a writer, having formally given it up, and having gone right on writing, I determined to test the matter once and for all. I arranged to go on half-time at Tulane, working there five afternoons a week, giving myself the mornings and evenings free. This went on for five months. In that time (I kept careful track) I wrote one hundred and twenty thousand words, of which I sold exactly one thousand two hundred, for twelve dollars, also to *The Dial*. Several of the stories sold for high prices after I won the Pulitzer Prize, one to a magazine which had formerly rejected it. A number of them were reprinted and have gone into anthologies, one got an O. Henry Prize, which doesn't mean much. I mention this because it illustrates the extent to which a writer depends on reputation, as all artists do, and the timidity of editors, similar to that of the people who buy pictures.

On the side I wrote about half of *Laughing Boy*. I had a bad conscience about this as it was a work which could not further my purpose, but I was unable to let it alone.

The five months went by, and a twelve-dollar sale was not enough. The final test came to an end. I had flunked it. Now there was no more room for doubt. I was twenty-seven; old enough to achieve success if I had it in me, and one per cent of all my output accepted indicated that what I had was nothing but a nice talent, useful on the side and for pleasure.

Then Tulane University canned me ignominiously, and matters grew serious. For a short time I was at Harvard, digging up the real, inside dope on the mutations of the letter *k* in the Mayan family. I also worried hard about my future, and only on rare occasions, as a special indulgence, did I allow myself to work on the novel. I had to get down to brass tacks.

Ferris Greenslet of Houghton Mifflin got in touch with me. He told me he had liked my Navajo short story in *The Dial*, and wondered if I had any idea of anything of book length along those lines. I joyfully outlined my novel. He said that Houghton Mifflin would like to see it. This word was like coming across a life-preserver when one was all but spent from swimming. It set me free and it gave me a new, incredulous hope.

So I went back to New Orleans and finished the book, making it my main occupation now, tasting for the first time the full delight of writing, the luxury of absorption. And they really did take it. Good Lord, the hope came true. A book, with a regular binding and a dust jacket and everything, and OLIVER LA FARGE on it, was sent to me. I put it on the mantelpiece and walked around studying it from all angles. With the conviction which that carried I upped my estimate of its probable sales to two thousand five hundred, which would make me more money than I had ever seen in one lump in my life. And, at last *I was a writer*.

No writer can form a valid opinion on his own work. I know only that I am dissatisfied with mine. Least of all can I judge *Laughing Boy*, for it was the product of a young man whom I have ceased to be and at the same time it is so loaded with associations as to make it impossible for me to approach it impersonally. I have a certain dislike for it because it has been so popular whereas my other books have done only fairly well. I grow sick of smiling fools who tell me, 'Oh, Mr. La Farge, I did so love your *Laughing Boy*, when are you going to give us another book?' Having written four other novels, a book of short stories and two non-fiction books, and being like all writers badly in need of more royalties, one can hardly avoid giving a short answer.

I know a woman whom I like for various reasons, but whom I should adore in any case simply because she prefers *Sparks Fly Upward*. I know a writer who was actually influenced by my style in another book. I prize such people. If anybody wants to seduce me into doing something for him, the most effective thing he could do would be to praise any book of mine other than that first success. Which is unfair to a perfectly honest novel, but a prejudice I can't help but feel. Other writers suffer from it, too.

That success set me free to return to the Southwest, and then began the process of education towards reality through my chosen medium of escape. My writing did not keep pace. My second novel was laid in Latin America, in an imaginary country, in the first half of the nineteenth century, which was making it about as remote as could be managed. The next dealt with privateers in the War of 1812. My Indian short stories mostly avoided what I was learning and continued to reconstruct the relatively untouched Indian country of *Laughing Boy* although a feeling of the disaster inherent in white contacts ran through them.

If I had stayed in New Orleans, or at least among artists, things might have developed quite differently. When I was still in the French Quarter I wrote a short story, not much good, which was almost straight reporting. At that time I saw the material for a novel in the life around me. I had not evolved a plot for it, but thought about the possibilities from time to time, liked them a lot, and thought that I should probably tackle the idea as soon as the decks were cleared of work in hand. I had no idea that this would be a big change, not merely in subject matter, but in the entire type of my work. I was near enough to freedom then for it merely to seem the handiest and most promising material.

Established in New York, I discarded the idea. It didn't appeal to me. Then, after several years, I decided one day to write a short story *against* Bohemia and the French Quarter. That, I decided, was the true interpretation of the material I had considered. I started out with that purpose in mind, laid out my story, and found it changing under me. At the same time the writing of it excited me much more than usual. What I produced was not autobiographical, but willy-nilly I set down honest observations on the life I had abandoned, I wrote, not against it, but passionately for it, and in clear, easily interpreted symbols I stated the flat truth about the choice I had made.

This was most disturbing. The logic of character and situation, I explained to myself, prevented me from turning the story the way I wanted it to go. I had stated a special case. The symbolism I flatly denied. As a man I succeeded in avoiding the implications of what, as a writer, I had been unable to help doing. Some day I should write the answering, 'true' story. From time to time I fiddled around with that intention, but somehow I could never cook up a convincing idea. Oh, well, it had been a youthful stage and I was concerned with Indians.

One day it occurred to me that I was in a rut. Analysis of my writings showed that I had one theme and one fundamental love story. I had rewritten the theme from every angle, the only new treatment I could see for the love story would be to set it up between homosexuals. The stories sold, the books made money. If I didn't change pretty soon all hope of growth, all hope of eventually achieving at least once the kind of work I had set out to do, was gone. The only thing to do was to change right now. This meant that the flow of money would stop. Editors had me ticketed for Indian stuff with a romantic turn to it, so had the public. I hardly knew what it felt like to write about white folks, and I intended to experiment. There would be no more thousand-dollar checks, at least for a while. The big money days would go for good, and I'd better make up my mind to it.

At the same time I saw that in my writing I had run away steadily from the present-day realities which occupied most of my thoughts in connection with Indians. For the first time I felt a desire to tackle those realities. I should write a counterpart to *Laughing Boy*, a real study of what his son would be up against today. I did, and I still think *The Enemy Gods* is my first nonescape writing though the critics don't agree with me.

But *The Enemy Gods* was still about Indians, it was still the thing observed rather than the thing experienced. Writing about white folks still came hard. Back at last in contact with myself, my education was falling into coherence inside me, but I had taken the most essential experiences of my life and walled them up behind a solid wall the very existence of which I had denied.

All my life I have been lucky, and of all my luck the greatest has been in the calibre of my friends. Now at a critical time a friend stepped in, a woman of unusual quality, great perception, and remorseless persistence. Finally she forced the word, 'Bop,' across my unwilling lips. I was thirty-six; I had not spoken that word since I left School. The central stone, the key, came out with a loud bop! and the wall began to crumble. The first decent writing I ever did about the important things known to me of my own knowledge was about little boys at school. Then, and only then, I ceased to be afraid, and then at last I slew the Groton Boy.

So in effect I'm beginning again, which is perhaps the real reason behind the various ones I perceive for writing this account. My last novel is in many ways a first novel. I'm curious to see what I'll think of it ten years from now. I'm even more curious to see where I'll go from here, providing there is any going at all from now on for a luxury profession such as mine.

This kind of arbitrary shift points up my remark that if an artist wants to marry he should find a woman who doesn't mind doing her own housework. I don't see how the women stand for it. At least the wife of a mechanic doesn't have her husband tell her one day that he's going to quit his good job because he's getting into a rut. Artists' wives are remarkable people; the requirements are extra special. Thinking over the ones I know, I'm surprised to note that their marriages are as durable as those of other people.

They have to have enough of the artist in themselves, plus enough character, to be genuinely more interested in the production of good work by their husbands than in comfort or security. It takes more than a little not only to accept but to further the man's decision that he must abandon a profitable but exhausted line; some women can't take it, those who can are the kind who don't just take it, but see the reasons and are all for it. When a man is seized by as cockeyed an idea as writing this book she does not stop to consider that it's not likely to make money or that the project involves telling things about himself which will cause some people to go 'tchk, tchk!' She considers first and exclusively whether in her opinion it will produce good writing, and if she thinks it will, makes preparations to alter year before last's dresses again and urges her husband on. In return for which she gets his excessive mood-swing, his irregular habits, chronic trouble over bills, and lots of practice washing dishes. Women like that don't grow on every bush. I like artists, but their wives I find magnificent.

You write. You spend your life in pursuit of something you will never catch. Καλος, ἀγαθος ... the good, the beautiful, and the true. They are all one. I suppose a painter would choose the second word for the name of the perfect union of the three, a writer finds ultimate beauty and goodness in ultimate, absolute truth, a brilliance of which the human mind can catch no more than glimpses. It lies in your idea, in your intention. In the story you are about to write you see the gleam of one fragment of universal truth, you see the possibility of that beauty. And you write. And you haven't caught it. Perhaps later. Perhaps if I become more skillful and learn to shed my inadequate self more completely. Perhaps if I write enough books, enough stories, somewhere in one of them I shall actually lay hands on the absolute and have my moment of greatness. You don't really believe this, but you have seen something — not really seen it but caught a fugitive glimpse, and that is enough. You haven't heard it but you have an idea of what is meant by the music of the spheres and a longing has been set up in you which will never cease. You can never give up hunting for it nor will you ever be satisfied; though in the end your juices may dry up, your vision and your memory of vision be clouded, and another man than the one you used to be may become satisfied.

I suppose everyone must visualize his objective in his own way. The crystal comparison is the one I think of most, the completely clear, flashing crystal which is also, in different terms and under different conditions, the goal of science and of religion. The crystal hidden in a medicine bag. Inadequate, but then, no visualization or metaphor will serve. You simply know that it exists and that you are shooting at the North Star with a popgun.

And now comes War, just as I have cleared my personal Main Line and made ready to get going down it. Now, as the result of inner compulsions too convincing to need analysis at the time, I wear a uniform and I do more steady, drudging work than ever in my life before, I have before me the promise of some excitement and a slight element of risk, and what writing I may do — other than occasional, leisure activity — is as one officer said, 'for a very select audience.' Sometimes for an audience of one. Literary flights are not indicated.

What makes men go to war? Many good reasons are given, all true, but all together are still incomplete. There is something the civilian feels (as I well know) when he is among soldiers in wartime. The feeling gets dulled under some circumstances, there are men whose obtuse souls remain unaffected, but the average, virile civilian feels a mixture of envy and inferiority when he confronts men in uniform. This is one reason why it is important to give badges or uniforms to merchant sailors, war workers, civilian flyers and such.

The feeling has nothing to do with the man's own knowledge of the relative value of his own and the soldier's contributions to the war. It goes down into the ancient make-up of men, into fundamentals of the fact of being a man which all our civilization has not changed. Tolstoy has sketched it to some extent. Knowing that war is destructive and evil, still even a war lacking the profound moral justifications and flat necessity of this one has an appeal. It is one of man's proper occupations, it is a restatement and fulfillment of himself as a man which calls to him deeply, blindly, far within his voiceless, essential being. He knows intuitively the group loyalty of men in a common uniform and the solidarity which a soldier indicates when he speaks of his 'outfit.' This, too, alternating with the equal requirement of individual freedom, is a necessary spiritual vitamin from which civilized life has largely cut him off.

The average American, being neither a primitive savage nor a Nazi, does not go to war merely because of these impulses, although he responds to them restlessly. He volunteers or accepts the draft because of his convictions. But he does so with a certain satisfaction, a willingness, which comes out of his nature as a man. This does not mean that he doesn't hate war, is not determined that there must be no more of it, and will not return from war even more determined to see to that. But when war does come and his conscience tells him that the cause is righteous, these other forces are released.

In the first months after Pearl Harbor I was offered several opportunities for civilian service. The positions were interesting, some involved foreign travel, most were well-paid. They left me unsatisfied. When the Ferrying Command offered me a chance at a commission I jumped at it. It was a job I could do, it would be useful, and it promised to be interesting.

I made my application, took my physical examination, and went home to wait. The notice was a month in coming. It was brief and to the point.

My application was rejected because I was 'unfit for military service, including limited service, because of old miliary tuberculosis, pulmonary.'

I've no more had tuberculosis than I've been pregnant. I had myself X-rayed, and found that for whatever cause, I had a chest the Army would have no part of. If they ever got around to drafting me, one look at my X-ray and I'd be 4-F. Yes, the explorer and horseman, the hard-living man who hunted with the Indians at timberline and swung a mean machete in the low tropics would be too delicate to go to war. I was safe as a church. The State Department wanted to send me to Uruguay. Everything was just dandy.

It was possible to get the idea across, first to appropriate officials in the Ferrying Command (which in the meantime had become the Air Transport Command), then to the Flight Surgeon at the Albuquerque Air Base, that if the official diagnosis were correct, then I must have died years ago, probably of a hemorrhage induced by violent exertion at an altitude at which flyers wear oxygen masks. After delays, I took a new examination. My case history was written into the record. The conclusion was 'Waiver recommended. Qualified for military duty.'

Driving home, my wife asked me how I felt.

Without reflection, out of my heart I said, 'I feel as if my balls had been given back to me.'

So out of basic, male naïveté I got myself completely blocked off from my own main line. Nothing of the kind. Not even if I were young enough to qualify for combat action. Helping to restore a world in which free writing can exist strikes me as one of a writer's prime functions, but that's only part of it. I never believed much in the ivory tower. If the evolution I've traced in this book has really occurred, I'm at a prime moment for recharging myself with realities. The loss of a few years of production in return for a share in the greatest experience of our time is an excellent swap.

I am assigned to a fascinating outfit, made up to an exceptionally high degree of men bent on outdoing themselves in a tremendous undertaking. In my Command discipline is joined with informality and flexibility in a most effective union, and the bond between man and man is strong. I've had many lucky breaks in my life. Of these, next to being accepted by my wife, this is the biggest of all. I have fallen in love with a bomber; quite literally, a new world has been opened to me.

THE END

www.ingramcontent.com/pod-product-compliance
Lightning Source LLC
Chambersburg PA
CBHW022111150426
43195CB00008B/354